publication PN°1
Bibliothek der Provinz

LANDES
GALERIE

Objekt : Video

OÖ. LANDESGALERIE

VORWORT

FOREWORD

The link between the ancient medium of sculpture and the younger – but no longer the youngest – medium of video is the theme of the exhibition "Objekt : Video". However, this does not mean that the term "video sculpture", which has nearly taken on the character of an artistic genre designation in recent years, is to be examined for possible genre definitions. Rather, this exhibition presents an artistic phenomenon that is intended to be experienced in its current manifestation in multifaceted innovations and connections to other artistic traditions. Aside from the fact that most of the artists participating in this exhibition come from other fields of art (sculpture, painting, photography, theatre, film) and are not interested themselves in being classified as "video artists", the exhibited works are convincing in the congruity between the tactility of the static object and the movement of the flowing image.

The exhibition does not aspire to gather together the most well-known works – or names – yet again, but rather to assemble a section-like overview of three generations of artists, to cite early works, to show new works from the generation of "pioneers" and to present current pieces from a younger and the youngest generation; the intention is to convey an impression of the development, of the way in which an artistic form of expression and the use of transmedial possibilities have been transformed within a short period of time.

The criteria of technical sophistication was not a basis for designing this exhibition. Only those artworks were sought out and considered, that are convincing and whose confrontations and constellations join to form a broad spectrum of intensive artistic creation.

Peter Assmann / Gottfried Hattinger

Die Verbindung des uralten Mediums Skulptur mit dem jungen – aber nicht mehr jüngsten – Medium Video ist Thema der Ausstellung „Objekt : Video". Keinesfalls soll jedoch der Begriff „Videoskulptur", der in den letzten Jahren fast den Charakter einer künstlerischen Gattungsbezeichnung angenommen hat, auf mögliche Gattungsdefinitionen untersucht werden. Die Ausstellung präsentiert vielmehr ein künstlerisches Phänomen, das in seinen vielfältigen Innovationen bzw. Verbindungen zu anderen Kunsttraditionen in seiner aktuellen Erscheinungsform erfahrbar gemacht werden soll. Ungeachtet des Faktums, daß die meisten der an der Ausstellung beteiligten Künstlerinnen und Künstler aus anderen künstlerischen Bezirken (Bildhauerei, Malerei, Fotografie, Theater, Film) stammen und selber gar keinen Wert auf die Klassifizierung als „Videokünstler" legen, überzeugen die ausgestellten Werke durch ihre Kongruenz zwischen der Haptik des statischen Objekts und der Bewegung des fließenden Bildes.

Die Ausstellung verfolgt nicht die Ambition, die bekanntesten Arbeiten – und Namen – einmal mehr zusammenzustellen, sondern führt in einem ausschnitthaften Überblick drei Künstlergenerationen zusammen, zitiert frühe Werke, zeigt neue Arbeiten der 'Pionier'generation und aktuelle Stücke der Jungen und Jüngsten, um einen Eindruck der Entwicklung zu vermitteln, wie sich eine künstlerische Ausdrucksform und der Umgang mit transmedialen Möglichkeiten innerhalb eines kurzen Zeitraumes gewandelt hat.

Das Kriterium der technischen Avanciertheit spielte bei der Gestaltung der Ausstellung keine Rolle. Die Suche und das Interesse galt allein überzeugenden Kunstwerken und ihren Konfrontationen bzw. Konstellationen, die sich zu einem breiten Spektrum intensiven künstlerischen Gestaltens zusammenfügen.

Peter Assmann / Gottfried Hattinger

Über die Ästhetik und Museologie der Neuen Medien

CHRISTINE VAN ASSCHE

Nicht eine Welt schaffen,
die Möglichkeit einer Welt schaffen,
eine Möglichkeit durch das Drehbuch schaffen, und erst die Kamera ermöglicht diese Arbeit –
Dieses Mögliche schaffen.

Jean-Luc Godard, „Scénario du film Passion"

Dieser Artikel versucht, einen Überblick über die Beziehungen zu geben, die zwischen Künstlern, verschiedenen Institutionen und Kritikern und jenen Arbeiten bestehen, die für technisch reproduzierbare Trägermedien konzipiert wurden, also in erster Linie für Kino, Diapositiv, Video, Hypermedien und VR-Technologien. So weit es möglich ist, werden wir sie auch in einen globalen Zusammenhang stellen. Wir können in diesem Rahmen natürlich keinen erschöpfenden Überblick über die internationale Situation geben, sondern nur versuchen, jene Haltungen zu skizzieren, die bei Künstlern, Kritikern und Institutionen in Europa und Nordamerika während der letzten drei Jahrzehnte beobachtbar waren. Da die Entwicklungen in Asien, Australien und Südamerika weniger bekannt sind – wir wissen zwar, daß sich dort eine intensive künstlerische Aktivität entfaltet hat –, können wir sie hier nicht berücksichtigen.

1. DIE ÄSTHETIK MECHANISCH REPRODUZIERBARER WERKE

Uns interessiert hier die Frage, ob wir von einer für Medienkunstwerke spezifischen Ästhetik sprechen können oder ob sich diese Werke in die allgemeine zeitgenössische Ästhetik einreihen lassen.

Die Künstler haben sich der neuen technischen Trägermedien seit deren Erscheinen auf dem Markt bedient. Die Photographie war sicherlich die erste Technik zur Schaffung mechanisch reproduzierbarer Werke, die im 20. Jh. aufgekommen ist und die sich Künstler zunutze gemacht haben. Im Anschluß daran ist dann ein Medium nach dem anderen gekommen: Film, Video, Hypermedien und die aktuellen Technologien des Virtuellen (die sich aber erst in der Beobachtungsphase befinden). „Um neunzehnhundert hatte die technische Repro-

ON AESTHETICS AND THE MUSEOLOGY OF THE NEW MEDIA

Not to create a world,
to create the possibility of a world,
a possibility created by a script,
though the camera alone can make it tangible –
This is the Possible we create.

Jean-Luc Godard

This article will attempt to provide an overall view of the relationships which exist between artists, different institutions, critics and those pieces of work conceived for technically reproducible communications media, that is to say, primarily for cinema, slide projection, video, hypermedia and VR-technology. We will also put these, in as far as this is possible, in their global context. It is, of course, impossible to paint an exhaustive picture of the international situation within the constraints of this article; we can only attempt outline in the positions of artists, critics and institutions in Europe and North America observable over the last thirty years. As the developments in Asia, Australia and South America are less well-known – although we are quite aware of their recently developed, intense artistic activities – we cannot take them into consideration here.

I. THE AESTHETICS OF MECHANICALLY REPRODUCIBLE WORKS OF ART

The question that is of interest for us is whether one can speak of a specific aesthetics for media art, or whether these works can be included within the general contemporary aesthetics.

Artists have been using the new technical communications media ever since they first appeared on the market. Photography was undoubtedly the first technical means of creating mechanically reproducible works of art to rear its head in the 20th century and to be made use of by artists. It was followed by one medium after another: film, video, hypermedia and the contemporary technology of virtual reality (which, however, is still in the observation phase). "Around 1900, technical

duktion einen Standard erreicht, auf dem sie nicht nur die Gesamtheit der überkommenen Kunstwerke zu ihrem Objekt zu machen und deren Wirkung den tiefsten Veränderungen zu unterwerfen begann, sondern sich einen eigenen Platz unter den künstlerischen Verfahrenweisen eroberte."[1] In unserem Kontext interessiert uns allerdings nur der zweite Teil von Walter Benjamins Behauptung.

Die Zielsetzungen der Künstler, die sich der verschiedenen Reproduktionstechniken bedienen, sind jedoch nicht identisch: Manche verfolgen von Anfang an ihre künstlerischen Ziele, ohne sich von der Technik einengen zu lassen, andere sehen es für notwendig an, mit der Technik an sich zu experimentieren.

Diese doppelte Perspektive kann man immer dann feststellen, wenn ein neues Medium zur Bildspeicherung bzw. Bildwiedergabe aufkommt, denn von diesem Moment an geschieht die Bezugnahme auf zeitgenössische Kunstströmungen auf unterschiedliche Weise. Und wir müssen uns fragen, ob es vom theoretischen Standpunkt her gerechtfertigt ist, eine Kunstform nach ihrer technischen Spezifizität zu benennen.

Die erste Gruppe von Künstlern eignet sich ein technisches Medium an – manchmal übrigens gleich mehrere – und verwendet es als ein Mittel künstlerischen Schaffens unter vielen, ohne sich speziell mit dem Werkzeug an sich auseinanderzusetzen. Sie adaptieren das Medium an ihr Konzept, ohne die Besonderheiten des Mediums wirklich zu erforschen. Diese Haltung nehmen in erster Linie die meisten Fluxus-Künstler, Happening- und Performance-Künstler sowie Konzeptkünstler ein.

Nehmen wir das Beispiel von Vito Acconci: Bei seinen Arbeiten kommen eine ganze Reihe verschiedener Medien zur Anwendung: vom traditionellsten Medium bis zu Film, Tonband und Video, ja, sogar bis hin zum Virtuellen, und das in einer historischen Logik und konzeptuellen Kontinuität.

In einem Interview, das er im November 1984 Florence Gilbard für „Afterimage"[2] gegeben hat, spricht Vito Acconci zwei für die Kunst am Ende der sechziger Jahre wichtige The-

reproduction had reached a level on which it began, not only to take the entirety of traditional art as its object, subjecting its effects to profound alterations, but also to achieve status as a distinct and separate means of artistic procedure."[1] In our context, however, it is only the second part of Walter Benjamin's contention that interests us.
The aims of the artists who make use of the various reproduction techniques are, however, by no means identical: Some pursue their own artistic aims from the beginning, without letting the technique restrict them, while others feel it is necessary to experiment with the technological technique per se.
This double perspective always becomes apparent when a new medium for image storage or reproduction comes on the scene, for, from that point on, the interaction with contemporary artistic movements happens in a number of ways. Thus we must ask ourselves if we are justified, from a theoretical point of view, in labeling an art form according to its technical specifications.
The first group of artists appropriate a technical medium – sometimes several, incidentally – and use it as one of many means of artistic creation, without engaging specifically with the tool itself. They adapt the medium to suit their concepts, without really exploring its distinctive features. This is the line taken primarily by most Fluxus artists, Happening and Performance artists as well as conceptual artists.
Let us look at the example of Vito Acconci: He employed a whole series of different media in his work, from the most traditional medium to film, tape and video, even including virtual reality, and all this with historical logic and conceptual continuity.
In an interview given in November 1984 to Florence Gilbard for "Afterimage"[2], Vito Acconci addresses two subjects that are highly relevant to art at the end of the Sixties: "One question was particularly acute at that time, and that was whether the concept of a work of art as a unique piece was in need of

revision (..) Does art reside solely in this unique piece of art, that only a few people have seen, or also in the photographs and articles ?" Following Walter Benjamin, Vito Acconci speaks of calling into question the cultural value of a work of art, of the loss of its aura, of its increased social function. In the same interview, he also raises the question as to the necessity of transition between one medium and another: "I think that at the time I began to use the medium of film (I worked with film even before I worked with video), there was one aspect that particularly interested me: the conventional concept of the frame. It separates, in quite an obvious way, that which is outside the screen from that which is being filmed. It was like a hall of meditation. On the screen I can be alone with myself. One cannot avoid becoming involved with oneself, concentrating on oneself." The point of these works of art is not a preoccupation with the medium itself, but rather the realization of a concept. The necessity of being able to check up on the image in the moment of filming resulted in the use of the medium of video. "That was at the time that I was given the opportunity of working with video. This was how I approached the problem: OK, up till now I have worked with direct performance, I have used photography. What can I do with video that I couldn't have done in the media I have used so far ? At first I concentrated on what immediately suggested itself: on the fact that I could see the action at the moment of its realization, instantaneous feedback, in other words (..) Then I very soon thought of the possibility of involving the spectator in my space (..) The question that preoccupies me is why so many pieces which imply an 'I' were realized as films, while works that involve other people have been produced as videos." [3] The idea of involving the spectator in the work itself made it necessary for the artist to use a medium other than film. So the linear video was gradually transformed into installations which used a number of different elements.

men an: „Eine Frage war damals besonders virulent, und zwar die Frage, ob der Begriff des Kunstwerkes als einzigartiges Werk nicht zu revidieren sei. (...) Liegt die Kunst in diesem einzigartigen Kunstwerk, das nur wenige Personen gesehen haben, oder in den Photographien oder Artikeln?" Im Gefolge von Walter Benjamin spricht Vito Acconci vom Infragestellen des kulturellen Wertes eines Kunstwerkes, vom Verlust der Aura, von seiner verstärkten sozialen Funktion. In diesem Interview schneidet er auch die Frage nach der Notwendigkeit des Übergangs von einem Medium zu einem anderen an: „Ich glaube, daß mich damals, als ich begonnen habe, das Medium Film zu benützen (ich habe den Film sogar vor dem Video benützt), ein Aspekt besonders interessiert hat: der konventionelle Begriff des Rahmens. Dieser trennt auf sehr offensichtliche Weise das, was sich außerhalb der Bildfläche befindet, von dem, was gefilmt wird. Es war wie in einem Meditationssaal. In der Bildfläche kann ich allein mit mir selbst sein. Da kann ich gar nicht anders, als mit mir selbst zu arbeiten, mich auf mich selbst zu konzentrieren." Sinn und Zweck dieser Arbeiten ist nicht eine Beschäftigung mit dem Medium an sich, sondern die Realisation eines Konzeptes. Die Verwendung des Mediums Video ergibt sich aus der Notwendigkeit, das Bild im Moment des Drehens selbst überprüfen zu können. „Das war zu der Zeit, als ich die Gelegenheit bekam, mit Video zu arbeiten. Ich ging auf folgende Art und Weise an dieses Problem heran: OK, bis jetzt habe ich direkte Performances realisiert, ich habe die Photographie benutzt. Was kann ich mit Video machen, was ich mit den bis jetzt verwendeten Medien nicht hätte tun können? Zuerst habe ich mich auf das Naheliegendste konzentriert: auf die Tatsache, daß ich die Aktion simultan zur Realisation sehen konnte, also unmittelbares Feedback. (...) Dann habe ich sehr schnell an die Möglichkeit gedacht, den Betrachter in meinen Raum einzubeziehen. (...) Die Frage, die mich beschäftigt, ist, warum zahlreiche Arbeiten, die das „Ich" implizieren, als Film realisiert wurden, während Arbeiten, die andere Personen miteinbeziehen, als Video produziert wurden."[3] Die Idee, den Betrachter ins Werk mit einzubeziehen, machte für diesen Künstler den Umstieg auf ein anderes Medium als das des Films notwendig. So verwandelte sich das lineare Video schließlich in Installationen, die mehrere Elemente umfaßten.

Nam June Paik, ein unbestrittener Vertreter des Fluxus, hat sich die Videotechnik in allen ihren Feinheiten angeeignet und sie zuerst in seine Klang- und Musikperformances eingebaut. Später hat er damit seine Fernsehbänder und -sendungen entwickelt und schließlich immer komplexere Videoinstallationen gestaltet. Computertechnologie ist immer mit im Spiel, sei es auf dem Niveau der Bearbeitung der Bilder, der Verdichtung des Schnitts oder dem Einbinden mehrerer Bilder und Klänge im Raum der Installationen. Auch wenn Nam June Paik manchmal als Vater der „Videokunst" tituliert wird, so war und bleibt er, was seine Haltung und Produktionsweise betrifft, in erster Linie ein Fluxus-Künstler. Die Verwendung des Begriffs „Videokunst" hat bei diesem Werk umso weniger Sinn, als sich diese Kunstform nicht über eine Technik definiert (die wesentlich komplexer ist, als diese Bezeichnung es vermuten ließe), sondern über klare ästhetische Kriterien.

Eine konzeptuelle Notwendigkeit, ähnlich der bei Vito Acconci begegneten, liegt auch so unterschiedlichen Werken wie denen von James Coleman, Hollis Frampton, Dan Graham, Robert Morris, Bruce Nauman, Andy Warhol usw. zugrunde. Die meisten dieser Künstler bedienen sich verschiedener Formen künstlerischen Ausdrucks: Performance, Film, Video, Musik, Malerei oder Skulptur. Die Medien sind Teil eines ganzen Komplexes evolutiver Praktiken, sie sind eingebettet in einen globalen Prozeß.

Ganz anders ist die Herangehensweise bei jenen Künstlern, die das Bedürfnis verspüren, die vielfältigen Möglichkeiten eines Mediums zu hinterfragen, indem sie die Grenzen des technisch

Nam June Paik, indisputably a representative of the Fluxus movement, appropriated video technology in all its detail and, at first, integrated it into his sound and music performances. Later, he used it to develop his television tapes and programs, and, finally, to create ever more complex video installations. Computer technology always plays a part, be it on the level of manipulating the images, improving editing precision or integrating several images and sound into the installation space. Even if Nam June Paik is sometimes hailed as the father of "video art", he was and is, as far as his attitude and methods of working are concerned, primarily a Fluxus artist. The use of the term "video art" in regard to his work has even less meaning when one considers that this art form is not defined by a technique (much more complex than that definition would make it appear), but by clear aesthetic criteria.

A necessity of conception similar to that which we encountered with Vito Acconci is also the basis of such divergent work as that of James Coleman, Hollis Frampton, Dan Graham, Robert Morris, Bruce Naumann, Andy Warhol and so on. Most of these artists make use of different means of artistic expression: performance, film, video, music, painting and sculpture. The media are simply a part of a whole complex of previously evolved practices, they are embedded within a global process.

The approach of those artists who feel the need to question the many possibilities of a certain medium by constantly straining the limits of the technically possible is quite a different matter. Naturally, some of these artists have also dedicated themselves to another medium in the course of their artistic development. It is seldom the case that an artist restricts him- or herself to a single medium for the course of their entire career. Michael Snow, for instance, has restricted himself in his work – though he uses a number of different techniques – primarily to the machine "film camera" and to the possible resulting variations in perception; in his work, he insistently poses the question as to the role of the viewer. Michael Snow developed his work independently of all other artistic movements of his time, independently, above all, of minimalism and the recent questioning of formalism in North America. It may be precisely because he realized his main projects by means of the communications medium of film that he remained aloof from any aesthetic movement. An "extended" history of art, however, might well compare his work with that of the American minimalists.

The experiments of Peter Campus in the Seventies, too, which ran parallel to the those of certain artists working with the medium of film, sounded out the various possibilities of video tape and all the then achievable effects, both with regard to video and to installations within a closed system.

Campus was intrigued by the following paradigms: light as a material, dissolve and superposition as a language of editing, simultaneity of recording and broadcasting, the screen as a window, the glass as an opaque yet simultaneously transparent mirror, perspective and view-point, the spectator as watcher and doer and so on.

This meticulous work corresponds to the aims of the minimalists, who explored a diversity of industrial materials and their relationships to space and the spectator. The achievements of a Peter Campus might thus be placed in the historical perspective of contemporary art, for the artist used video art as one of precisely those materials of the industrial era which was utilizable for the artist within the critical context of the time.

Nevertheless, Peter Campus' s works were created in isolation and without contact with visual artists using more "traditional" materials, and this for a good ten years. Later he applied himself to photography, and today employs electronic means as well.

Under Bill Viola's aegis, the general interest moved to other areas, that also touch upon phenomenological questions, both in regard to

Machbaren bei jedem Werk weiter hinausschieben. Manche dieser Künstler haben sich freilich im Zuge ihrer Entwicklung auch einem anderen Medium zugewandt. Es ist tatsächlich nur selten der Fall, daß sich ein Künstler während seiner gesamten Laufbahn auf ein einziges Medium beschränkt.

Michael Snow zum Beispiel hat sich in seinen Arbeiten – auch wenn er sich dabei mehrerer Techniken bedient – in erster Linie auf die Maschine „Filmkamera" und die sich dadurch ergebenden Variationen in der Wahrnehmung konzentriert und stellt damit auf sehr eindringliche Weise die Frage nach dem Platz des Zuschauers. Michael Snow hat sein Werk unabhängig von allen anderen künstlerischen Bewegungen seiner Zeit entwickelt, vor allem unabhängig vom Minimalismus und der neuerlichen Infragestellung des Formalismus in Nordamerika. Vielleicht blieb er gerade deswegen außerhalb jeder ästhetischen Bewegung, weil er seine Hauptwerke mittels des Trägermediums Film realisiert hat. Eine „erweiterte" Geschichte der Kunst könnte seine Arbeiten aber in die Nähe der amerikanischen Minimalisten rücken.

Auch die Untersuchungen eines Peter Campus in den siebziger Jahren, die parallel zu den Experimenten gewisser Künstler im Medium Film stattfanden, loteten die verschiedenen Möglichkeiten des Videobandes und alle damals erlaubten Effekte aus, sowohl was das Video als auch Installationen in geschlossenem System betraf.

Campus hat sich für folgende Paradigmen interessiert: das Licht als Material, Überblendung und Überlagerung als Schnittsprache, die Simultaneität von Aufnahme und Sendung, der Bildschirm als Fenster, das Glas als undurchsichtiger und gleichzeitig transparenter Spiegel, die Perspektive und der Standpunkt, der Zuschauer als Akteur und Beobachter usw.

Diese minutiöse Arbeit entspricht auch den Anliegen der Minimalisten, die die unterschiedlichsten industriellen Werkstoffe und deren Beziehung zu Raum und Betrachter erforschten. Das Werk eines Peter Campus könnte sich also in die historischen Perspektiven der Gegenwartskunst einreihen, denn der Künstler hat das Videoband als eines jener Materialen der industriellen Ära benutzt, das für die Künstler im kritischen Kontext der Zeit verwertbar war.

Peter Campus hat aber trotzdem seine Arbeiten isoliert betrieben, ohne Kontakt mit bildenden Künstlern, die „traditionellere" Materialien verwendeten, und das während gut zehn Jahren. Später hat er sich der Photographie zugewandt, wobei er heute auch elektronische Mittel einsetzt.

Unter der Ägide von Bill Viola hat sich dann das Interesse auf andere Bereiche verlagert, die auch phänomenologische Fragen berührten, und zwar sowohl was die Dreharbeiten (Objektivwechsel, Übergang vom Scharfen zum Verschwommenen ...) und den Schnitt (Überblendung, Überlagerung, Auflösung) betraf als auch die Stellung des Betrachters, z. B. bei Installationen. Dabei ging es immer um die Paradigmen Bildschirm, Raum, Bild, Ton.

Gleichzeitig experimentierte Gary Hill, der am Anfang seiner Laufbahn traditioneller Bildhauer war (das von ihm benutzte Material war formbarer Stahl), in einer Serie von Videobändern mit der Gegenüberstellung von geschriebenen bzw. gesprochenen Worten und Bildern. Auf der Suche nach einer akzentuierteren Kommunikation mit dem Betrachter bezog er diese Gegenüberstellung auch in seine Mehrschirminstallationen ein, was es ihm erlaubte, die verschiedenen Möglichkeiten der Immaterialität von Bild und dessen Hardware (Monitor, Videoprojektor, Lautsprecher) zu erforschen.

Diese beiden grundlegend modernen Strömungen haben es dem Medium erlaubt, sein Potential zu entwickeln und sich einen Platz unter jenen künstlerischen Materialien zu sichern, die imstande sind, Sinn zu produzieren, mit Metaphern umzugehen und einer zeitgemäßen Vision der Welt Ausdruck zu verleihen. Sie sind aber auch heute noch isolierte ästhetische Formen, die noch immer auf ihren Platz in einer „erweiterten" Geschichte der Kunst warten.

the filming itself (change of lenses, transition from clear to blurred images ..) and the editing process (dissolves, superpositions, contrast) as well as to the spectator's position, i.e. in installations. Here, the relevant paradigms are always screen, space, image, sound. At the same time, Gary Hill, who was a sculptor working with malleable steel at the start of his career, was experimenting with the juxtaposition of written or spoken words and images in a series of video tapes. In the search for an accentuated form of communication with the viewer, he also integrated this juxtaposition into his multiple-screen installations, allowing him to explore the various possibilities of the non-materiality of the image and its hardware (monitor, video projector, loudspeakers).

These two fundamental movements have allowed the medium to develop its potential and secure a place among those artistic materials capable of producing meaning, dealing in metaphor and expressing a contemporary vision of our world. Yet even today, they are isolated aesthetic forms, still awaiting their place in an "extended" history of art.

In the meantime, we have learned that we can easily place the forms of expression of other multimedia artists within a historical perspective. Yet this integration into history is less obvious with those works that experiment with the technological technique itself, particularly if we are dealing with modern technology (computer graphics, VR etc.). The main reasons for this momentary isolation are that these technological systems are in a constant state of flux and further development, and that this research, furthermore, is carried out by technicians or scientists, who have complete control over the different areas of application, but often know nothing at all about the current artistic context. We may be justified in asking whether this relative innocence is actually necessary for successful experimentation.

Perhaps it really is time we defined new criteria for this kind of work, analyzed the degree of hybridization (if this is indeed the case) and examined which elements are leading to breakthroughs, which are continuing a tradition, as well as undertaking precise analysis and criticism. Up until now, we have been able to establish that whenever a new kind of technology appears, critics avoid thorough analysis of the works of art that have been thus produced – an analysis whereby, sooner or later, new criteria might be established. The very fact that an artist or experimenter is using a reproductive technique seems to exempt him or her from the critical gaze. This means that contemporary critics of technical experiments either merely take stock or else completely and utterly reject them. As far as I know, no analytical, critical approach to these fields exists, which consequently take no further interest in any kind of artistic debate and isolate themselves in technical complacency. The symposium held in Karlsruhe in May 1995 was one of the first attempts at laying down new criteria. "We take a model of the eye and ear as our starting-point, in order to move towards models of mental processes, of the conceptual structure of the brain. This will give conceptual art a whole new meaning", writes Bill Viola[4]. It is evident that throughout the various phases of artists' appropriation of the media, critics have done their best to describe these projects and to perceive only their positive aspects; it is equally evident that they have made no effort to compare and contrast these pieces of work with those from other artistic fields or to place them in a wider aesthetic context, or even to lay down general assessment criteria.

II. INSTITUTIONAL STRUCTURES

After discovering the media for themselves, the artists of the Sixties and Seventies began to move into museums of modern art. The museums of Europe and North America (Kölnischer Kunstverein, Köln; Folkwang Museum, Essen; Everson Museum, Everson; MOMA, New York; ICA, London and Boston;

Seit damals wissen wir, daß wir ohne Schwierigkeiten auch die Ausdrucksformen anderer Multimedia-Künstler in eine historische Perspektive einbeziehen können. Diese Einbeziehung in die Geschichte ist bei jenen Arbeiten weniger offensichtlich, die mit der Technologie selbst experimentieren, vor allem wenn es sich um moderne Technologien (Computergraphik, VR usw.) handelt. Die Hauptgründe für diese vorübergehende Isolierung liegen darin, daß diese Technologien sich in stetem Fluß befinden und noch in der Entwicklung stehen und auch darin, daß diese Forschungen von Technikern oder Wissenschaftlern betrieben werden, die die verschiedenen Anwendungen zwar perfekt beherrschen, aber oft nichts über den aktuellen künstlerischen Kontext wissen. Wir können uns also die Frage stellen, ob diese relative Unschuld für ein erfolgreiches Experimentieren notwendig ist.

Es ist jetzt vielleicht doch an der Zeit, neue Kriterien für diese Art von Arbeiten zu definieren, den Grad an Hybridisierung (falls dies überhaupt der Fall ist) zu analysieren und die Elemente zu untersuchen, die zu einem Bruch führen bzw. die Kontinuität wahren, sowie eine minutiöse Analyse und Kritik vorzunehmen. Bis jetzt haben wir nämlich feststellen können, daß immer dann, wenn eine neue Technologie aufkommt, die Kritik es unterläßt, die damit entstandenen Arbeiten einer echten Analyse zu unterziehen, wodurch sich nach und nach aber neue Kriterien entwickeln könnten. Die Tatsache, daß der Künstler oder Experimentator eine Technik der Reproduktion anwendet, scheint ihn vom kritischen Blick auszunehmen. So liefert die aktuelle Kritik der technischen Experimente entweder nur eine Bestandsaufnahme, oder aber sie lehnt sie in Bausch und Bogen ab. So weit ich informiert bin, gibt es zur Zeit keine analytische, kritische Annäherung an diese Bereiche, die sich infolgedessen auch nicht an der künstlerischen Auseinandersetzung beteiligen und sich in technischer Selbstzufriedenheit isolieren. Das im Mai 1995 im ZKM in Karlsruhe abgehaltene Symposium war einer der ersten Versuche, neue Kriterien festzulegen.

„Wir gehen von einem Modell des Auges und des Ohres aus, um uns auf Modelle des geistigen Prozesses, der konzeptuellen Struktur des Gehirns hinzubewegen. Die Konzeptkunst wird dadurch einen neuen Sinn bekommen", schreibt Bill Viola[4].

Während der verschiedenen Phasen der künstlerischen Aneignung der Medien haben wir feststellen können, daß die Kritik sich zwar bemüht hat, die Werke zu beschreiben und nur deren positive Aspekte wahrzunehmen, jedoch nicht versucht hat, diese Werke in einen Dialog mit solchen aus anderen Kunstsparten in bezug zu setzen oder sie in einen erweiterten ästhetischen Kontext zu stellen bzw. allgemeine Kriterien festzulegen.

II. INSTITUTIONELLE STRUKTUREN

Nachdem die Künstler die Medien in den sechziger und siebziger Jahren für sich entdeckt haben, haben sie auch in den Museen moderner Kunst Einzug gehalten. Die europäischen und nordamerikanischen Museen (Kölnischer Kunstverein, Köln; Folkwang Museum, Essen; Everson Museum, Everson; MOMA, New York; ICA, London und Boston; Long Beach Museum, Long Beach; Palais des Beaux-Arts, Brüssel; Musée d'art moderne d'Ottawa, Kanada; Musée national d'art moderne, Paris usw.) waren die ersten, die sich für diese zeitgenössische Kunstform interessierten. Je nach Institution erfolgte die Annäherung aber auf sehr unterschiedliche Art und Weise.

Gewisse Museen haben spezielle dafür verantwortliche Abteilungen geschaffen; es wurden neben den Abteilungen für Malerei, Bildhauerei oder Graphik Abteilungen für Photographie, Film und Video geschaffen. Das MOMA z. B. hat im Jahre 1935 ein Department „Film" eingerichtet, das die wichtigste und umfangreichste Filmsammlung beherbergt und nicht nur Experimental- und Kunstfilme umfaßt, sondern auch Spiel- und Dokumentarfilme. Diese Abteilung funktioniert unabhängig von allen anderen Bereichen des Museums und entwickelt ihre

Long Beach Museum, Long Beach; Palais des Beaux-Arts, Brussels; Musé d' art moderne d' Ottawa, Canada; Musé national d'art moderne, Paris, and so on) were the first to become interested in this contemporary art form. The different institutions, however, approached the field in a variety of ways. Certain museums created specific sections; alongside the departments of painting, sculpture and graphics, they created departments for photography, film and video. The MOMA, for instance, created a film department in 1935 which now contains the single most important and comprehensive collection of films, not only experimental and art films, but also feature and documentary films.
This department functions separately from all other areas of the museum, and develops its own thematic focuses and touring exhibitions. Later on, video art was given its own subdivision within the department. This decision had important consequences, in as far as the compilation of the video collection of the MOMA was concerned. Films and video tapes were collected, but the MOMA could not purchase video installations and similar structures, for this is actually impossible for a department centered around films and working according to the rules of cinema. Quite apart from this, one must realize how very few truly interdisciplinary projects, in which the context would have been productive for such works, existed at that time. And one must note that projects based on modern technology are equally underrepresented today.
The project of the Musé national d'art moderne in Paris might have followed the same pattern. Thanks to the associations with other contemporary art forms in the field of video, however, the museum succeeded in forming an impressive collection of video installations, and in expanding these further in the direction of those technological techniques that are still being created today. This opening for future works took place without clashing, either on an institutional

or an aesthetic level, with those works conceived for other media, while still providing the possibility of expansion necessary for an understanding of contemporary artists and their work.

Smaller institutions, such as the Long Beach Museum in Long Beach (Los Angeles) or the Palazzo dei Diamanti in Ferrara (Italy), have succeeded, thanks to their size and to the personal enthusiasm of those responsible, not only in forming collections and organizing events, but also in producing in their own studios and supporting artists in their work.

Other museums have no desire to create separate departments at all, but have nevertheless organized events connected to the media and formed collections which include representative technically reproducible pieces. This type of structure tends to have caught on in museums whose dimensions allow it. The Stedelijk Museum in Amsterdam, the MOCA in Los Angeles and the Walker Art Center in Minneapolis have organized a number of monographic and theme exhibitions on film or video artists and integrated reproducible art into their collections and festivals. There, however, there are no specialized departments; instead, there are curators responsible for those fields, which they supervise along with other areas. Edy de Wilde, the director of the Stedelijk Museum, stated in his introduction to the catalogue „The Luminous Image“ [5] in 1984 that the museum continually takes note of the medium of video, though not because the medium per se has any inherent artistic value, but because so many important artists have occupied themselves with it.

Without wishing to draw any final conclusions at this stage, one might say that in general, large, museum-like structures that are organized into departments or sections tend to form collections around a specific communications medium, while failing to purchase or exhibit hybrid works or to integrate current, more sensitive developments in the area of media art. Specialists,

eigenen Themenschwerpunkte und Wanderzyklen. Videokunst wurde später als Unterabteilung dem Department Film angeschlossen. Diese Entscheidung zog wichtige Konsequenzen nach sich, was die Zusammenstellung der Video-Sammlung des MOMA betrifft. Es wurden nämlich in diese Sammlung Filme und Videobänder aufgenommen, aber das MOMA konnte keine Videoinstallationen und ähnliches erwerben, denn dies ist in einer für Film zuständigen, nach den Regeln des Kinos funktionierenden Abteilung tatsächlich unmöglich.

Außerdem kann man feststellen, daß nur sehr wenige interdisziplinäre Projekte aus der Zeit, in der der Kontext solchen Arbeiten förderlich war, existieren. Und heute müssen wir bemerken, daß Projekte, die auf den modernen Technologien basieren, ebenfalls sehr unterrepräsentiert sind.

Das Projekt des Pariser Musée national d'art moderne hätte dem gleichen Szenario folgen können. Dort jedoch ist es dank der Verknüpfung mit zeitgenössischen Kunstformen im Bereich Video gelungen, eine bedeutende Sammlung von Videoinstallationen aufzubauen und diese in Richtung jener Technologien zu erweitern, die heute erst im Entstehen begriffen sind. Diese Öffnung für zukünftige Werke hat stattgefunden, ohne daß es auf institutioneller oder ästhetischer Ebene zu einem Bruch mit den für andere Medien konzipierten Werken gekommen wäre, sie bietet aber jene Erweiterung, die für ein Verständnis der zeitgenösisschen Künstler und ihrer Werke notwendig ist.

Kleinen Strukturen, wie es z. B. das Long Beach Museum in Long Beach (Los Angeles) oder der Palazzo dei Diamanti in Ferrara (Italien) sind, ist es dank ihrer Größe und des Engagements der Verantwortlichen gelungen, nicht nur Sammlungen einzurichten und Veranstaltungen zu organisieren, sondern in hauseigenen Studios auch selbst zu produzieren bzw. Künstler in ihrer Arbeit zu unterstützen.

Andere Museen wollten überhaupt keine eigenen Abteilungen schaffen, haben aber trotzdem Veranstaltungen mit

Medienbezug organisiert und Sammlungen aufgebaut, in denen technisch reproduzierbare Werke vertreten sind. Dieser Strukturtypus hat sich vor allem dort durchgesetzt, wo es aufgrund der Dimensionen des Museums möglich war. Das Stedelijk Museum in Amsterdam, das MOCA in Los Angeles und das Walker Art Center in Minneapolis haben etliche monographische und themenzentrierte Ausstellungen über Film- oder Videokünstler organisiert und reproduzierbare Kunstwerke in ihre Sammlungen und Veranstaltungen integriert. Dort gibt es aber keine spezialisierten Abteilungen, sondern Kuratoren, die für diese Bereiche zuständig sind, daneben aber auch noch andere Aufgaben wahrnehmen. Edy de Wilde, der Leiter des Stedelijk Museum, hat 1984 in der Einleitung zum Katalog „The Luminous Image"[5] festgehalten, daß das Museum dem Medium Video kontinuierlich Beachtung schenkt, aber nicht deswegen, weil das Medium als solches irgendeine künstlerische Bedeutung hätte, sondern weil zahlreiche wichtige Künstler sich damit beschäftigt haben.

Ohne nun irgendeinen endgültigen Schluß ziehen zu wollen, können wir doch festhalten, daß große, nach Abteilungen organisierte museale Strukturen am Trägermedium orientierte Sammlungen aufbauen, aber keine hybriden Werke erwerben oder ausstellen und auch die aktuelleren sensiblen Entwicklungen im Bereich der Medien nicht integrieren. Dagegen sind Spezialisten die Garanten dafür, daß Fragen der Restaurierung, der Aufbewahrung und Präsentation eine Lösung finden.

Bescheidenere Musuemsstrukturen hingegen haben die Möglichkeit, Werke zu fördern, die zwischen den Kunstformen angesiedelt sind und von Künstlern stammen, die Brücken zwischen den Kunstformen schlagen und sich den „richtigen" Ort suchen, nämlich einen, an dem sich die verschiedenen Ausdrucksformen begegnen können.

„Denn der Ort, von dem Godard zu uns spricht, von dem er uns mahnt, ist gewiß nicht der sichere Ort einer Berufssparte, ja, nicht einmal der eines persönlichen Projektes; es ist ein Ort,

on the other hand, can guarantee that solutions are found for questions of restoration, collection and presentation.

More modest museum structures, for their part, have the opportunity of encouraging works situated between artistic genres and produced by artists engaged upon forging connections between art forms, searching for an place which feels „right" for them; one where different forms of expression can meet.

„For the place from which Godard speaks to us, from which he admonishes us, is by no means the safe environment of a definite profession, why, not even that of a specific personal project; it is a place which lies between two or even three areas, an uncomfortable place, which includes photography (the art of the 19th century) as well as cinema (the art of the 20th century) and television (the art of the 21st century)" – Serge Daney writing on Jean-Luc Godard.[6]

The questions which remain unanswered, however, are the museological ones concerning presentation in- and outside the framework of the museum as an institution. Faced with the new technological techniques flooding the market at present, we must be prepared to question things we have always taken for granted, the presentation of works in the museums themselves, for instance, the passive attitude of the audience or the now definitively passé question as to the unique nature of a piece of art.

The system of selection, too, is in for some changes. Works of art will no longer be chosen as separate pieces, but according to whether or not they form a coherent ensemble. New spaces in which such ensemble collections are accessible – whether these be video tapes, hypermedia or digital films – will correspond to the availability of the audience, their wish to obtain information on their own and the ability to manipulate works themselves. This model is that of the library. Alongside this model, however, the model of the exhibition will continue to exist, be it for extant or future works of art.

III. EDUCATIONAL ISSUES

In France, no training for media curators exists. Neither at the Ecole du Patrimonie nor at the Ecole du Louvre is there any course of education that concerns itself with the conservation or restoration of media art. Today, all one can do is arrange one' s own curriculum, graduating in an all-round course of study for art historians or art aesthetes, supplementing this with courses at schools specializing in media or computer art and practical experience at an institution or with artists who appreciate the problem.
In the face of the multiple developments in the field of media art, it is imperative to create a course of education specializing in this particular art form, with regard to both conservation and restoration.

IV. FESTIVALS AND EVENTS

There were and are a number of different events dedicated to media art. While in the field of more traditional art forms, a update on recent artistic creations and available pieces is provided by means of collective or single exhibitions, more alternative events or trade fairs, mechanically reproducible works are either presented in the context of festivals, organized like film festivals, or of exhibitions, conceived like exhibitions on plastic arts.

A. FESTIVALS

Different festivals in a number of countries regularly provide an overall perspective on current artistic creation in the field of media art, be this film, video, installations, hypermedia or new technologies. The festivals which have so far played a vital role for the artists themselves and their integration into collections and museum exhibitions include: the "Festival international du Jeune Cinéma" in Hyères, the "International Film Festival" in Knokke/Heist, the "National Video Festival"

der zwischen zwei oder sogar drei Bereichen liegt, es ist ein unbequemer Ort, der sowohl Photographie (die Kunst des 19. Jh.) als auch Kino (die Kunst des 20. Jh.) und Fernsehen (die Kunst des 21. Jh.) umfaßt", schreibt Serge Daney über Jean-Luc Godard [6].

Ungelöst sind allerdings noch museologische Fragen, die die Präsentation inner- oder außerhalb des Rahmens der Institution Museum betreffen. Angesichts der neuen Technologien, die zur Zeit auf den Markt drängen, müssen wir uns darauf gefaßt machen, daß in Zukunft gewisse für uns selbstverständliche Gegebenheiten in Frage gestellt werden, z. B. die Präsentation von Werken in den Museen selbst, die passive Haltung des Publikums oder die nun definitiv überholte Frage nach der Einzigartigkeit eines Kunstwerkes.

Auch das Selektionssystem wird sich dadurch in Zukunft verändern. Die Werke werden nicht mehr als Einzelwerke ausgewählt, sondern danach, ob sie ein kohärentes Ensemble bilden. Neue Räume, in denen solche Werkensembles zugänglich sind – seien es nun Videobänder, Hypermedia oder digitaler Film – entsprechen der Verfügbarkeit des Publikums, seinem Bedürfnis, sich Informationen eigenständig beschaffen und Werke selbst manipulieren zu können. Das Modell dahinter ist das Modell der Bibliotheken. Daneben wird aber auch das Modell „Ausstellung" weiter seine Funktion behalten, sei es für bereits existierende oder auch zukünftige Werke.

III. PÄDAGOGIK

In Frankreich existiert keine Ausbildung für Medien-Kuratoren. Bis heute gibt es weder an der Ecole du Patrimoine noch an der Ecole du Louvre eine Ausbildung, die sich mit Konservierung oder Restaurierung von Medienkunstwerken beschäftigen würde.

Es ist heute lediglich möglich, sich sein eigenes Curriculum zusammenzustellen, indem man ein allgemeines Studium für Kunsthistoriker oder Kunstästheten absolviert und als Zusatzausbildung Kurse an Schulen, die sich auf Medien- oder Computerkunst spezialisiert haben, belegt und Praktika in einer Institution oder bei Künstlern, die dieser Problematik Aufmerksamkeit schenken, absolviert.

Angesichts der vielfältigen Entwicklungen im Bereich der Medienkunst wäre es aber dringend notwendig, eine auf diese Kunstform spezialisierte Ausbildung, und zwar sowohl was Konservierung als auch Restaurierung betrifft, zu schaffen.

IV. VERANSTALTUNGEN

Verschiedene Arten von Veranstaltungen waren bzw. sind der Medienkunst gewidmet. Während im Bereich traditionellerer Kunstformen kollektive oder Einzelausstellungen, alternative Veranstaltungen oder kommerzielle Messen einen gewissen Stand des künstlerischen Schaffens und der verfügbaren Werke dokumentieren, werden die mechanisch reproduzierbaren Werke entweder im Rahmen von Festivals präsentiert, die nach dem Muster von Filmfestivals organisiert sind, oder bei Ausstellungen, die wie Ausstellungen über bildende Kunst konzipiert sind.

A. FESTIVALS

Verschiedene Festivals in mehreren Ländern geben regelmäßig einen Überblick über das aktuelle Kunstschaffen im Bereich Medien, seien das nun Film, Video, Installationen, Hypermedien oder neue Technologien. Die Festivals, die bisher eine wichtige Rolle für die Künstler selbst und deren Integration in Sammlungen und Museumsausstellungen gespielt haben, sind unter anderem: das „Festival international du Jeune Cinéma" („Internationales Festival für jungen Film") in Hyères, das „International Film Festival" in Knokke/Heist, das „National Video Festival" des American Film Institute in Los Angeles, das „Festival de Vidéo et Télévision" in Montbéliard, die „Videonale" in Bonn, das „Videofest Medien Operative" in Berlin, das „World Wide Video Festival" in La

of the American Film Institute in Los Angeles, the "Festival de Vidéo et Télévision" in Montbéliard, the "Videonale" in Bonn, the "Videofest Medien Operative" in Berlin, the "World Wide Film Festival" in La Haye, the "Semaine internationale de Vidéo" in Geneva, the "WRO" in Wroclaw, the video department of the "Festival international" in San Sébastian, the "Festival nacional de Video" in Madrid, the "Ars Electronica" in Linz, the "Art Futura" in Barcelona, the "Imagina" in Monte Carlo, the various "ISEA" and so on. (There have also been other festivals, which are mainly for television production or graphic applications, however.)
These festivals supplied or still do supply a useful overall view of artistic creativity being implemented at a particular moment in time. These numerous festivals, which tend to have limited life-spans, take over from each other or evolve gradually by beginning to include, bit by bit, other technological techniques. The current tendency of these events is towards inclusion of all kinds of technological techniques for the creation of mechanically reproducible works of art – video, new technologies, installations, hypermedia etc.

B. EXHIBITIONS

International, theme exhibitions have had a fundamental impact on the progress in theoretical reflection and artistic creation per se.
The term "alternative", current in the 60s and 70s (artists seized upon film and video as a reaction to the overpowering influence of capitalism, to the influence and omnipresence of television); the belief in progress that dominated in the late 70s and early 80s (machines substantially improved human living conditions); the alarming increase of "spectacle" in the society of the 70s and 80s and the disillusionment that followed in the 90s as a result of the economic recession and major geopolitical changes (which had no influence on the intensified research on new

communications techniques, however) – those are the aspects that determine the history of technically reproducible art, and at the same time, the development of an aesthetic theory of contemporary art. This double history of ideas, which, nevertheless, does not seem paradoxical, has brought about a certain number of events.

Irrespective of the position or non-position of the host institutions, international events such as the "Documenta V" or "Documenta VII" in Kassel, the "Prospect 71" and the biennials of Whitney, also including some of the Venice biennials – not to forget Harald Szeemann's inspirational 1969 exhibition "When attitude becomes form" – have presented media art and film/video, along with other works (installations, painting, sculpture).

Apart from a number of single exhibitions, there were two exhibitions in Europe in the 80s which established video and its related techniques as acknowledged and indisputable art forms: "The Luminous Image" in the Stedelijk Museum in Amsterdam (1984) and "Videoskulptur" in the Kunstverein of Cologne (1989).

In their wake, the necessity of intensifying the relationships between the contemporary plastic arts and media art became evident. It was this necessity that led to the 1989 exhibition "Passages de l' image" in the Musée national d'art moderne, which attempted to create some kind of connection between the plastic arts in general and photography, cinema, video, even – very cautiously – the latest technologies. The three curators – namely Raymond Bellour, Caterine David and myself – of this international exhibition, which also offered a cinema and video program, formulated their opinions a little late, in 1989 (the exhibition was conceived in 1985/86): "This exhibition came about as a result of the desire to understand what has happened in and between the images since the moment it became clear that one could no longer say "This is cinema,

Haye, die „Semaine internationale de Vidéo" („Internationale Woche des Video") in Genf, das „WRO" in Wroclaw, die Abteilung Video des „Festival international" in San Sébastien, das „Festival nacional de Video" in Madrid, die „Ars Electronica" in Linz, die „Art Futura" in Barcelona, die „Imagina" in Monte Carlo, die verschiedenen „ISEA" usw. (Es gab oder gibt auch andere Festivals, die aber in erster Linie für Fernsehproduktionen oder graphische Anwendungen gedacht sind.)

Diese Festivals lieferten oder liefern noch immer einen guten Überblick über das Kunstschaffen in dem Moment, in dem dieses Gestalt annimmt.

Diese zahlreichen Festivals, die im allgemeinen eine begrenzte Lebensdauer haben, lösen einander ab oder entwickeln sich, indem sie nach und nach auch andere Technologien mit einbeziehen. Die aktuelle Tendenz dieser Veranstaltungen geht dahin, sich allen Arten von Technologien zur Schaffung mechanisch reproduzierbarer Kunstwerke – Video, neue Technologien, Installationen, Hypermedien usw. – zu öffnen.

B. AUSSTELLUNGEN

Internationale Themenausstellungen haben wesentlich zum Fortschritt in der theoretischen Reflexion und im Kunstschaffen an sich beigetragen.

Der Begriff des „Alternativen" der sechziger und siebziger Jahre (die Künstler bemächtigten sich des Films und des Videos als Reaktion auf die Übermacht des Kapitalismus, auf die Macht und Allgegenwart des Fernsehens); der Fortschrittsglauben, der gegen Ende der siebziger und Anfang der achtziger Jahre herrschte (die Maschine verbessert die Lebensbedingungen des Menschen); das Überhandnehmen des „Spektakels" in der Gesellschaft der siebziger und achtziger Jahre und die Ernüchterung, die sich in den neunziger Jahren im Zuge der wirtschaftlichen Rezession und der geopolitischen Umwälzungen einstellte, was aber die Forcierung neuer Kommunikationstechniken nicht beeinträchtigte – das sind jene Aspekte, die die Geschichte der technisch reproduzierbaren Kunstwerke und parallel dazu die Entwicklung einer ästhetischen Theorie der zeitgenössischen Kunst bestimmten. Diese doppelte Geschichte der Ideen, die sich dennoch nicht als eine paradoxe Geschichte präsentiert, hat eine gewisse Anzahl an Veranstaltungen hervorgebracht.

Unabhängig von der jeweiligen Position oder Nicht-Position der Institutionen haben internationale Veranstaltungen wie die „Documenta V" oder „Documenta VII" in Kassel, die „Prospect 71" in Köln und die Biennalen des Whitney oder auch gewisse Biennalen von Venedig – nicht zu vergessen die wegweisende Ausstellung „When attitude becomes form" von Harald Szeemann im Jahre 1969 – Medienkunstwerke und Film/Video, eingestreut unter anderen Werken (Installationen, Malerei, Skulptur), präsentiert.

Abgesehen von vielen Einzelausstellungen, haben in Europa in den achtziger Jahren zwei Ausstellungen das Video und Arbeiten, die auf verwandten Techniken basieren, als seitdem unbestrittene Kunstform etabliert: „The Luminous Image" im Amsterdamer Stedelijk Museum (1984) und „Videoskulptur" im Kölnischen Kunstverein (1989).

Im Anschluß daran wurde die Notwendigkeit spürbar, die Beziehungen zwischen zeitgenössischer bildender Kunst im allgemeinen und Medienkunst zu vertiefen. Aus dieser Notwendigkeit heraus entstand 1989 die Ausstellung „Passages de l'image" im Musée national d'art moderne, die versuchte, einen Zusammenhang zwischen der bildenden Kunst allgemein und Photographie, Kino, Video und – noch sehr vorsichtig – den neuen Technologien herzustellen. Die drei Kuratoren dieser internationalen Ausstellung, die auch ein Kino/Video-Programm bot – Raymond Bellour, Catherine David und ich – haben schon etwas spät, nämlich erst 1989 (das Konzept für diese Ausstellung wurde 1985/86 erarbeitet) gemeint, „diese Ausstellung sei aus dem Wunsch entstanden, das zu verstehen,

that's photography or painting"; for it had finally come to a crisis of the image, which touched upon its very nature. This crisis began, as is well known, with photography, that is to say, with the mechanical reproduction of the world, and spread from there to the idea of art per se. With the appearance of new technical means of producing and reproducing images, this crisis has increased. And prompted one new question after another".[7]
In the same year, the American exhibition "A Forest of Signs (Art in the Crisis of Representation)" was opened at the MOCA in Los Angeles, an exhibition concerning itself more with the question of transforming reality into an ensemble of new signs. Anne Rorimer wrote in the catalogue text that "the artists of the 80s have profited by the methodology and theoretical innovations of their predecessors. Nevertheless, these artists have redefined the main works of their predecessors by taking reality as a direct experience as their starting point, for their work denies any immediate point of contact with existing reality and sees its own reality in representation itself (..) The artists of the 80s concern themselves with the unrealities of current reality by attempting to pin down meaning through a diversity of representational signs".[8]
In 1990, the Whitney American Museum of Art in New York organized the exhibition "Image World", which was concerned with the omnipresent influence of advertising and of the influence of the communications media on the contemporary artist:"...for they force the artist to enter into a relationship with media culture, to explore its ideological potential and its seductive materialism, in order to redefine art".
Exhibitions with a more historical bent, which dedicate themselves to specific artistic movements – for instance, "BLAM (The Explosion of Pop, Minimalsim and Performance 1958-1964)" in the Whitney in 1984; the exhibition "Fluxus", in the Walker Art

Center in Minneapolis in 1993; "L' Art conceptuel, une perspective" in the ARC, Musée d' art moderne de la Ville de Paris; or "Peinture/Cinéma/Peinture" in Marseille; the second biannual of contemporary art in Lyon in 1993, "Et tous ils changent le monde" (And all of them change the world) – just to mention a few – have created real connections and relationships between the separate art forms by newly placing the entirety of artistic efforts into the context of time.

It may seem that this area has been the subject of enough research; but it has a long way to go before being exhausted – both on a historical level (cross-references and re-adjustments have yet to be made) and on a contemporary level. Cross-connections can now be defined with greater precision.

A consolidation of the contact points between the plastic arts and "technically reproducible" art should give cause for a historically orientated showing that has, however, never yet been achieved. The history has yet to be written. The whole history of art has yet to be created.

was seit jenem Augenblick, in dem klar wurde, daß man nicht mehr wie früher sagen konnte 'Hier Kino, dort Foto oder Malerei', in und zwischen den Bildern passiert ist, denn es war endgültig zu einer Krise des Bildes gekommen, die das Wesen des Bildes selbst berührt. Diese Krise hat bekanntlicherweise mit der Photographie begonnen, d. h. mit der mechanischen Reproduktion der Welt, und sich dann auf die Idee der Kunst an sich ausgeweitet. Mit dem Aufkommen neuer Techniken zur Produktion und Reproduktion von Bildern hat sich diese Krise seit damals weiter verschärft. Und immer neue Fragen aufgeworfen." [7]

Im gleichen Jahr wurde im MOCA in Los Angeles die amerikanische Ausstellung „A Forest of Signs (Art in the Crisis of Representation)" eröffnet, die sich mehr mit der Frage der Transformation der Wirklichkeit in ein Ensemble neuer Zeichen beschäftigte. Anne Rorimer hat im Text zum Katalog geschrieben, daß „die Künstler der 80er Jahre von einer Methodik und von theoretischen Innovationen ihrer Vorgänger profitieren. Diese Künstler haben aber nichtsdestotrotz die wesentlichen Arbeiten ihrer Vorgänger neu definiert, indem sie von der Realität als direkter Erfahrung ausgehen, denn ihre Arbeit leugnet jeden unmittelbaren Berührungspunkt mit der existierenden Realität und sieht ihre eigene Realität in der Repräsentation. (...). Die Künstler der 80er Jahre beschäftigen sich mit den Unwirklichkeiten der aktuellen Wirklichkeit, indem sie versuchen, durch eine Vielfalt von Repräsentationszeichen einen Sinn festzumachen." [8]

1990 organisierte das Whitney American Museum of Art in New York die Ausstellung „Image World", die sich mit dem Einfluß der allgegenwärtigen Werbung und der Kommunikationsmittel auf die zeitgenössischen Künstler auseinandersetzte, „da sie die Künstler zwingen, Beziehungen mit der Medienkultur auszuhandeln, ihr ideologisches Potential und ihren verführerischen Materialismus zu erforschen, um die Kunst neu zu definieren."

Ausstellungen mit mehr historischer Ausrichtung, die sich künstlerischen Bewegungen widmen – z. B. „BLAM (The Explosion of Pop, Minimalism, and Performance 1958-1964" im Whitney im Jahr 1984, die Ausstellung „Fluxus", 1993 im Walker Art Center in Minneapolis, „L'Art conceptuel, une perspective" („Konzeptkunst, eine Perspektive") 1989 im ARC, Musée d'art moderne de la Ville de Paris, oder „Peinture/ Cinéma/Peinture" („Malerei/Kino/Malerei") in Marseille, die zweite Biennale zeitgenössischer Kunst („Et tous il changent le monde" – „Und alle verändern sie die Welt") in Lyon im Jahr 1993 – um nur einige anzuführen – haben echte Beziehungen zwischen den einzelnen Kunstformen aufgebaut, indem sie alle künstlerischen Bestrebungen neu in den Kontext der Zeit gestellt haben.

Obwohl es so scheint, als wäre dieses Gebiet ohnehin gut erforscht, ist es noch lange nicht erschöpft, weder auf geschichtlicher Ebene (Bezüge müssen noch hergestellt werden, Anpassungen vorgenommen werden) noch auf zeitgenössischer Ebene. Querverbindungen könnten nunmehr präziser definiert werden. Eine Vertiefung der Berührungspunkte zwischen bildender Kunst und „technisch reproduzierbarer" Kunst sollte eigentlich Anlaß für eine geschichtlich orientierte Schau sein, die bis dato aber noch nicht gemacht wurde. Die Geschichte muß noch gemacht werden. Die ganze Geschichte der Kunst muß noch gemacht werden.

1 Walter Benjamin, Das Kunstwerk im Zeitalter seiner technischen Reproduzierbarkeit, edition suhrkamp, Frankfurt 1963, S.11

2 Interview mit Vito Acconci in: Videoworks 1970-78, Afterimage, Rochester, November 1984

3 ebenda

4 Bill Viola, Y aura-t-il copropriété dans l'espace des données? in: Vidéo, Communications, Nr. 48, Paris 1988

5 The Luminous Image, Katalog des Stedelijk Museum Amsterdam, 1984

6 Serge Daney, Le Terrorisé, in: La Rampe, ed. Cahiers du Cinéma, Paris 1983

7 Raymond Bellour, Catherine David, Christine Van Assche, Vorwort zu: Passage le l'image, Musée national d'art moderne, Centre Georges Pompidou, Paris 1989

8 Anne Rorimer, Photography – Language – Context: Prelude to the 1980s, in: A Forest of Signs (Art in the Crisis of Representation), MOCA, Los Angeles 1989

Video, Bilder, Ambiente, Objekte

VITTORIO FAGONE

VIDEO, IMAGES, AMBIANCE, OBJECTS

Birth and Genesis of a New Art

VIDEO ART

The 30 or so years that video research has been conducted – depending on whether we consider the exhibition at Parnass Gallery in Wuppertal (1963) as the starting point, or the film that Nam June Paik produced with the PortPack from Sony in New York (1965) – may be regarded today as the extraordinary and still creatively productive era that determined the genesis and rapid development of a new art genre.

On the other hand, it appears that of all the avant-garde forms that characterized the artistic scene of the 60's and 70's, "videography" is the only one that still shows no signs of fatigue or interruption. It was probably not even avant-garde in the narrow sense of the word – exclusive and aggressive – or else it was not only avant-garde, but rather a varied type of interaction – on the side of communicative expression, with the technological changes in the creation and distribution of images that was no longer to be checked.

Three generations of artists with their differently oriented creative work may illustrate the three decades of video art. The first generation is that of Nam June Paik and Wolf Vostell: this is the generation that first tried out the possibilities of working on an electronic image, of large-scale communication by means of a clever game of manipulation, even before there was access to autonomous instruments of video production. They led iconoclastic strategies to a new area of research, strategies engaged in a dialogue tending toward an innovative multimedia horizon: this was the generation of the "Fluxus Movement". The second generation, including artists such as Bill Viola, Gary Hill and many others on both sides of the Atlantic, intended to plumb the depths of

Geburt und Genesis einer neuen Kunst

DIE VIDEO-KUNST

Die 30 (oder etwas mehr) Jahre, die die Video-Forschung nun zählt – je nachdem, ob man als Ausgangspunkt die Ausstellung in der Galerie Parnass in Wuppertal (1963) oder den Film nimmt, den Nam June Palk mit dem PortPack von Sony in New York (1965) hergestellt hat, können heute als jene angesehen werden, außerordentlich und auf kreativer Ebene noch produktiv, die die Genesis und schnelle Entwicklung einer neuen Kunstgattung ausgemacht haben.

Auf der anderen Seite erscheint es evident, daß von den Avantgarde-Formen welche die künstlerische Szene in den sechziger und siebziger Jahren ausgemacht haben, die „Videographie" die einzige ist, die keine Zeichen von Müdigkeit und Unterbrechungen zeigt. Wahrscheinlich war sie auch keine Avantgarde im engeren Sinne des Begriffs, exklusiv und aggressiv, oder sie war nicht nur eine Avantgarde, sondern eher eine unterschiedliche Art der Interaktion, auf der Seite des kommunikativen Ausdrucks, mit der nicht eindämmbaren technologischen Veränderung beim Ausformen und Verbreiten von Bildern.

Die drei Jahrzehnte der Video-Kunst können auch die verschiedene Orientierung der kreativen Arbeit von drei Künstlergenerationen aufzeigen. Die erste, die von Nam June Palk und Wolf Vostell, die die Möglichkeit der Arbeit am elektronischen Bild der großen Kommunikation durch ein weises Spiel der Manipulationen schon vor dem Zugriff auf autonome Instrumente der Video-Produktion ausprobiert hat, führt die ikonoklastischen Strategien zum neuen Bereich der Forschung, Strategien, die einen Dialog in Richtung auf einen multimedial innovativen Horizont führen: Es handelt sich um die „Fluxus-Bewegung". Die zweite, von Bill Viola, Gary Hill und vielen anderen Künstlern diesseits und jenseits des Atlantik, recht bedacht darauf, die ungeheuren sprachlichen Substanzen des neuen Mediums auszuloten, die sich im Struktur vermittelnden Spiel des jeweiligen Ambientes und der Einrichtungen feststellen lassen.

Die dritte, schließlich, die nicht weniger umfangreich und bedeutungsvoll in dieser Ausstellung dargestellt wird, mit einer kompositionellen Verdichtung gegenüber der üblichen Sphäre der visuellen Künste, aktiv seit den 80er Jahren, mit der Absicht produktive Verbindungen zwischen verschiedenen expressiven und medialen Kodices herzustellen und den Gebrauch des elektronischen Mediums in Hinblick auf eine direkte kommunikative Effizienz zu radikalisieren. Die drei Linien, verschieden durch die Auswahl der operativen Kriterien mehr noch als durch die Generationenschichtungen, leben zusammen und beleben, in einem lebhaften Verhältnis von Austausch und Begegnung, die Experimentzone, die heute allgemein als Video-Kunst bezeichnet wird.

FLUXUS UND DER BEITRAG VON NAM JUNE PAIK

Nam June Paik, der international anerkannte Meister der Video-Kunst, war niemals ein Gefangener der technologischen Fetischismen, er hat die Maschinen nie zum Idol emporgehoben. Viel eher hat er ihnen einen Widerstand entgegengesetzt, indem er ihnen neuen Gehalt gegeben hat. Ich erinnere an die Installation des koreanischen Künstlers, der den Ausstellungsrundgang im wichtigen O'Hara-Museum in Tokyo eröffnet: Innerhalb des Chassis eines Fernsehers, in einem Raum, der normalerweise vom Bildschirm ausgefüllt wird, thront eine einfache Kerze.

Das elektronische Bild war für Paik nie ein kaltes Element, sondern ein aktives Feld, voll von mobilen Erleuchtungen, ein Ort, wo die Berührung zwischen Realitäten, Verhaltensweisen

the incredible linguistic substances of this new medium, substances determined in the structure mediated by the interplay of specific ambiance and furnishings.

Finally, the third generation, which is no less comprehensively and significantly represented in this exhibition, has attempted a compositional compression contrary to the common spheres of visual arts; since the 80's, these artists have been actively working to forge productive links between various expressive and mediated codices, and to radicalize the use of the electronic medium in terms of directly communicative efficiency.

These three lines, differing more in their selection of operative criteria than in the make-up of the generations, survive together and vitalize the experimental zone that is usually referred to as video art today in a lively relationship of exchange and encounter.

FLUXUS AND THE ROLE OF NAM JUNE PAIK

Nam June Paik, the internationally celebrated master of video art, has never been a prisoner of technological fetishes, he has never set machines on a pedestal as idols. On the contrary, he has resisted them by providing them with a new form. I remember an installation by this Korean artist at the beginning of an exhibition at the important O'Hara Museum in Tokyo: inside the chassis of a television, in a space normally occupied by an entire screen, a simple candle was enthroned.

The electronic image was never a cold element for Paik, but rather an active field full of mobile illuminations, a place where the contacts between realities, behaviors and language codices appear definitive and productive. In 1965, Paik was the first person to use Sony's new portable camera with a clear and artistic intention. This camera enabled artists to steer clear of the almost unconquerable inhibiting factors of televisual studies, which, in this western society, are biased against any type of experimentation with the electronic medium. Paik was also the first to transcend the frontier of that 'obstacle' which compares the videomatic object, material and perceivable as the television set, with an expansion and transformation of the electronic image within a simultaneously plastic and luminous flux. The artist realized video sculptures which multiplied these image and dynamics within the opposing and well-balanced presence of a number of other, congruent "places of appearance".

Today, at a moment in time when games of simulation are again disturbing the slumber of the illusion of complete mimesis, Paik emphasizes that he is not interested in the mimetic reproduction of reality, but in the fantastic mobilization of forms of communication.

As we have mentioned, Wuppertal, 1963 and New York, 1965 are the places which are now credited with the historical genesis of video research; and this as a result of the work of two protagonists of the Fluxus movement: Nam June Paik and Wolf Vostell. In their installations in the Galerie Parnass in Wuppertal, Paik and Vostell deconstructed the new televisual instrument, whose enormous potential for mass education they well perceived, by dividing the mechanical and electronic supports of the system into a new kind of self-evidence.

In 1965 in New York, Paik experimented with a decisive change in his research, and, for the first time, with the possibility of setting up a synthesis that might redefine the electronic image.

In order to achieve any real understanding of the video research that was carried out in this period, these two starting-points must be juxtaposed: this may be achieved by retaining, as consistently recognizable constants the critical deconstruction of the established elements of televisual communication and the creation of a new image, dialectically opposed to that of figurative convention.

und Sprachkodices definierend und produktiv erscheint. Paik ist im Jahre 1965 der erste, der mit klarer künstlerischer Intention die von Sony eingeführte tragbare Kamera einsetzt, die es den Künstlern erlaubt, die fast absolute Hemmschwelle der televisiven Studien zu umschiffen, die in der westlichen Welt gegen jeden Typ von Experiment mit dem elektronischen Medium bestehen. Paik ist auch der erste, der die Grenze des „Hindernisses" überwindet, welches die videomatische Sache, materiell und wahrnehmbar, als den Fernseher einer Erweiterung und einer Umformung des elektronischen Bildes innerhalb eines gleichzeitig plastischen und leuchtenden Fließens gegenüberstellt. Der Künstler realisiert Videoskulpturen, die das Bild und die Dynamismen dieses in der gegensätzlichen und ausgewogenen Präsenz von verschiedenen und kongruenten „Orten der Erscheinung" vervielfältigen.

Paik betont heute, zu einem Zeitpunkt, an dem die Spiele der Simulation die Illusionen der absoluten Mimesis wieder aufzuwecken scheinen, nicht an der mimetischen Reproduktion der Wirklichkeit interessiert zu sein, sondern an der phantastischen Mobilisierung der Ausdrucksmittel der Kommunikation.

Wuppertal 1963 und New York 1965 sind, wie schon erwähnt, die Orte, denen man jetzt den historischen Aufbruch der Video-Forschung zuerkennt: Und zwar durch das Werk von zwei Protagonisten der Fluxus-Bewegung: Nam June Paik und Wolf Vostell. Paik und Vostell destrukturieren in den Installationen in der Galerie Parnass in Wuppertal das neue televisive Instrument, dessen enorme Potentialität der Massebildung sie wahrnehmen, indem sie die mechanischen und elektronischen Stützen in einer verschiedenen Evidenz aufgliedern.

Paik experimentiert 1965 in New York mit einer entscheidenden Veränderung der Forschung und da erstmals mit der Möglichkeit eine Synthese aufzustellen, die das elektronische Bild neu definiert. Die zwei Anfangsmomente müssen für ein reales Verständnis der Video-Forschung dieser Jahre überkreuzt sein, und zwar in der Weise, als kritische Destrukturierung der feststehenden Elemente der televisiven Kommunikation und Schaffung eines neuen Bildes, dialektisch gegenüber dem der figurativen Konvention, immer erkennbare Konstanten bleiben müssen.

Eine Strategie dieses Typs gelangt zu einer Übereinstimmung mit der dichterischen Qualität von Fluxus, die zwei grundlegende Ziele hat. Ein neues soziokulturelles Ambiente zu schaffen, welches nützlich ist für rasche Zirkulation auf jedem Niveau einer neuen ästhetischen Komunikation, die imstande ist, die Distanz zwischen Künstlern und Publikum zu verringern, indem der gegenseitige Einsatz innerhalb eines Feldes von kreativen linguistischen Beziehungen gefordert wird. Weiters den Mustern und Konventionen der institutionalisierten Kunst neue und offene Modelle entgegenzusetzen, die imstande sind, eine Totalität aufzustellen, die die ästhtischen Verhaltensweisen neu bestimmt. Dieses offene Programm der Forschung hat die visuellen Künstler angespornt, sich ohne Unterwerfung mit dem neuen elektronischen Instrument zu messen, als einem Mittel, das benützt wird zur Erweiterung der Dimension visueller Bilder, und geeignet, in einen virtuellen Raum einzudringen: Historische und innere Zeit der künstlerischen Arbeitsamkeit in der neuen Dimension der realen Zeit.

Wenn Paik und Vostell erklären, daß die Schlüssel des Verständnisses der Gründe und Entwicklungen der Video-Forschung in der umfassenden und freien Poetik – aber es wäre exakter von Strategie zu sprechen – der Fluxus-Bewegung erkannt werden müssen, geben sie einen Hinweis der nur schwer zur Diskussion gestellt werden kann. Nur muß man den grundsätzlichen Beitrag bedenken, der von diesen beiden Autoren bei der Geburt der Video-Kunst gegeben wurde, oder den Wert der Neudefinition bei der Berührung zwischen verschiedenen künstlerischen Sprachen und Modellen der neuen Kommunikation, unterstützt und praktiziert wenigstens in den

Such a strategy leads one to an agreement with the poetical quality of Fluxus, which has two distinct aims. The one is to create a new socio-cultural ambiance which is useful for rapid circulation on every level of a new aesthetic communication, capable of reducing the distance between artists and their audience by encouraging mutual involvement in a field of creative linguistic relationships. But further, to counter the conventional patterns of institutionalized art with new, open models capable of establishing a totality which may redefine our aesthetic behavior. This open research program has spurred visual artists on to measure themselves with, not submit to, the new electronic tool as a useful medium, competent to lead us – assuming an expansion of the dimension of visual images – towards a virtual space: historical and internal time of artistic work within the new dimension of real time.
Paik and Vostell explain that the key to an understanding of the motives and developments of video research lies within the comprehensive free poetics (although it may be more exact to use the term "strategies") of the Fluxus movement, and this is a hint that is surely irrefutable. However, one must take into consideration the fundamental contribution of these two authors at the time of video art's genesis, and of the value of the new definitions created by the points of contact of differing artistic languages and models of the new communicative medium, which were supported and practiced – in the first few years, at least – by the artists of the new movement itself.
If one accepts this fact as incontestable, then one must be clear about three other, no less relevant elements:

1. Fluxus came into being in the late 50s in the USA, where it was regarded as an intellectual manifestation of late dadaism, which had leanings toward "dangerous", anarchic communist utopias, and was hence viewed with enmity and marginalised. In

Europe, on the other hand, and particularly so in Germany, the actual dialectic and innovative start of the movement hit upon open spheres of activity and – I hope I am not generalizing – positive recognition on the part of the critics.

2. One must regard 1974 as the end of the actual life and historical inherence of the Fluxus movement, the year in which George Maciunas died, and with him, the theoretical pressure and critical self-awareness of the movement. Some individuals among the circle of "Fluxus artists", of course, still continued their work after that date.

3. Throughout the Sixties and well into the Seventies, it appears that the most receptive, if not the preferred area of the various avant-garde experiments was that of those visual arts which allow, and, many cases, further encourage an active exchange between the medial expressions of the new means of communication: the conventional visual arts and performance art. If one takes all these facts into consideration, then video research begins to assume the connotations of a dialectical progression, rather than of an undefined, guileless and unhistoric peripheral space, hanging in the air, like a kind of limbo, somewhere between artistic expression with highly expressive intensity and models of the new method of communication which are luke-warm and inactive, if not completely cold, according to McLuhan's understanding. To put it more clearly: The thirty years which separate the most recent pieces by Paik and the two following generations of artists, which are presented in an exemplary fashion in this exhibition, from those in the Galerie Parnass in Wuppertal, have not developed any kind of clear linear perspective. The lively dynamics of the new research movement, characterized by a real and constant internationalism, reveal moments only, attitudes and differing strategies, that must needs be isolated today for a correct

ersten aktiven Jahren von den Künstlern der neuen Bewegung. Indem man dieses Faktum als etwas nicht anzugreifendes aufnimmt, muß man sich dreier Elemente im Klaren sein, die nicht weniger relevant sind.

1. Fluxus entsteht am Ende der fünfziger Jahre in den Vereinigten Staaten, wo es als eine intellektualistische spätdadaistische Manifestation angesehen wird, die sich an „gefährlichen" anarchisch-komunistischen Utopien anlehnt und deshalb feindlich gesehen und an den Rand gedrängt wird. In Europa hingegen, und vor allem in Deutschland, findet die tatsächliche dialektische und innovative Einstellung der Bewegung offene Räume des Wirkens und – soweit nicht generalisiert – positive Anerkennung von Seiten der Kritik.

2. Das reale Leben, und die historische Inhärenz, der Fluxus-Beweung muß im Jahre 1974 abgeschlossen betrachtet werden als George Maciunas stirbt und mit ihm auch der theoretische Druck und das kritische Bewußtsein der Bewegung. Jenseits dieses Datums setzen sicherlich einzelne Künstler ihre Arbeit im Geiste des Fluxus fort.

3. In den sechziger Jahren und wenigstens bis zur Hälfte der siebziger Jahre erscheint das am meisten bereite Feld, wenn nicht sogar das bevorzugte, der verschiedenen Experimente bezüglich Avantgarde jenes der visuellen Künste, die einen aktiven Austausch zwischen den medialen Ausdrücken der neuen Komunikationsweisen annehmen und in vielen Fällen weitertragen: Visuelle Künste der Konvention und der Performance-Künste. Wenn man das Insgesamt dieser Fakten berücksichtigt, dann nimmt die Video-Forschung die Konnotationen einer dialektischen Progression an, eher als die Undefiniertheit eines arglosen und unhistorischen peripheren Raumes, in der Luft hängend, in einer Art Limbus, zwischen künstlerischem Ausdruck mit hoher expressiver Dichte und

Modellen der neuen Kommunikation, die lauwarm-untätig, wenn nicht sogar kalt sind, wie McLuhan annahm.

In klareren Worten gesagt: Die dreißig Jahre, die die jüngsten Werke von Paik und der zwei darauffolgenden Künstlergenerationen, die in dieser Ausstellung beispielhaft vorgestellt werden, von jenen in der Galerie Parnass in Wuppertal unterscheiden, entwickeln keine eindeutig lineare Perspektive. Die lebhafte Dynamik der neuen Forschungsbewegung, charakterisiert von einer realen und konstanten Internationalität, zeigt Momente, Einstellungen und verschiedene Strategien, die man heute für ein korrektes Verständnis des Phänomens in seiner Geschichte und Aktualität isolieren muß.

VIDEO. INSTALLATIONEN, AMBIENTE, SKULPTUREN

Das Verhältnis von Video und Ambiente-Kunst in der zweiten Hälfte der sechziger und in den siebziger Jahren, ist, wie bekannt, reichlich eng. Das Video registriert nicht nur die Dimension der neuen Modelle und Parameter der Kunst in einem offeneren und durchlaufbaren räumlichen und über das Sprachliche hinausgehenden Feld, sondern wird auch selbst ein Bereich der Erweiterungen aktiver und produktiver Gleitmechanismen der Bedeutung. In dieser Perspektive konnte man den Terminus „Videoambiente" mit der neuen Bezeichnung „Videoinstallation" zusammentreffen lassen. Die Nichtverdoppelbarkeit und die Unmöglichkeit der Transferierbarkeit einer spezifischen ambientalen Determination, in der das Video im allgemeinen eingebaut werden konnte wie eine „Kontrollkammer", ein regelrechtes Kontrollorgan, ließ Platz für eine linguistische Betriebsamkeit, die mehr mit der Notwendigkeit einer Erweiterung des Video-Bildes und mit seinen möglichen redefinitorischen Kombinationen und Kontaminationen verbunden war, als mit der kritischen Zurschaustellung einer Räumlichkeit, die zugleich geöffnet und komplex ist. Von hier aus verstärkt sich in den achtziger Jahren die Lage

understanding of the phenomenon in the context of its history and its actuality.

VIDEO, INSTALLATIONS, AMBIANCE, SCULPTURES

The relationship between video and ambiance art in the second half of the Sixties and the Seventies is, as is well-known, a exceedingly close one. The video does not only register the dimension of the new models and parameters of an art which loves to present itself in an more open and transversable field which transcends the level of language, it becomes itself an area for the expansion of active and productive flexible mechanisms of meaning. From this point of view, one might allow the term "video ambiance" to collide with the new term "video installation". The fact that a specific ambiental determination, in which the video in general could be built in, like a "control room", a proper controlling body, cannot be duplicated or transferred, left room for a different linguistic activity; this had more to do with the necessity of expanding the video image and its possible redefinitive combinations and word blendings than with the critical exhibition of a simultaneously open and complex space. In consequence, the position of the video sculpture is reinforced: it is a phenomenon which may be classed among the ranks of video installations, but should not be confused with that of the video ambiance. If one does not apply such a distinction, one runs the risk of losing track of the meaning behind the innovatory research carried out by many young authors in the last ten years. The firm plastic consistency of the sculpture and the oscillating, but not inconsequential definition of the video image combine to realize a new visual form in which the virtuality of appearances connects to limits, stability and order of positionings as well as to changes of perspective, with a particular emphasis on the temporal dimension. The link between sculpture and time, traditionally a fundamental one, acquires a new value and becomes the end, not only of the constitution of the plastic structure, but also of the viewer's understanding and aesthetic recognition.

In more recent studies, encounters between the electronic image of the video and the methodology of computer science, between interactive access procedures and the modulation of complessive icons, underline the mobility, but also the all-encompassing presence of image and time. With its mutable, yet not open structures, the new technological complexity of the video leads onward to a new dimension of the video image as a structured, concrete and interactive image-object.

der Videoskulptur, ein Phänomen, das auch in die Rubrik der Videoinstallationen eingereiht werden kann, aber das nicht verwechselt werden darf mit jener des Videoambientes. Wenn eine solche Unterscheidung nicht angewandt wird, läuft man das Risiko den Sinn der Innovation der Forschungen zu verlieren, die in den letzten zehn Jahren viele junge Autoren unternommen haben. Eine feste plastische Konsistenz der Skulptur und eine oszillierende, aber nicht unkonsequente Bestimmung des Video-Bildes, die sich verbinden, realisieren eine neue visuelle Form, in der Virtualität der Erscheinungen und der Grenzen, Stabilität und Abfolge von Positionierungen und Veränderungen des Gesichtspunktes zusammenfließen, und zwar innerhalb einer Betonung der zeitlichen Dimension. Die Verbindung von Skulptur und Zeit, traditionell eine grundlegende Verbindung, erwirbt einen neuen Wert und ist Endpunkt nicht nur der Konstitution der plastischen Struktur, sondern von Erkundung und ästhetischer Anerkennung für den, der sie betrachtet.

Die Berührung in den jüngsten Forschungen zwischen elektronischem Bild des Videos und Bearbeitungstechniken der Informatik, von interaktiven Prozeduren des Zugangs und Modulierung der komplessiven Ikone, unterstreicht die Mobilität, aber auch die Präsenz des Insgesamt von Bild und Zeit. In seiner veränderbaren, aber nicht offenen Strukturierung führt die neue technologische Komplexität des Videos zu einer neuen Dimension des Video-Bildes als ein gegliedertes, konkretes und dialogbereites Bild-Objekt.

Kunst und neue Technologien – warum eigentlich?

DIETER DANIELS

Fragen aus den 1960ern und Antworten der 1990er

In mehrfacher Hinsicht werden in den 1990ern Themen wieder aufgegriffen, die erstmals in den 1960ern aktuell waren. Hierzu gehören das Verhältnis von Kunst und Technologie ebenso wie die soziale und politische Wirkung von Kunst. Aber auch im Bereich der Pop- und Jugendkultur erinnert manches an die swinging sixties, von neo-psychedlischen Technovideos bis hin zur Plateausohle und Hosen mit Schlag. Man könnte behaupten, daß die 90er an den ungelösten Themen der 60er Jahre arbeiten, jedoch zeigt ein genaueres Hinsehen, daß auch die Fragen neu gestellt werden.

Warum sollen oder wollen Künstler überhaupt neue Technologien verwenden? Solch grundsätzliche Themen wurden in den 1960ern heftig diskutiert, als die Künste sich mittels neuer Medien aus dem als einengend empfundenen Kontext der bürgerlichen Kultur befreien wollten. Die Frage muß angesichts der Omnipräsenz der elektronischen Medien heute anders herum gestellt werden: Warum sollen Künstler *nicht* mit neuen Medien arbeiten, wie fast alle anderen Berufe, bzw. wie lange können sie der digitalen Revolution noch sinnvoll widerstehen? Im Unterschied zur politischen und ästhetischen Debatte der 60er werden im technologisch und industriell bestimmten Medieneifer der letzten Jahre solche Grundsatzfragen jedoch kaum noch gestellt. Gewiß haben sich Thesen der 1960er weitgehend als utopisch erwiesen: Die wesentlichen Mechanismen der Kunstwelt und des Kunstmarktes haben die letzten dreißig Jahre unbeschadet überstanden. Es ist wenig zu bemerken von einer damals von Mc Luhan bis Nam June Paik prognostizierten Ersetzung aller traditionellen Mittel der Kunst durch neue Medien, die zugleich eine neue gesellschaftliche Rolle der Kunst bestimmen sollte.

Erweist sich die allgemein proklamierte Haltung, daß Kunst am Ende des 20. Jahrhunderts der Herausforderung der neuen digitalen Techniken nicht ausweichen kann, als trügerische

ART AND NEW TECHNOLOGIES – WHY?
1960's Questions and 1990's Answers

In many ways, issues that were current in the 1960's are being re-addressed now in the 1990's. Among these issues are the relationship between art and technology and the social and political effect of art. Even in the realm of pop and youth culture, though, there is much that is reminiscent of the swinging sixties, from neo-psychedelic techno-videos to platform shoes and bell bottoms. One could maintain that the 90's are working on the unresolved issues of the 60's, but a closer look reveals that the questions are being rephrased.

Why should artists use new technologies at all, or why would they want to? Fundamental questions of this nature were discussed heatedly in the 1960's as the arts endeavored to use new media to liberate themselves from what was perceived as the corseting context of bourgeoisie culture. In light of the omnipresence of electronic media today, the question must be asked the other way around: why should artists not work with new media in the same way that all other professions do, or how long can artists reasonably withstand the digital revolution? Unlike the political and aesthetic debates of the 60's, however, these kinds of fundamental questions are rarely asked today in the midst of a media fever dominated by technology and industry. On the whole, the positions of the 1960's have proven to be largely utopian: the essential mechanisms of the art world and the art market have survived the past thirty years unscathed. There is little to be seen of the traditional tools of art being replaced by new media, as was predicted by theorists and artists from McLuhan to Nam June Paik; this expected shift has hardly defined a new role for art in society.

Does the widely proclaimed belief that art at the end of the 20th century will not be able to avoid the challenge of new digital technologies prove to be an illusory truism? We can

Selbstverständlichkeit? Voraussichtlich wird sich die gesamte Alltags- und Arbeitswelt durch die digitalen Techniken einschneidend ändern. Die Verschmelzung von Fernsehen, Computer, Video und Telefon zu einem einzigen Multimedia-Massenmedium enthält ein enormes Potential zur Veränderung unseres Weltbildes. Aber muß dies auch die Kunst in ihren Grundfesten erschüttern oder sollte sie sich nicht gerade jetzt auf die „ewigen Werte" berufen? Soll die Kunst vielleicht als Ort der Besinnung dienen, um in der Umwandlung aller Techniken und medialen Formen die Bedeutung der Inhalte und der ästhetischen Grundsätze zu betonen?

Solche Fragen sind nicht neu, denn sie haben die Diskussion um den Paragone von Kunst und Technik seit Anfang des 20. Jahrhunderts bestimmt. Als zentraler Stimulans dieser Debatte erweist sich dabei ein Minderwertigkeitskomplex der Künste gegenüber der Innovationskraft von Technik und Naturwissenschaft.

Das auf den 11. Feb. 1910 datierte Manifest der futuristischen Maler verkündet: „Genossen! Wir erklären euch hiermit, dass der triumphale Fortschritt der Naturwissenschaft so große Veränderungen in der Menschheit hervorgerufen hat, daß sich ein Abgrund auftut zwischen den willfährigen Sklaven der Vergangenheit und uns Freien, die wir der strahlenden Herrlichkeit der Zukunft gewiß sind."

Die Futuristen sind in ihrer künstlerischen Produktion vielleicht nicht ganz den von ihnen selbst so hoch gesteckten Erwartungen gerecht geworden, doch dieses Schicksal teilen sie mit vielen folgenden Generationen von Künstlern, die sich mit dem Fortschritt von Technik und Naturwissenschaft messen wollten. Tatsächlich sind die Futuristen aber die ersten, die mit dieser Deutlichkeit ausgesprochen haben, daß im 20. Jahrhundert die Kunst bei weitem nicht mehr den Platz an der Spitze der menschlichen Kultur hat, wie sie ihn zum Beispiel in der Renaissance einnahm. Dieser Minderwertigkeitskomplex der Künste gegenüber Technik

expect that the entire world of everyday life and work will be significantly changed by digital technology. The merging of television, computer, video and telephone to a single multimedia mass media bears an enormous potential for changing our world view. But must this necessarily shake the foundations of art, or should it be more the case that art, particularly now, evokes the „eternal values"? Should art perhaps serve as an instance of recollection, in which it may emphasize in the transformation of all technologies and media forms the significance of content and aesthetic foundations?

Questions of this nature are not new; they have characterized discussions surrounding the respective roles of art and technology since the beginning of the 20th century. In this context, the inferiority complex of the arts in relation to the innovative power of technology and natural science has shown itself to be a central stimulant in these debates.

The Manifesto of Futurist Painters, dated from February 11, 1919, proclaims: "Comrades! We declare herewith that the triumphant progress of science has brought forth such great changes in humanity that an abyss has opened up between those meek slaves of the past and us free men, who are secure in the bright magnificence of the future."

Although the Futurists may not have entirely met the great expectations they set for themselves, they share this fate with the many subsequent generations of artists attempting to measure their work against the progress of technology and science. However, the Futurists were indeed the first to state so unequivocally that art in the 20th century no longer has anywhere near the position at the pinnacle of human culture that it had in the Renaissance, for example. This inferiority complex of the arts in comparison with technology and science is still today, almost 90 years after the Manifesto of Futurist Painters, the central issue of the topic "art and new technologies". Today, the questions could be phrased in this way: Can new technologies contribute to the repair of the broken link between the avant-garde and mass culture? May new technologies lead contemporary art out of its "self-imposed" marginal existence? Do artistic visions still possess the power to create new symbols in the midst of a general lack of orientation in the field of new technologies?

In the initial phase of media art in the 1960's, a strong utopian element originating from these questions provided an important motive for misusing the brittle world of electronic appliances for the purpose of exploring artistic forms. The motto was: "new media for a new audience". If television had become the most important factor in our visual world-view, it seemed to be obvious and self-evident that artists must work with video. It was both hoped and demanded that these new art forms should have a share in the attention and widespread effects of the electronic mass media. However, it was precisely this link that failed: support and interest on the part of television and industry were minimal. And just as with the Futurists, these artistic products were not always able to meet the goals they had set for themselves. Thus, an attempt to overcome the marginal position of art in society resulted in the course of the 1970's in "Video Art", an enclave of contemporary art with an even more marginal position than that of the artistic field it belongs to. Finally in the mid-1980's, the postmodernist revival of painting made it possible to believe that the link between art and electronic images had been a dead-end in art history.

In the last 10 years since then, circumstances have nearly reversed themselves again. As was predicted by media artists such as Nam June Paik and theorists like McLuhan, the replacement of a major portion of all traditional media by electronics has become part of our daily lives. There is no longer any doubt that new image media not only produce new visual effects, but that they are also changing western culture's understanding of images

und Wissenschaft steht auch heute, fast 90 Jahre nach dem Manifest der Futuristen, immer noch im Brennpunkt des Themas „Kunst und neue Technologien".

Die Fragen lassen sich heute so formulieren: Können die neuen Technologien dazu beitragen, die abgebrochene Verbindung von der Avantgarde zur Massenkultur wieder herzustellen? Führen neue Technologien die zeitgenössische Kunst aus ihrer „selbstverschuldeten" Marginalität? Haben künstlerische Visionen noch die Kraft, neue Symbole in der allgemeinen Orientierungslosigkeit im Bereich der neuen Technologien zu schaffen?

Am Anfang der Medienkunst, in den 1960er Jahren, war ein aus den genannten Fragen entspringendes, stark utopisches Element wichtiges Motiv dafür, die spröde Welt der elektronischen Geräte für die Zwecke der künstlerischen Formfindung zu mißbrauchen. „Neue Medien für eine neues Publikum" hieß die Devise. Es schien naheliegend und selbstverständlich, daß Künstler mit Video arbeiten müssen, wenn das Fernsehen der wichtigste Faktor unseres visuellen Weltbildes ist. Daß diese neuen Kunstformen dann auch an der Aufmerksamkeit und Breitenwirkung der elektronischen Massenmedien partizipieren würden, war ebenso Hoffnung wie Forderung. Doch genau diese Verbindung scheiterte: Unterstützung und Interesse von Seiten des Fernse-hens und der Industrie waren minimal. Auch die künstleri-schen Produkte konnten, wie schon bei den Futuristen, nicht immer dem selbst gestellten Anspruch genügen. Aus einem Versuch, die Marginalität der Kunst in der Gesellschaft zu überwinden, entstand so im Laufe der 1970er die „Videokunst", eine Enklave in der zeitgenössischen Kunst, noch marginaler als ihr künstlerisches Umfeld. Schließlich konnte man Mitte der 1980er angesichts des postmodernen Revivals der Malerei glauben, daß die Verbindung von Kunst und elektronischem Bild ein Irrweg der Kunstgeschichte gewesen sei.

Seitdem haben sich die Verhältnisse im Laufe der letzten 10 Jahre fast ins Gegenteil verwandelt. Die in den 1960er Jahren von Medienkünstlern wie Nam June Paik und Theoretikern wie McLuhan prognostizierte Ersetzung eines Großteils aller traditionellen Medien durch die Elektronik ist mittlerweile Teil des Alltags geworden. Es ist längst klar, daß die neuen Bildmedien nicht nur neue visuelle Effekte erzeugen, sondern den Bildbegriff der abendländischen Kultur ebenso tief verändern wie die Einführung der Fotografie. Diese Erkenntnisse sind von der intellektuellen und künstlerischen Avantgarde mittlerweile bis zu den politischen Entscheidungsträgern durchgesickert. In Deutschland wurden Anfang der 1990er mehrere Hochschulen bzw. Institute mit einem Schwerpunkt auf der künstlerischen Arbeit in digitalen Medien gegründet. Das deutsche öffentlich-rechtliche Fernsehsystem ist in Auflösung begriffen und sucht angesichts des explodierenden Weltmarkts der Telekommunikation seine Zukunftshoffnung in einer kulturellen Wegfindung durch den digitalen Informationsdschungel. Sogar die Industrie hat bei unaufhaltbar fallenden Preisen für ständig bessere Hardware den identitätsstiftenden Faktor des Ästhetischen entdeckt. Wo der technische Innovationsprozess schneller verläuft, als das Verständnis oder gar Bedürfnis der Kundschaft nachwächst, ist über Kunstsponsoring manchmal vielleicht mehr zu erreichen – vor allem wenn die Künste sich der firmeneigenen Produktpalette bedienen.

Heutzutage kommen die Vorbehalte zu einer glücklichen Verschmelzung von künstlerischem, technischem und wirtschaftlichem Fortschritt eher von der Seite der Kunst: Niemand möchte sich für die im rasenden Tempo der medientechnischen Entwicklung liegengebliebenen Aufgaben der Sinnfindung verantwortlich erklären. Es wird abgestritten, daß die Kunst zur Ausbesserung der kulturellen Defizite der Mediengesellschaft dienen könne. Es ist unvergessen, daß in den 1960er und 1970er Jahren der Versuch einer Grenzerwei-

just as radically as the introduction of photography did. These insights have meanwhile permeated through the intellectual and artistic avant-garde all the way to the political decision makers. In the early 1990's in Germany, a number of art schools and institutes were founded with an emphasis on artistic work in digital media. The German public-institutional television system is in the process being disbanded and, in light of the exploding world market of telecommunications, is seeking future directions in paving cultural paths through the digital information jungle. Faced with constantly falling prices for continuously improved hardware, now even industry has discovered the identity-forming factor of aesthetics. Where the process of technical innovation outruns the understanding or even demands of the customers, sometimes more may be achieved through sponsoring art – especially when the arts take advantage of the product range provided by the company in question.

Nowadays, reservations regarding the happy union of artistic, technical and economic progress are more likely to be heard from the side of art: no one wants to accept responsibility for the task of making sense, which has been left behind at the enormous speed at which media-technical developments have been taking place. No one wants to accept that art could serve to balance out the cultural deficiencies of media society. For no one has forgotten that the attempts of the 1960's and 1970's to expand the boundaries of the art world into media finally failed, because the mediating structures of museums, galleries and the art market proved to be far more stable than expected. What remains is a distrust of claims of being able to change the conditions, although – or perhaps precisely because – the failed attempts to expand the boundaries on the level of society as a whole, did in fact succeed within the realm of art (e.g. award of the Biennale of Venice for Nam June Paik, Bill Viola and Garry Hill).

On the whole, the issue is: should the

ambiguous construct of the term media art refer merely to an intersection of two otherwise independent areas; in other words, is this the lowest common denominator for two worlds that are to be taken for granted as such? If the hopes of touching a central issue in the development of culture, that have been pinned to the link between art and new technologies, are not to be disappointed, then there must be more to the discussion than a provisional union of two disjunct entities. The real significance of the intersection of art and media is that these two areas are in a position to fundamentally challenge one another. Thus it may be possible to counterbalance the individualism of art with the universalism of media, or to dampen the enthusiasm of media technology with the arrogance of art. Once this type of exchange of paradigms has taken place, similar to that which Paul Feyerabend successfully applied to art and science, then it may become apparent that both of the fields "art" and "media" are in the midst of a process of revision. According to media theorists such as Friedrich Kittler, the current heated discussion about the differences between individual media will soon burn itself out: when there is but one single multimedia fluidum, then the separate media terms for written words, images and sound can no longer be meaningfully maintained. Thus, if the term „media" is a transitional phenomenon, then perhaps it is equally possible to rethink the term "art", as it has evolved in western thought since the Renaissance.

Examples for the thesis of "art" as a transitional phenomenon may be found in Japan. The term art, which has been imported from the western world, meaning an elite area removed from the sphere of everyday life, is partly disintegrating again in the field of electronic media: there are young people working in software companies and the experimental laboratories of the television companies, who are identified on their business cards as "artist". Although there is

terung der Kunstwelt in die Medien daran scheiterte, daß sich die Vermittlungsstrukturen durch Museen, Galerien und Kunstmarkt als viel unumstößlicher erwiesen als gedacht. Deshalb bleibt ein Mißtrauen gegenüber der behaupteten Veränderung der Verhältnisse, obwohl – oder gerade weil – die gesamtgesellschaftlich gescheiterte Grenzüberschreitung dennoch innerhalb der Kunst durchaus von Erfolg gekrönt ist (Anerkennung auf der Biennale von Venedig für Nam June Paik, Bill Viola und Garry Hill).

Die generelle Problematik lautet: soll es im zwiespältigen Konstrukt des Begriffs Medienkunst nur um eine Schnittmenge zweier ansonsten unabhängiger Bereiche gehen, also um einen kleinsten gemeinsamen Nenner von zwei Welten, die als solche nicht in Frage stehen? Wenn die auf die Verbindung von Kunst und neuen Technologien gesetzte Hoffnung, eine Schlüsselstelle in der Kulturentwicklung zu berühren, nicht enttäuscht werden soll, dann muß mehr als eine provisorische Vereinigung des Unvereinbaren zur Debatte stehen.

Die Chance an der Schnittstelle von Kunst und Medien liegt darin, daß die beiden Bereiche sich wechselseitig grundsätzlich in Frage stellen. Dadurch kann es gelingen, den Individualismus der Kunst durch den Universalismus der Medien zu relativieren oder die Euphorie der Medientechnik durch die Borniertheit der Kunst zu dämpfen. Erst durch einen solchen Austausch von Paradigma, wie ihn Paul Feyerabend zwischen Kunst und Wissenschaft erfolgreich angewendet hat, kann hervortreten, daß beide Felder, „Kunst" und „Medien", in einem Revisionsprozeß stehen.

Die derzeit so heftig geführte Diskussion über die Unterschiede der einzelnen Medien wird sich laut Medientheoretikern wie Friederich Kittler in absehbarer Zeit von selbst erledigen: wenn es nur noch ein einziges, multimediales Fluidum gibt, lassen sich die Begriffe einzelner Medien für Schrift, Bild und Ton gar nicht mehr sinnvoll aufrecht erhalten. Wenn der Begriff „Medien“ also ein Übergangsphänomen ist, kann man vielleicht auch über den Begriff „Kunst“, der sich in seinem abendländischen Verständnis seit der Renaissance gebildet hat, neu nachdenken.

Beispiele für die These von „Kunst“ als einem Übergangsphänomen lassen sich in Japan finden. Der aus der westlichen Welt importierte Begriff der Kunst als eines elitären, vom täglichen Umgang abgekoppelten Bereichs löst sich im Feld der elektronischen Medien gerade wieder auf: in Softwarefirmen und in den Experimentierlabors der TV Anstalten arbeiten junge Leute, deren Visitenkarte sie als „artist“ ausweist. Ohne das für den Besucher irgendwelche Kunstwerke sichbar werden, sind sie im Entwicklerteam z.B. eines Videospiels einfach für den künstlerischen Anteil zuständig. George Maciunas, der Gründer und Motor der Fluxus-Bewegung – 50 Jahre nach dem Futurismus vielleicht die letzte intermediale Kunstbewegung des 20. Jahrhunderts – sah in dem anonymen Kunstwerk als Massenware für jedermann sein eigentliches Ziel, auch wenn dies von seinen Fluxuskollegen kaum geteilt wurde. Innerhalb des auf Autoren und Objekte fixierten Systems der Bildenden Kunst mußte diese Vision notwendigerweise scheitern – gerade weil Maciunas sein Ziel über die Distribution von Objekten in Form von Multiples erreichen wollte.

Im effizientesten Distributionssytem der Menschheitsgeschichte, dem weltumspannenden Datennetz, wo jeder Zugriff auf alles hat, werden die Grenzen zwischen Autorschaft und Anonymität fließend. Interessanterweise treten derzeit immer mehr Pseudonyme und Gruppennamen auf, hinter denen Künstler ihre Autorenschaft verbergen, die mit Telekommunikation und Netzwerken arbeiten (Van Gogh TV, The Thing, Knowbotic Research, HILUS, Handshake...). Offenbar sind die fundamentalen Kriterien von „Kunst“ im Feld der Medien erneut in Bewegung geraten – das beste Zeichen für eine interessante Zukunft.

no visible art work that may be presented to visitors, these artists are members of a team of developers, for example, for a video game, where they are responsible simply for the artistic section. George Maciunas, founder and motor of the Fluxus movement – perhaps the last intermedial art movement of the 20th century, 50 years after Futurism – regarded the anonymous art work as mass-produced goods for everyone as his real goal, even though this view was hardly shared by his Fluxus colleagues. Within a system of fine arts that adheres to authors and objects, this vision was necessarily doomed to failure – precisely because Maciunas wanted to achieve this goal through the distribution of objects in the form of multiples.

In the most efficient distributions system in human history, the global data network where everyone has access to everything, the boundaries between authorship and anonymity converge. It is interesting to observe that more and more pseudonyms and group names are appearing that disguise the authorship of artists working with telecommunications and networks (Van Gogh TV, The Thing, Knowbotic Research, HILUS, Handshake ...). It appears that the fundamental criteria for "art" are being set in motion again in the field of media – the best sign of an interesting future.

The question posed at the beginning, why, if at all, artists should use new media usually becomes a question of power under the premises of the so-called bourgeoisie understanding of art: may the arts be permitted to allow their autonomy that is protected by the guardians of aesthetics to become dependent on technological progress? And on the other hand, under the premises of art's social responsibility as it was characterized in the 1960's, the question becomes one of morality: may the arts be permitted to simply ignore the radical changes in the entire media world, or must they accept a cultural responsibility to find solutions to problems they have not created? Neither of these paths leads to conclusive results, but rather lead the argument over the priority of art vs. technology into a discussion similar to that of the chicken and the egg. Not until the current terms of "art" and "media" and "technology" are understood as transitional phenomenon, will a stance that is independent of all questions of priority be possible – a stance illustrated by the following statement from Masaki Fujihata on his project "Impressed Velocity" from 1994.

"For this project, I climbed Mt. Fuji in the summer of 1992 and 1993, equipped with a GPS (Global Positioning System), which enables me to determine my position around the world according to longitude, latitude and elevation above sea level. I did this first of all and especially because an instrument such as GPS exists. I let this fact set off my imagination ... I find products that are made unconsciously, for no clear reason, and technologies that are not created for a specific purpose much more interesting than a situation where first there is a concept, and then you look for a technology to implement that concept."
(ICC News, Tokyo Summer 1994)

This attitude needs no social or aesthetic imperative, no external force, to bring the arts and technology together. It is not a question of art fulfilling an obligation to explicate the world or to attempt to keep up with the changes in the world due to technology. Rather, Fujihata paraphrases a statement made by E. P. Hillary, when he was asked why he climbed Mt. Everest: "Because it's there."
This matter-of-fact way of dealing with the wonders of technology overcomes the inferiority complex that art has had in relation to science and technology since the beginning of this century by regarding technology as a „second nature" that does not need to be changed or improved and certainly not deterred. The task of art is rather to raise this "second nature" to a reflective level. The Futurists were the first to use this term and

Die anfangs gestellte Frage warum und ob überhaupt Künstler die neuen Technologien nutzen sollen, wird unter den Prämissen des sogenannten bürgerlichen Kunstbegriffs meist zu einer Machtfrage: Dürfen die Künste ihre durch die Wächter der Ästhetik gehütete Autonomie in Abhängigkeit vom technischen Fortschritt bringen? Und umgekehrt wird unter der Prämisse der sozialen und gesellschaftlichen Verantwortung der Kunst, wie sie in den 1960ern geprägt wurde, daraus eine Moralfrage: Dürfen die Künste die radikale Veränderung der gesamten medialen Umwelt ungestraft ignorieren oder müssen sie eine kulturelle Verantwortung zur Lösung von Problem übernehmen, die sie nicht selbst geschaffen haben?

Beide Wege führen zu keinem endgültigen Ergebnis, sondern nähern den Prioritätsstreit von Kunst und Technologie letztlich dem von Henne oder Ei. Erst wenn die derzeitigen Begriffe von „Kunst" und „Medien" und „Technologie" als Übergangsphänomene aufgefaßt werden, wird eine solche Haltung jenseits aller Prioritätsfragen möglich, wie bei folgendem Statement von Masaki Fujihata zu seinem Projekt „Impressed Velocity" von 1994:

„Für dieses Projekt erstieg ich den Mt. Fuji im Sommer 1992 und 1993 ausgerüstet mit einem GPS (Global Positioning System) welches mir erlaubt, meine Position weltweit in Längengrad, Breitengrad und Höhe über Meer zu bestimmen. Zunächst und vor allem habe ich dies gemacht, weil es ein solches Instrument wie das GPS gibt. Ich ließ meine Imagination von diesem auslösen. ... Ich finde Produkte, die unbewußt, ohne klares Selbstverständnis gemacht werden und Technologien, die nicht für einen bestimmten Zweck gemacht werden, viel interessanter als eine Situation, wo zuerst ein Konzept existiert und man dann nach einer Technologie sucht, um dieses Konzept zu realisieren." (ICC News, Tokyo Sommer 1994)

Diese Haltung bedarf keiner sozialen oder ästhetischen Notwendigkeit, also keines äußeren Zwangs, um die Künste mit der Technologie zusammenzubringen. Es geht nicht um eine Pflichterfüllung der Kunst bei ihrer Erklärung von Welt oder bei ihrem Versuch, mit der Veränderung der Welt durch die Technologie Schritt zu halten. Fujihata paraphrasiert vielmehr einen Auspruch von E. P. Hillary, der auf die Frage warum er den Mt. Everest bestieg antwortet: „Weil es ihn gibt."

Diese Selbstverständlichkeit des Umgangs mit den Wundern der Technologie überwindet den seit Beginn des Jahrhunderts akuten Minderwertigkeitskomplex der Künste gegenüber Technik und Wissenschaft, indem sie die Technik als „zweite Natur" begreift, die von der Kunst nicht verändert, verbessert oder gar verhindert werden muß, sondern durch die künstlerische Leistung vielmehr erst auf die reflexive Stufe gehoben wird. Schon die Futuristen prägten diesen Begriff der „zweiten Natur" und sahen sich der Technik gegenüber als die „Primitiven einer neuen Sensibilität". So wie dem Ureinwohner oder prähistorischen Kulturen die Distanz zur Natur fehlt und sie deshalb in ihrer Kunst nicht Thema werden kann, so muß der Technologie gegenüber erst die Stufe des kulturellen Überlebenskampfes überwunden werden, damit wir uns als selbstvertändlichen Teil einer technologischen Welt begreifen, in der den Künsten die Rolle zuwachsen kann, gegenüber dem großenteils völlig unbewußten und unkontrollierbaren Entstehungsprozeß dieser technologischen Welt die Arbeit an der Entstehung eines kulturellen Selbstbewußtseins zu beginnen.

Der Aufsatz erschien erstmals in: RAM Realität – Anspruch – Medium, Kunstfonds, Bonn 1995 und wurde vom Autor für diese Publikation überarbeitet.

saw themselves in relation to technology as the "primitives of a new sensibility". Just as aborigines or prehistoric cultures lack a distance to nature and are thus unable to make it a theme of their art, in relation to technology we must first overcome the phase of a cultural battle for survival in order to see ourselves as an inherent component of a technological world. Then the arts may take on the role of initiating the development of cultural awareness in a process of accelerating technological growth that is as yet largely unconscious and uncontrolled.

Über das Skulpturale in der Videoskulptur

PETER ASSMANN

THE SCULPTURAL ASPECT OF VIDEO SCULPTURE

It is obvious that video sculpture is different from traditional sculpture in the way that artistic work with the medium of video is integrated into each project. What video sculpture and traditional sculpture have in common, on the other hand, includes the same broad spectrum as the whole field of artistic projects that are usually labeled video sculpture. Video sculpture ranges from installation art and artistic work with "new" media to the categorizations of sculpture and object: it seems that video sculpture must be regarded as a categorization of the in-between. Addressing here the aspect of sculpture presupposes that the artistic work focuses on the aspect of corporeal volume. Of course, there is no way of determining a precisely quantifiable boundary based on focus and attention, however, the primary artistic intention of each particular project may serve to characterize the respective structural orientation.
Video sculpture is always the convergence that results when creative work on an object is linked to creative work on an image. The medium video makes it possible to work on an individual image or on a filmic sequence of images, but it also implicitly presupposes the technical specifications for presenting the image; these, in turn, determine the details of the sculptural formation of the specific work. Whether a video projection is involved or a monitor – the technical devices that are required respectively, decisively determine the final appearance of the work.

The most direct effects of these specifications for forming the work may be found in those video sculptures, in which the external form of the work is defined by the form or form combination of the TV monitor, which is used either alone or in combination to achieve an independent sculptural effect. The block-like appearance of the "object" video in the form of the monitor as an apparatus for presenting

Was Videoskulptur von traditioneller Skulptur unterscheidet ist offensichtlich die im jeweiligen Werkprojekt integrierte künstlerische Arbeit mit dem Medium Video. Was sie jedoch verbindet, ist so vielfältig und offen wie das weite Feld der künstlerischen Projekte, die üblicherweise mit dem Etikett „Videoskulptur" versehen werden. Eingespannt zwischen die Pole Installationskunst, künstlerische Arbeit mit „neuen" Medien und den Zuordnungen zu Skulptur und Objekt ist Videoskulptur wohl nur als Zwischenbereichszuordnung zulässig.

Von Skulptur zu sprechen, setzt die künstlerische Arbeit konzentriert auf den Aspekt des Körpervolumens voraus. Eine exakt quantifizierbare Grenze ist hier natürlich in keiner Weise zu eruieren. Als Strukturierungsmerkmal mag jedoch die jeweilige hautpsächliche Ausrichtung des Kunstwollens jedes Werkprojektes gelten.

Videoskulptur formuliert immer ein Zusammenführen der künstlerischen Arbeit am Gegenstand verbunden mit einer solchen am Bild. Das Medium Video ermöglicht sowohl die Arbeit an einem Einzelbild wie an einer filmischen Abfolge von Bildsequenzen, impliziert jedoch in jedem Fall technische Voraussetzungen der Präsentation des Bildes, die sehr detaillierte Vorgaben an die skulpturale Ausformulierung des jeweiligen Werkstückes geben. Ob Videoprojektion oder Monitor – die jeweils benötigten technischen Apparaturen sind für das Erscheinungsbild des Werkprojektes absolut entscheidend.

Die direktesten Umsetzungen dieser Gestaltungsvorgaben erfolgen bei jenen Videoskulpturen, bei denen die äußere Form des jeweiligen Werkstückes sich aus der Form bzw. Formkombination des Fernsehmonitores definiert, der – entweder als Einzelobjekt bzw. in Kombination mehrerer solcher Monitore – zu eigenständiger skulpturaler Wirkung geführt wird. Dieses blockhafte Erscheinungsbild des „Objekts" Video als jenes des Videopräsentationsapparates Monitor rekurriert auf skulpturale Traditionen einer geometrienahen Körperkonstruktion, auf die entsprechende Prägung des Betrachterblickes durch formale Konstruktion der Skulptur und ihre in der Tradition entwickelte meditative Zuordnung.

Eine gleichsam kontrapunktische Erweiterung dieser skulpturalen Tradition setzt die Videoskulptur im auf den Monitor erscheinenden Bild. Pezoldo alias Friederike Pezold arbeitet seit den späten sechziger Jahren sehr konzentriert in diesem Spannungsfeld. Ihr großes künstlerisches Anliegen ist hier die Propagierung der Langsamkeit des Blickes, stets verbunden mit der bildhaften Auseinandersetzung mit dem weiblichen Körper. In ihrem Ausstellungsbeitrag formuliert die Künstlerin in diesem Sinne visuell prägnante, präzise gesetzte Skulpturen: Vier schwarze Monitore werden auf schwarzen Holzsockel übereinander angeordnet und die so entstehenden Körper in einer strengen Reihe aufgestellt. Auf den vier Monitoren präsentiert die Künstlerin in kaum wahrnehmbarer Veränderung des Bildes Teilbereiche des Körpers von Frauen aus Tibet, Afrika und Südamerika, wobei sich diese Details zumeist auf das flächenhafte Ornament des Gewandes beziehen.

Die auratische Arbeit an der Langsamkeit verbindet sich hier mit der kunsthistorischen Tradition der transzendierenden Bedeutung einer Bildfläche. Das Körpervolumen der gezeigten Frauen, ja ihre gesamte Körperlichkeit wird ausschließlich über eine partielle Segmentierung zitiert. Pezoldo unterläuft daher jegliche Form des Voyeurismus, der die Formen des weiblichen Körpers im ausschließlichen Hinblick auf ihre erotisch wirksame Körperlichkeit betrachtet. In der Vergangenheit hat die Künstlerin für ähnliche Werkstücke zumeist die Bezeichnung „Göttin" gewählt, hier also bewußt kulturell transzendente Beziehungen hergestellt, die die stelenartigen Formulierung ihrer Videoskulpturen im Sinne eines Totems vorstellen.

video reverts to the sculptural tradition of body construction based on geometry, the corresponding conditioning of the viewer's gaze marked by the formal construction of the sculpture, and the meditative associations developed through the course of traditional viewing.

At the same time, video sculpture extends this sculptural tradition counterpunctually through the image that appears in the monitor. Friederike Pezold, alias Pezoldo, has strongly focused her work in this field of contrasts since the late sixties. Her main artistic aim here is to propagate the slowness of the gaze; this aim is constantly associated with using images to explore the female body. Thus, in this exhibition, the artist forms visually striking, formally precisely set sculptures: four black monitors are placed one on top of the other on black wooden pedestals, and the figures created this way are presented in a strict series. On the four monitors, the artist presents partial views of the bodies of women from Tibet, Africa and South America; the images are continuously, but barely perceptibly changing, and the details usually reflect the surface ornamentation of the clothing.
Here, the aural work with slowness combines with the art historic tradition of the transcendental significance of an image surface. The corporeal volume of the women shown on the monitors, their very bodily existence, is conveyed exclusively through a partial segmentation. In this way, Pezoldo effectively subverts any form of voyeurism that would view the female body only in terms of the erotic effect of corporeality. For works of this type in the past, the artist has frequently used the term "Goddess"; in other words, she consciously forms culturally transcendent relationships that represent the stelar-shaped form of her video-sculptures as being similar to totems.

A strong likeness to Pezoldo's work may be found in Ulrike Rosenbach's "Requiem für eine

Eiche". In this case, however, the upright stele is not formed by monitors stacked on top of one another, but rather by steel constructions. The front surface of these constructions is formed by a monitor and stretched tissue paper, behind which the shadows of tree branches may be seen. The filmic representation of a flickering fire on the monitor combines with the constantly flickering light of the presentation technique of the monitor image. The shapes of roots and branches, which are perceived as shadow images, are formed on the surface of the object, which serves as a projection surface – although it is clearly a statue at the same time. A direct connection is drawn here again between the technique of the work and animistic cultural forms.

A spectrum emerges that extends from the body formed by light, here with the additional aspect of the relationship between the lighting technique of the monitor and the projection technique – the relationship between the digital (monitor) and analog (tissue paper) technique – to the massive external casement. And from this spectrum, sign-like formations arise that point to a broad field of associated terms.

Here, as in the first work, there is a certain proximity to a memorial, to a totem as the link between different worlds. Technical logic and bio-logic are utilized to reveal signs of a larger reality that overreaches both logics. Within the fixed framework of an object, a body-image is displayed that constantly refers to transcendence, because it is formed by light. Contrary to the every-day use of the medium video displaying a fleeting, superficial scan of a world of images, Rosenbach's video sculpture paradigmatically emphasizes a concentration of reality/realities.

Helmut Mark's creative work focuses on video sculpture as a way of using media to expand on an artistic sculptural tradition: the monitor is used as raw material, just like any other material that is formed and used in a sculptural work. The image element represented by the

Ulrike Rosenbachs *Requiem für eine Eiche* ist hier durchaus ähnlich zu sehen. Die aufragende Stele wird in diesem Falle allerdings nicht aus aufeinandergestapelten Monitoren geformt, sondern von Stahlkörpern, deren frontale Oberfläche sowohl vom Monitorbild als auch von aufgespanntem Seidenpapier, hinter dem sich die Formen von Baumgeäst abzeichnen, gebildet wird. Die filmische Abbildung flackernden Feuers am Monitor verbindet sich kongenial mit dem beständig flackernden Licht der Präsentationstechnik des Monitorbildes. Die im Sinne eines Schattenbildes erfahrbaren Wurzel- bzw. Geästformen bilden sich an der Oberfläche des Objektes, die als Projektionsfläche dient – gleichsam im Sinne eines Standbildes – ab. Auch hier wird die Technik in direktem Zusammenhang mit animistischen Kulturformen gesetzt.

Das Spannungsfeld zwischen einem über Licht formulierten Körper, hier in der zusätzlichen Spannung zwischen der Lichttechnik des Monitores und der Projektionstechnik – zwischen der digitalen (Monitor) bzw. analogen (Seidenpapier) Projektionstechnik – und einem massiven äußeren Gehäuse lassen zeichenhafte Werkformulierungen entstehen, die auf einen weiten begrifflichen Assoziationsraum verweisen.

Die Nähe zum Mahnmal, einem Totem als Verbindung verschiedener Welten, ist auch hier gegeben. Technische Logik und Bio-Logik werden eingesetzt, um zeichenhaft auf eine größer und über beide Logiken hinausragende Wirklichkeit zu verweisen. Innerhalb eines festen Objektrahmens zeigt sich ein Bildkörper, der durch seine Formulierung über das Licht stets auf Transzendenz verweist. Gegen ein flüchtiges oberflächiges Abtasten von Weltbildern, wie es der Alltagsgebrauch des Mediums Video zeigt, setzt Rosenbachs Videoskulptur in beispielhafter Weise auf eine Konzentration der Wirklichkeit(en).

Videoskulptur als mediale Erweiterung einer künstlerischen Skulpturtradition ist der Schwerpunkt der künstlerischen Arbeit von Helmut Mark: Der Monitor wird zum Gestaltungsmaterial wie andere bildhauerisch verwendete und geformte Materialien auch. Das durch ihn repräsentierte Bildelement wird stets als die Konstruktion des haptisch greifbaren Körpers erweiternde Bewegungsformulierung gestaltet. Sinnliche und mediale Präsenz von Formkonstrukten stellen ein gemeinsames Ordnungssystem vor, eine durch Proportion konzentrierte Ordnungsstruktur.

Körpervolumen wird in bewußter Massivität der Erscheinung gestaltet. Skulptur ist so eher zeichenhafte Repräsentation einer für sich stehenden Form, die – im absoluten Gegensatz zum sonstigen Einsatz des Fernsehmonitors – in keiner Weise literarisch oder wirklichkeitsabbildend fungiert.

Ist die Skulptur von Helmut Mark stets ein auratisches Gebilde, das bei aller haptischer Präsenz letztlich Distanz einfordert und diese formuliert, so provoziert die *Videoschwelle* von Gudrun Bielz und Ruth Schnell einen direkten Körperbezug zum Betrachter. Die in Betonmodule integrierten Monitore zeigen Wahrnehmungshürden an. Sie formulieren den Widerstand gegen den selbstverständlichen Ablauf, sei es der eigenen Körperbewegung wie der eigenen Blickbewegung.

Der Monitor in der Funktion eines Fernsehers zumeist in oder über Kopfhöhe des Betrachters montiert, nähert sich mit seinen Bildsequenzen hier von unten. Er lenkt so die Aufmerksamkeit durch die Bildbewegung hin zum direkten visuellen Bodenkontakt. Das Werkstück operiert nicht nur mit einer Alltagsform, die zur speziellen auch ästhetischen Aufmerksamkeit geführt wird, sondern verweist zugleich auf das Körperhafte als Phänomen eines Hindernisses der Blickrichtung. Der Raum über den Monitoren mit seinen Lichtbildstrahlen (im übertragenen Sinn) mutiert in gleicher Weise zu einem Volumenshindernis wie die massiv ausgeführte Betonschwelle.

monitor is always constructed as a formulation of movement extending the haptic, tangible body of the work. Constructs of form with a sensuous and a mediated presence represent a joint system of order, a structure of order based on concentrated proportion.
In Mark's works, corporeal volume is consciously formed to present a massive appearance. In this way, sculpture is more of a sign-like representation of a self-sufficient form, which – totally unlike any other use of the TV monitor – has no literary or literal function whatsoever.

Whereas Helmut Mark's sculptural work is always an aural configuration that ultimately requires viewers to keep their distance despite its haptic quality, Gudrun Bielz and Ruth Schnell's "Videoschwelle" provokes a direct bodily relationship between the work and the viewer. The monitors integrated in the cement modules show obstacles to perception. They formulate resistance to the processes that are taken for granted, whether they involve the movement of one's own body or the movement of one's own glance.
A monitor functioning like a television is usually mounted at or just above eye-level, but in this case, the monitor approaches the viewer with a sequence of images from below. In this way, the movements of the images attract the viewer's attention to establish direct visual contact with the ground. This piece does not only work with an ordinary form that is evolved into a specific, even aesthetic awareness, but also refers to corporeality as the phenomenon of an obstacle in the path of viewing. The space above the monitors, with rays of light images (in a figurative sense), is transformed into an obstacle mass in a way similar to the massive formation of the cement obstacle.
There is a striving here for direct bodily contact that displays parallels to similar tendencies in the field of sculpture in general, for instance in Franz West's work: the haptic perceptibility of a sculptural work is no longer

restricted to the possibility of a tactile exploration of the work with one's fingertips, but rather the work becomes a "mold". It seeks a confrontation with the whole body, which is at once a provocation of the entirety of tactile perceptibility.

In Gundi Berghold's work "cut 1/2", the confrontation takes place primarily between two video monitors fixed in an open circular frame, with the screen surfaces positioned exactly opposite one another. The circular construction, which is actually tangible, opens exactly at the point where the two monitors face one another. Each monitor image reflects the form of the circle as a light structure; thus, a light connection is created between the two monitors. Thus the light connection also defines a bodily space and refers through this definition to another fundamental element of video sculpture: not only does the video monitor enable an image-like suggestion of a body – whether in a film-like or statuesque representation –, the video monitor not only presents itself as a body, but the light rays emanating from the surface of its screen also create the impression of corporeal volume. This is not presented in the form of a physical resistance, but rather as the perception of light beams.

The formation of a corporeality in this sense is expressed with particular clarity where two monitors are placed facing one another, so that the space between them defines a separate corporeal space. Bill Viola's striking work "Heaven and Earth" is exemplary in this context: in this case, the contents of the images displayed by the monitors additionally define the space between them as representing the nexus of human life.

In comparison, Gundi Berghold's work dissolves a tactilely perceptible interface – the open body of the circle – functioning as a separator; the way she uses the two monitors joins the circle to create a totality of movement. The moving form of the circle is represented on several different levels of perception as a

Die direkte Körperkonfrontation, die hier gesucht wird, läßt Parallelen zu ähnlichen Tendenzen im Bereich der Skulptur erkennen, z.B. im Werk von Franz West: Die haptische Erfahrbarkeit eines skulpturalen Werkes beschränkt sich nicht mehr auf ein mögliches Ertasten des Gegenstandes mit den Fingerspitzen, sondern das Werkstück wird zum „Paßstück". Es sucht die Konfrontation mit dem ganzen Körper, der in seiner gesamten taktilen Erfahrbarkeit herausgefordert wird.

In Gundi Bergholds Werkstück *cut 1/2* ereignet sich Konfrontation vor allem zwischen zwei Videomonitoren, die eingespannt in einen offen gehaltenen Kreisrahmen mit der Oberfläche ihres Schirmes genau gegenüber positioniert sind. Der faktisch greifbare Kreiskörper ist genau an jener Stelle geöffnet, an der sich die beiden Videomonitore gegenüberstehen. Beide Monitorbilder nehmen die Form des Kreises als Lichtkörper auf; es entsteht eine Lichtverbindung zwischen beiden Monitoren, die ebenfalls Körperraum definiert und in dieser Definition auf ein grundsätzlich Element der Videoskulptur verweist: Der Videomonitor ermöglicht nicht nur das bildhafte Zitat eines Körpers, sei es in filmischer Ansicht oder in der Ansicht eines Standbildes, der Videomonitor präsentiert sich nicht nur selbst als Körper, sondern die von seiner Oberfläche ausgehende Lichtstrahlung schafft ebenfalls den Eindruck von Körpervolumen, wenngleich nicht in der Form eines Massewiderstandes, sondern als Strahlungswahrnehmung.

Besonders deutlich kommt eine Körperformulierung in diesem Sinne zum Ausdruck, wenn zwei Monitore gegenübergestellt werden und so der Raum zwischen den beiden Monitoren einen eigenen Körperraum definiert. Es sei in diesem Zusammenhang auch auf Bill Violas markante Arbeit *Heaven and Earth* verwiesen, die mit zusätzlicher inhaltlicher Determinierung einen solchen Strahlungsraum zwischen zwei Monitorbildern als Schnittstelle des menschlichen Lebens vorstellt.

Gundi Bergholz Arbeit hingegen löst eine taktil wahrnehmbare Schnittstelle – den offenen Kreiskörper – in ihrer Trennungsfunktion auf, durch den Einsatz der beiden Monitore verbindet sie den Kreis zu einem Insgesamt an Bewegung. Auf mehreren Wahrnehmungsebenen wird hier die Bewegungsform des Kreises als durchgängiges Bewegungsmotiv vorgestellt, das somit gleichnishaft für Bewegung an sich steht.

Die Permanenz von Bewegung ist auch das künstlerische Hauptthema von Leo Schatzls Ausstellungsbeitrag. Sein Werkstück *Oxo* verbindet Geruchs- und Geschmacksimpulse mit einem Videobild zur gemeinsamen Erfahrung von Bewegung. Die Steuerung des Videobildes der dampfenden Suppe erfolgt durch die Dampfmenge, die von zwei quasi Antennen des Monitors, die mit Verdampfungsmeßgeräten ausgestattet sind, erfaßt wird. Es entsteht somit der Eindruck einer closed circuit-Videoinstallation. Die biologische Abhängigkeit und dadurch Öffnung dieses quasi closed circuit ist jedoch klar durch die Suppe gegeben: Nur solange die Suppe kocht, ist auch die Interaktion mit dem Monitor gegeben und nur solange ist auch das Bild im Monitor zu sehen.

Leo Schatzls Arbeit formuliert Beziehungskonstellationen zwischen einzelnen Sinneswahrnehmungen. Ähnlich wie zuvor bei Gundi Berghold die Strahlung des Monitors, so ist auch hier der von den Kochtöpfen aufsteigende Dampf integriertes skulpturales Element. Ende und Anfang einer skulpturalen Wahrnehmung sind hier ebenso in einen Graubereich geführt, wie Anfang und Ende einer auf bestimmte sinnliche Bereiche fixierten Wahrnehmungseinheit.

Der Aspekt von Video als Echtzeit-Phänomen, also der möglichen Gleichzeitigkeit von visueller Wahrnehmung und Wahrnehmung dieser visuellen Wahrnehmung, ist hier ebenso verarbeitet. – Dieser Aspekt markiert ja in großer Deutlichkeit den zentralen Unterschied zwischen Film und Video, der auch in der Frühzeit der Videokunst z.B. von Friderike Pezold klar

consistent motif of movement, thus becoming a simile for movement itself.

The permanence of movement is also the main theme of Leo Schatzl's work for this exhibition. His piece „Oxo" combines smell and taste impulses with a video image to create an overall experience of movement. The video image of steaming soup is controlled by the amount of actual steam that is registered by two antenna-devices on the monitor, which are equipped with an apparatus for measuring the amount of steam. In this way, an impression of a closed-circuit video installation is created. However, the soup demonstrates the biological dependency and thus the opening of the closed circuit. Interaction with the monitor only takes place as long as the soup is cooking, and only then may the image be seen in the monitor.

Leo Schatzl's work formulates the constellations of relationship among individual senses of perception. The steam rising here from the pots is an integrated sculptural element, similar to the light beams in Gundi Berghold's work described above. The end and the beginning of sculptural perception trail off into a gray area here, just like the beginning and the end of perceptual units fixed on a certain area of the senses.

The aspect of video as a real-time phenomenon, specifically the possible simultaneity of visual perception and the perception of this visual perception, is treated here as well. This is also the aspect that most clearly characterizes the central difference between film and video; this difference was recognized and clearly stated even in the early phases of video art by Frederike Pezold, among others. In addition, Schatzl's work also refers to the question of the "Gesamtkunstwerk", an synthetic art work that addresses all the senses, which has been discussed over and over throughout centuries of art history and has been imbued accordingly with new impulses in today's art discourse in light of virtual reality. Schatzl approaches this question in a wholly sculptural statement.

If Leo Schatzl's exhibited work is characterized by a massive reference to the multi-dimensionality of the human senses, including the experience of corporeal sculpture, then Andrea van der Straeten's work "Videohemd" ("Video Shirt") marks a complete turn-around from video-technical factors to a practically organic effect. The shirt woven from video tapes is an absolutely ironic statement of the boundaries of a fundamental video-sculptural effect. On the basis of the material conditional state of the magnet tapes, a possible video image is led to the massiveness of a haptic corporeal volume through the structure of weaving that is thousands of years old. Matter is thus defined as concentration.

The relationship to the human body stated here should also be understood in this sense: clothing in the sense of a protective covering, but also as decoration or a culturally associated tradition is merely a remote reference here, which is used to reveal a bodily determined limitation of video perception. Lacking the corresponding apparatus, the video tape is reduced to its exclusively material condition, separating it entirely from its usual function as an image transporter. Theoretically, the video tape in "Videohemd" still contains the prospect of an image, but that image is no longer perceptible. The artist uses the irony of the piece to indicate the separation (which still exists, although it is repeatedly negated) of human perceptions. Although the optical medium of video enables the citatory conjunction of divergent sensuous impressions on an optical level to a previously unknown extent, these cannot at all replace actual sensuous impressional qualities.

To continue the line of thought stated in this work, video sculpture shows itself to be a border area of sculpture and thus its opportunity for expansion. The sculptural question of the form and perception of corporeal volume is extended through the image's citation of

erkannt und formuliert wurde. – Außerdem verweist Schatzls Arbeit auf die über viele Jahrhunderte in der Kunstgeschichte immer wieder diskutierte Frage nach dem Gesamtkunstwerk, das alle Sinne anspricht; eine Frage, die in der heutigen Kunstdiskussion um virtuelle Realität einen entsprechenden Neuimpuls erhalten hat. Schatzl nähert sich dieser Frage in absolut skulpturaler Formulierung.

Verwies schon sein Ausstellungsbeitrag sehr massiv auf die Mehrdimensionalität menschlicher Sinnlichkeit, auch in der Erfahrung des körperhaft Skulpturalen, so markiert Andrea van der Straetens Arbeit *Mein Video ist mein Hemd* eine totale Rückführung von videotechnischen Faktoren zu einer quasi organischen Wirkung. Das aus Videobändern gewobene Hemd ist eine absolut ironische Formulierung der Grenze einer grundsätzlichen videoskulpturalen Wirkung. Das mögliche Videobild in seiner materiellen Bedingtheit des Magnetbandes wird durch eine jahrtausendealte Webstruktur zur Massivität eines haptischen Körpervolumens geführt. Materie definiert sich somit als Ballung.

Der hier formulierte Bezug zum menschlichen Körper ist ebenfalls in diesem Sinne zu verstehen: Kleidung im Sinne eines Schutzes auch als Dekoration bzw. in kulturellen Zuordnungstraditionen ist hier nur entfernt zitiert, um eine körperhafte Grenzbestimmung der Videowahrnehmung aufzuzeigen. Ohne entsprechende Apparatur ist das Videoband ausschließliche auf materielle Bedingungen zurückgeführt, die es völlig von seiner üblichen Funktion als Bildträger abtrennen.

Das Videoband im „Video-Hemd" trägt zwar nach wie vor die Möglichkeit des Bildes in sich, dieses Bild ist jedoch nicht mehr wahrnehmbar. Über die Ironie des Werkstückes verweist die Künstlerin auf die (stets vorhandene, wenn gleich immer wieder negierte) Trennung der menschlichen Sinneswahrnehmungen. Im optischen Medium Video sind zwar in zuvor nicht bekannter Art und Weise zitathafte Zusammenführungen der verschiedensten Sinneseindrücke auf einer optischen Ebene möglich, diese ersetzen jedoch in keiner Weise tatsächliche sinnliche Eindrucksqualitäten.

In dieser Arbeit formulierte Gedanken aufnehmend, erweist sich Videoskulptur als Grenzsituation der Skulptur, daher auch als ihre Erweiterungsmöglichkeit. Die skulpturale Frage nach der Gestaltung und Wahrnehmung von Körpervolumen erweitert sich durch das Bewegungszitat des Bildes sowie dem ästhetischen Eigenwert technischer Apparaturen, die in spezieller Weise die Grenze zwischen dem Werk und seiner Inszenierung fließend erscheinen lassen.

movement and the independent aesthetic value of the technical apparatus, which particularly allows the borderline between the work itself and its staging to appear fluid.

Objekt: Video. Eine Bild-Störung

GOTTFRIED HATTINGER

OBJECT : VIDEO. A PICTURE DISTORTION

When Wolf Vostell proclaimed that ART=LIFE, he was certainly not referring to life in front of a television set. The first artistic works that were identified as "video art" critically explored the medium of television, and they were created at a time when the TV industry was developing at an enormous pace, the sales of TV sets were skyrocketing and people were spending more and more time watching television. At the time, television was hailed as a democratic medium of communication, somewhat similar to Internet propaganda today, which is accepted – as it appears to me – with a certain degree of naiveté, even on the part of many artists. The current, wide-spread affirmative attitude regarding this new medium runs counter to the attitude of artists' in the 60's, who stated their criticism and ridicule in radical ways. As early as the mid-50's, the philosopher Günther Anders, in his book "Die Antiquiertheit des Menschen" ("The Antiquated Mind of Man"), debunked the global flood of images as "post-literary illiterateness" and the alleged participation in the events of the whole world as "merely gaping at images of the world". It was probably the same perspicacity that led the artists of the Fluxus and Happening movements to critically examine the medium of television even before the first video recorders and cameras were available. The same Wolf Vostell mentioned above wrapped barbed wire around television sets and then buried them ("TV Funeral", 1963). Vostell continued to formulate this attitude well into the 80's, when he enclosed television sets in cement and exhibited them in ensembles of up to thirty objects and several turkeys under the title "Endogenous Depression".
The Korean artist Nam June Paik created an ironic view of television culture with a sculpture composed of TV sets in the form of a cross representing a new altar of the media society. Between 1974 and 1982, he exhibited a series of "TV Buddha's" that are among his

Als Wolf Vostell seine Gleichung KUNST=LEBEN proklamierte, meinte er sicherlich nicht ein Leben vor dem Fernsehapparat. Die ersten künstlerischen Arbeiten, die als „Videokunst" deklariert sind, setzen sich mit dem Medium Fernsehen auseinander und fallen in eine Zeit, in der sich die Tv-Industrie mit immenser Rasanz entwickelte, der Verkauf von Geräten boomte und die Menschen immer mehr Zeit vor den Bildschirmen verbrachten. Fernsehen wurde damals allgemein als demokratisches Kommunikationsmittel begrüßt, was ein wenig an die heutige Internet-Propaganda erinnert, die mit – wie ich zu erkennen glaube – einiger Naivität angenommen wird – auch von vielen Künstlern. Die gegenwärtige, fast durchwegs affirmative Haltung dem neuen Medium gegenüber kontrastiert die Haltung der Künstler in den sechziger Jahren, die ihre Kritik und ihren Spott in radikaler Weise formulierten. Der Philosoph Günther Anders entlarvte in „Die Antiquiertheit des Menschen" bereits Mitte der fünfziger Jahre die globale Bilderflut als „post-literarisches Analphabetentum", und die suggerierte Teilnahme an der ganzen Welt als „bloßes Angaffen von Weltbildern". Diese Hellsichtigkeit war es wohl auch, die die Künstler der Fluxus- und Happeningbewegung zur Auseinandersetzung mit dem Medium führte, bevor die ersten Videokameras und Recorder erhältlich waren. Der bereits erwähnte Wolf Vostell umwickelte Fernsehapparate mit Stacheldraht und beerdigte sie anschließend („TV-Begräbnis", 1963). Diese Haltung thematisierte Vostell bis in die achtziger Jahre hinein, wo er Fernsehgeräte zubetonierte und sie in Ensembles mit bis zu dreißig Objekten und einigen Truthähnen unter dem Titel „Endogene Depression" ausstellte.

Der Koreaner Nam June Paik ironisierte die Fernsehkultur mit einer Skulptur aus Tv-Geräten in Kreuzform, womit er einen neuen Altar der Mediengesellschaft schuf. Zwischen 1974 und 1982 stellte er eine Serie von „TV Buddha's" aus, die zu seinen bekanntesten Videoskulpturen gehört. Eine Buddha-Statue sitzt vor einem Monitor und meditiert vor seinem eige-

Nam June Paik: Magnet-TV, 1965, Fernsehapparat, Eisenmagnet

Wolf Vostell: Endogene Depression II (Ausschnitt), 1980

nen Abbild. Eines der ersten Video-Objekte von Nam June Paik ist jeoch das „Magnet TV" von 1963. Über einem Fernsehgerät ist ein starker Eisenmagnet befestigt, der das laufende Bild stört und in ein Ornament verwandelt. Diese „Ornamentierung" von Tv-Programmen setzt er bis heute fort, indem er Sendungen beliebig in seinen Schnittplatz holt und die Bilderflut zu rasanten Mustern manipuliert, wobei die Anzahl der Montiore und die räumlichen Ausmaße der Werke immer größere Dimensionen angenommen haben.

Gewissermaßen als Referenz an die Tv-Arbeiten Paiks ist in der Linzer Ausstellung eine Arbeit des jungen Künstlers Jaap de Jonge zu sehen, der in „Kristallen Bol" auf ähnliche Weise die globalen Tv-Sender anzapft. Mittels zweier Satellitenempfänger holt er etwa neunzig verfügbare Programme aus dem Äther und fokussiert sie sämtlich in eine Glaskugel. Er verzichtet also auf die Darstellung des Gleichzeitigen in überdimensionierten „Video Walls", sondern reduziert die Masse des Verfügbaren auf eine bewegliche Kugel an der Wand, die es erlaubt, mit einer einzigen Handbewegung durch den Bilderkosmos zu jagen, der ebenfalls nur noch als Ornament wahrgenommen wird. Der Titel „Kristallen Bol" ist eine Anspielung auf den Anschein des Wahr-Sagens der Medien.

Die künstlerischen Ausdrucksformen und ästhetischen Kriterien haben sich innerhalb der letzten dreißig Jahren selbst-

most well-known video sculptures. One Buddha statue sits in front of a screen meditating before his own image. However, one of Nam June Paik's first video objects was the "Magnet TV" from 1963. A strong iron magnet was mounted above a television set, which continuously interfered with the picture and transformed it into an ornament. He has continued this "ornamentation" of TV programs up to the present by arbitrarily pulling broadcasts into his editing station and manipulating the flood of images to form hectic patterns, whereby the number of monitors and the spatial extent of his works has taken on larger and larger dimensions.

In the exhibition in Linz, one work by the young artist Jaap de Jonge may be seen as a kind of reference to Paik's TV works: in "Kristallen Bol", de Jonge taps into global television broadcasts in a similar way. Using two satellite receivers, he retrieves about ninety available programs from the ether and concentrates them all in a glass ball. Thus, rather than representing simultaneity in overdimensional "Video Walls", he reduces the mass of available programs to a moveable ball on the wall, with which one may race through a cosmos of images, and which is also perceived as a mere ornament. The title "Kristallen Bol" is a play on the seeming clairvoyance of the media.

Of course, artistic forms of expression and

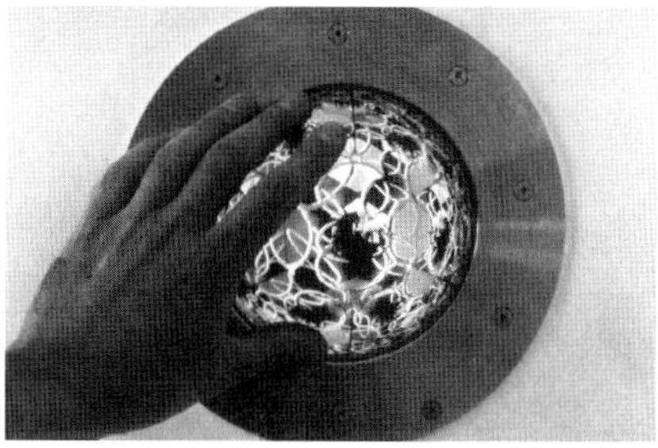

Nam June Paik: TV Trichter, 1984, 99 Fernsehapparate, Höhe 16m, größter Ø 11,6 m.

Jaap de Jonge: Kristallen Bol, 1996, 2 Satellitenantennen, Computer, Videomischpult, Sensor, Glaskugel, Ø 18 cm

aesthetic criteria have changed over the course of the past thirty years. The immediacy of the involved political gestures predominant in the 60's (the generation of '68) has given way to a more relaxed, almost nonchalant attitude of a younger and the youngest generation of artists; this does not necessarily mean, however, that a critical reflection of media presence, manipulation and consumerism has lost its significance. This is exemplified here in the work "tv-tod" by Richard Kriesche, born in 1940, and the object "Schleuderstern" by Dieter Kiessling, born in 1957. "tv-tod" presents a television with a gunshot hole as an exhibition object: this is a relict of an action that took place in 1975 at the Kunstverein in Cologne, in which Kriesche addressed the idea of "real" reality as opposed to "electronic" reality. The artists was filmed by a video camera and the image was transmitted to a monitor. This monitor was filmed by another camera, and its image was seen by the audience in a different room. An assistant shot at the monitor with a gun, which gave the viewers the impression that the artist had been shot. What remains of the shot television as an item from an art exhibition is the vivid manifestation of an action previously carried out: a television set with a gunshot hole.

In comparison, Dieter Kiessling's artistic gesture seems rather laconic; it is not marked by ambitions of enlightenment, of contrasting two realities, but rather it simply denies the television its function. The screen serves as a surface for an engraving work with the title "Schleuderstern" and thus becomes an

verständlich verändert. Die Unmittelbarkeit einer engagiert-politischen Geste der Sechziger (Achtundsechziger) ist einer gelasseneren, fast nonchalanten Haltung der jüngeren und jüngsten Generation gewichen, was aber nicht notwendigerweise zur Folge hat, daß kritische Bezugnahmen auf Medienpräsenz, Manipulation und Konsumismus an Bedeutung verloren hätten. Als Beispiel stehen in der Ausstellung die Arbeit „tv-tod" des 1940 geborenen Richard Kriesche, und das Objekt „Schleuderstern" des 1957 geborenen Dieter Kiessling gegenüber. „tv-tod" stellt als Ausstellungsobjekt einen Fernseher mit einem Einschußloch dar, das Relikt einer Aktion, die 1975 im Kölnischen Kunstverein stattgefunden hat und in der sich Kriesche mit der „wirklichen" Wirklichkeit gegenüber der „elektronischen" Wirklichkeit auseinandersetzt. Der Künstler wurde von einer Videokamera gefilmt und in einen Monitor übertragen. Dieser Monitor wurde mit einer anderen Kamera aufgenommen, dessen Bild in einem anderen Raum, in dem sich das Publikum befand, zu sehen war. Ein Assistent schoß mit einem Gewehr in das Monitorbild, wodurch den Beobachtern der Eindruck vermittelt wurde, daß der Künstler getroffen worden sei. Vom erschossenen Fernseher als Exponat der Kunstausstellung bleibt nur die eindringliche Manifestation einer zuvor ausgeführten Handlung: ein Fernsehapparat mit einem Einschußloch.

Die Geste von Dieter Kiessling nimmt sich daneben lakonisch aus, hat auch nicht mehr die aufklärerische Ambition, zwei Wirklichkeiten gegeneinander zu setzen, sondern verweigert dem Fernsehapparat schlichtweg seine Funktion. Der Bild-

Richard Kriesche: tv-tod, 1975, Fernsehapparat mit Einschußloch

Dieter Kiessling: Schleuderstern, 1992

schirm fungiert als Oberfläche für eine Gravurarbeit mit dem Titel „Schleuderstern", wird zum ästhetischen Objekt entfremdet und verlangt nach Neudefinition. Von Prägnanz und genauer Beobachtungsgabe zeugt eine zweite Arbeit von Dieter Kiessling in der Ausstellung: Vor einem Monitor ist eine rote Glühbirne befestigt, die von einer Kamera aufgenommen und in den Monitor übertragen wird. Die Übertragung wird wiederum aufgenommen und nochmals übertragen, welcher Prozeß solange fortgesetzt wird, bis eine Reihe von sechs Übertragungen der Glühbirne auf dem Bildschirm zu sehen ist. Durch das bläuliche Eigenlicht des Monitors wird die rote Farbe bei jeder Übertragung verfälscht, bis die letzte rote Glühbirne blau geworden ist.

Auch Kirsten Johannsen benützt in ihrem „Videopendel" das dem LCD-Bildschirme immanente Farbspektrum, allerdings ohne eingespieltes Bild. Durch die wechseln die Farben von grün über rot bis blau, und es ist auch eine Frage des Standortes, welche Farbe man wahrnimmt. In ihrer neuen Arbeit „Glasen" stellt sie das Verinnen der Zeit in zwei Monitoren dar, die als Sanduhr fungieren. Der Sand rinnt vom oberen Montor in den unteren. Hat sich der obere geleert, dreht ein Mechanismus die beiden Monitore wie eine Sanduhr um.

Das gesamte Werk von Friederike Pezold ist durchdrungen von gesellschaftlichen Utopien und gegenweltlichen Entwürfen, in denen die gegenwärtige Fernsehalltäglichkeit mit Vehemenz angegriffen wird. „Das Fernsehen hat seinen vorläufig technischen Höhepunkt und geistigen Tiefpunkt erreicht",

aesthetic object alienated from its original purpose and requiring a new definition.
Another work by Dieter Kiessling in this exhibition evinces conciseness and a talent for precise observation: a red light bulb is mounted in front of a monitor, filmed by a camera and transmitted to the monitor. The transmission is filmed and transmitted again, and this process is repeated until a series of six images of the light bulb may be seen on the screen. The bluishness of the light inherent to the monitor distorts the red color with each transmission until the last red light bulb has turned blue.
Kirsten Johannsen also uses the color spectrum inherent to the LCD monitor in her work "Videopendel", although she does not use a transmitted image. The colors shift from green to red to blue, and the colors a viewer perceives depend on the viewer's position. In her new work "Glasen", she represents time fleeting in the form of two monitors functioning as an hourglass. The sand runs down from the top monitor into the bottom monitor, and when the top one is empty, a mechanism turns both monitors around like an hourglass.
Friederike Pezold's entire work is permeated by social utopias and designs for counter-worlds, in which the every-day presence of television is vehemently attacked. "Television has provisionally reached its technical high point and its intellectual low point," as she states in her recently published monograph. As early as 1977, long before artistic television experiments were conceived anywhere else,

Friederike Pezold: RFU-Radio Freies Utopia, Fern- bzw. Nahsehprogramm „Nirwana", 1984

VA Wölfl: TV-Set, 1974

she founded her broadcasting station "RFU – Radio Free Utopia". All of the technical equipment for broadcasting and receiving could be carried on the artist's back. Where Nam June Paik presented a Buddha statue in deep meditation before its own image in the monitor, all Friederike Pezold needed for her last RFU programs "Nirvana" was pure light. In "Object: Video", Friederike Pezold exhibits three new video sculptures from her series of "Electronic Goddesses", which are based on the classic Three Graces. However, the ideal image of antiquity is discarded here – the goddesses come from the Third World, from Tibet, Guatemala and Africa.

The work "TV-Set" by VA Wölfl was created in 1974, in other words at a time when only two programs were available, even in Germany. He placed two TV sets, each broadcasting one of the two available programs, with the screens close together and wrapped them up with an iron band, so that no more than a weak glow escaped from the rigid encirclement. The medium suffices itself and closes the viewer out. In Linz, VA Wölfl recreates his work "Flagge" from 1984 as an "Austrian Version": three TV sets displaying the colors red-white-red are stacked on top of one another, and the screens are turned toward the wall, so that only the reflection remains visible. Perhaps it is a reference to another time, when there was still an end to broadcasts that was signaled by a flag and an anthem.

The question, "Who is afraid of video?", that Servaas posed in 1984, has even increased in

heißt es in ihrer jüngst erschienenen Monographie. Bereits 1977, also lange bevor anderswo an künstlerische Tv-Experimente gedacht wurde, gründete sie ihren Sender „RFU – Radio Freies Utopia", dessen gesamte technische Sende- und Empfängerausrüstung von der Künstlerin auf dem Rücken getragen werden konnte. Zeigte Nam June Paik noch eine Buddha-Statue, die sich in ihr eigenes Abbild im Monitor meditativ versenkte, benötigte Friederike Pezold nur noch reines Licht für ihre letzten RFU-Programme „Nirwana". Bei „Objekt:Video" zeigt Firederike Pezold drei neue Videoskulpturen aus ihrer Serie der „Elektronischen Göttinnen", die sich auf die klassischen drei Grazien bezihen. Das antike Idealbild wird jedoch verworfen – die Göttinen kommen aus der Dritten Welt, aus Tibet, Guatemala und Afrika.

Von 1974, also aus einer Zeit, in der auch in Deutschland nur zwei Programme zu empfangen waren, stammt die Arbeit „TV-Set" von VA Wölfl. Er stellte zwei Fernsehapparate, in denen jeweils eines der beiden Programme lief, mit den Bildschirmen aneinander eng zusammen und verband sie mit einem Eisenband, sodaß nur ein schwaches Leuchten aus der Umklammerung hervordrang. Das Medium genügt sich selber und schließt die Zuseher aus. In Linz rekonstruiert VA Wölfl seine „Flagge" von 1984 als „Österreich-Version", bei der er drei übereinander gestellte Tv-Geräte in die Farben rot-weiß-rot justiert und sie mit der Bildschirmseite so zur Wand dreht, daß nur mehr die Reflektion sichtbar ist. Vielleicht eine Referenz auf Zeiten, als es noch einen Sendeschluß mit Flagge und Hymne gab.

Die Frage: „Wer hat Angst vor Video?", gestellt von Servaas im Jahr 1984 hat angesichts des grassierenden „Infotainment" verstärkte Aktualität. In vier Kanälen der Installation laufen Tv-Berichte von verschiedenen Ereignissen. Wenn über besonders aggressive Szenen berichtet wird, löst sich innerhalb des Objektes eine Peitsche und bedroht die Betrachter. Servaas gestaltet seit Beginn der achtziger Jahre narrative Video-Installationen, die er vorzugsweise mit Pressluftelementen verbindet. Zum „Klassiker" der Videoskulptur ist seine Arbeit „Pfft..." geworden, die aus einer Flaumfeder vor einem Monitor besteht, in dem das Gesicht von Servaas zu sehen ist, der von Zeit zu Zeit die Feder anpustet, die sich daraufhin tatsächlich bewegt. Als Reaktion auf omnipräsente Medien- und Marktmechanismen entwarf Servaas 1990 seine Gegenstrategie und gründete unter dem Signet „Servaas/ Fi$h. Int." eine Firma, die seine Fisch- und Kunstprodukte vermarktet und vertreibt. Auf auf strategisch-subversive Weise benützt Servaas die professionellen Marktstrukturen als eine Art „Meta-Kunst".

Auch die Installation „A Virus of Sadness" von Lydia Schouten ist eine Reaktion auf Nachrichtensendungen im Fernsehen, die sie während ihres Aufenthaltes in New York dokumentierte. Sie reflektiert zwar einerseits die tatsächliche Situation der im Fernsehen vorgeführten Opfer, interessiert sich aber auch für die Opferrolle der Zuschauer, die ihre Zeit vor dem Bildschirm verbringen, um die moderne Einsamkeit in einer „Überdosis an Kanälen und Verbindungen". Lydia Schouten erzählt in ihren Arbeiten vielfach verflochtene Geschichten und benützt die in den Medien verbreiteten Klischees und den Kitsch der Plastikkultur für ihre opulenten Environments.

„Pinocchios Pipenose Householddilemma" von Paul McCarthy besteht aus einem Zimmer, einem Fernseher und einigen Stühlen. Im Monitor läuft ein Film über diverse Haushaltskatastrophen seines Helden Pinocchio, dessen Rolle

topicality in light of the rampancy of "Infotainment" today. TV reports of various events are broadcast on four channels in the installation. When there is a report of a particularly aggressive scene, a whip comes loose within the object and threatens the viewer. Servaas has been creating narrative video installations since the early 80's, which he frequently combines with pneumatic elements. One of the "classics" of video sculpture is his work "Pfft...", which consists of a feather fixed in front of a monitor that displays Servaas' face; the feather actually moves when the face in the monitor blows at it from time to time. In 1990, Servaas designed a counter-strategy as a reaction to the omnipresent mechanisms of media and the market: he founded a company with the insignia "Servaas/Fis$h" to market and distribute his fish and art products. Servaas uses professional market structures in a strategic-subversive way as a kind of "meta-art".

The installation "A Virus of Sadness" by Lydia Schouten is another reaction to television news broadcasts, which she documented during a stay in New York. On the one hand, she reflects on the actual situation of the victims presented on television, but on the other hand, she is also interested in the viewer's role as a victim, spending time in front of the screen to compensate modern loneliness with an "overdose of channels and connections". In her works, Lydia Schouten tells stories that are woven together in many ways, and she uses common media clichés and the kitsch of plastic culture to create opulent environments.

"Pinocchios Pipenose Householddilemma" by Paul McCarthy consists of a room, a television and several chairs. A film is played on the monitor about the various domestic catastrophes experienced by the hero, Pinocchio, who is played by the artist. The film is not shown to the viewers until they have costumed themselves in the Pinocchio costumes provided. In this way, McCarthy forces the audience to adopt an attitude of reception that at first appears comical – a flock of Pinocchios watching a Pinocchio film – but eventually leads to a feeling of something like suffocation inside the full mask. All the viewers look identical, and before they realize it, they have all become part of the spatial scene that Paul McCarthy has created.

In his object "The Hammer on the Anvil", Gusztáv Hámos explores the relationship between the medium and consumers, but also our behavior in response to annoyance. A complaining character in the monitor implores passersby to free him from the screen. If you want to get rid of this annoying stream of complaints, you have to hit the screen with the hammer on the anvil. Then it is quiet for a while, until the stream of complaints starts up again and the next visitor has the nerve to strike a blow.

Birgit Brenner's study of the processes of transformation, deformation and dissolution has led to "Selbstversuche" ("Self-experiments"), which she has conducted on the basis of careful research and precise calculations. The first experiment (1992) consisted of returning 390,000 tears to her own eyes using a drop device. The experiment now shown in Linz was the third, which was conducted in 1993; here the artist set herself the task of applying lipstick ("Rouge Essentiel 52"), kissing, and wiping her mouth, until the lipstick was entirely used up. The process may be observed through a wall telephone fitted with a small monitor, which is well smeared by the end of the procedure. Through the telephone receiver, viewers are requested to either stay or go away.

For her works, Susan Alexis Collins prefers public spaces and places, which she influences with small, intimate events in the form of video projections and sounds. People are taken by surprise as they come across her interventions by chance; passersby are usually left with a brief sensation of irritation in the midst of the hustle and bustle of everyday life.

vom Künstler gespielt wird. Der Film darf den Besuchern nur dann gezeigt werden, wenn sie sich zuvor mit den bereitliegenden Piocchiokostümen verkleidet haben. McCarthy zwingt die Zuschauer damit in eine Rezeptionshaltung, die im ersten Moment zwar komisch wirkt – wie sich eine Schar von Pinocchios einen Pinocchiofilm ansieht – aber mit der Zeit unter der Vollmaske zu leichten Atembeklemmungen führt. Die Zuschauer sehen alle identisch aus und finden sich unversehens als Teil einer Rauminszenierung von Paul McCarthy.

Die Beziehung zwischen Medium und Konsumenten, aber auch unser Verhalten angesichts einer Belästigung, thematisiert Gusztáv Hámos in seinem Objekt „The Hammer on the Anvil". Eine quengelnde Figur im Monitor fleht die Passanten an, ihn aus dem Bildschirm zu befreien. Will man das lästige Gequassel los werden, ist ein Schlag mit dem Hammer auf den Amboß erforderlich. Danach ist es für eine Weile ruhig, bis das Gequengel wieder beginnt und sich der nächste Besucher das Herz nimmt zuzuschlagen.

Birgit Brenners Auseinandersetzung mit Prozessen der Verwandlung, Deformation und Auflösung mündet in „Selbstversuche", die sie nach genauen Untersuchungen und Berechnungen eines Sachverhaltes durchführt. Der erste Versuch (1992) bestand darin, 390.000 Tränen mittels eines Tropfapparates in ihre Augen zurückzuführen. In dem in Linz gezeigten dritten Selbstversuch von 1993 unternimmt es die Künstlerin, sich mit einem Lippenstift („Rouge Essentiel 52") solange zu schminken, zu küssen und abzuwischen, bis der Stift aufgebraucht ist. Der Prozeß ist über ein Wandtelefon zu beobachten, in den ein kleiner Monitor eingelassen ist, der gegen Ende der Prozedur ziemlich verschmiert ist. Im Telefonhörer wird man aufgefordert, entweder hierzubleiben oder wegzugehen.

Susan Alexis Collins bevorzugt für ihre Arbeiten öffentliche Plätze und Räume, die sie mit kleinen, intimen Geschehnissen in Form von Videoprojektionen und Klängen beeinträchtigt. Auf ihre Interventionen stößt man überraschend und zufällig, meist hinterlassen sie bei den Passanten kurze Irritationen im alltäglichen Gedränge. In ihrer Arbeit „Introductory Exchanges" für eine Fußgängerunterführung unter der Themse in London projizierte sie einige Wasserlachen, die von den meisten Fußgängern tatsächlich übersprungen wurden. Im Linzer Hauptbahnhof installiert die Künstlerin ihre „Pedestrian Gestures", aus Animationsbildern von Händen, Mündern und Augen, um Pendler und Reisende in eine kurze Interaktion hineinzuziehen. Nähert man sich den Bildern, werden via Sensoren auch Klangbilder ausgelöst, für die Susan Collins österreichische Redensarten sammelte. Eine Überwachungskamera überträgt die Szenerie in die Landesgalerie, wo sie wie ein Bild zwischen den Ölgemälden projiziert wird. Für die Linzer Ausstellung entwarf sie „Touched", ein Stück für einen Korridor, in dem die Besucher von projizierten Händen „betatscht" werden. Susan Collins Arbeiten zielen auf eine aktive Kommunikation zwischen ihrer künstlerischen Arbeit und einem Publikum, das möglicherweise keine Kunstausstellungen besucht, an eine Form der Beteiligung, die sie als Künstlerin zwingt, ihre Rolle neu zu definieren.

Dies gilt in ähnlichem Sinn auch für die Arbeit von Paul Sermon, der in „Telematic Dreaming" an zwei entfernt liegenden Orten Betten installiert, in denen zufällige Begegnungen zwischen zufällig die Arbeit frequentierende Besucher stattfindet. Im Gegensatz zu Collins, die ihre Werke sehr wohl genau kalkuliert und strukturiert, spielt Sermon nur mehr die Rolle eines künstlerischen Gastgebers, der seine Herberge zur Verfügung stellt. Was in den Betten passiert, ist nicht mehr seine Angelegenheit.

Um die Rolle des Betrachtens, um eine voyeuristische Lust am Hinsehen geht es in der Arbeit von David Cerny und Milan Gustar in „Beasts". Knapp über Augenhöhe sind kleine Monitore in schlanke Säulen eingelassen. Um zu erfassen, was auf den Bildschirmen zu sehen ist, muß man näher herangehen

In Susan Alexis Collins' work "Introductory Exchanges" for a pedestrian tunnel under the Thames in London, she projected several puddles, which most pedestrians actually jumped over. The artist has installed her work "Pedestrian Gestures" at the main train station in Linz, which consists of animated images of hands, mouths and eyes and is intended to involve commuters and travelers in a brief interaction. When the images are approached, sensors trigger sound images, for which Susan Collins has collected Austrian dialects. A surveillance camera transmits the scene to the Landesgalerie, where it is projected like a picture among the oil paintings. For the exhibition in Linz, she designed "Touched", a piece for a corridor, where visitors are "touched" by projected hands. Susan Collins' works aim to achieve active communication between her artistic work and an audience that may never intentionally visit an art exhibition; she strives for a form of participation that forces her to redefine her own role as an artist.

In a way, this is also true for Paul Sermon's work. In "Telematic Dreaming", he places beds in two remote locations, where chance encounters may take place between chance visitors to these locations. Unlike Collins, who calculates and structures her works very precisely, Sermon plays the role of an artist-host, who simply makes his place of repose available to the guests. What happens in the beds is no longer his concern.

The role of the observer and a voyeuristic pleasure in looking are the focus of David Cerny and Milan Gustar's work in "Beasts". Small monitors are mounted in slender columns just above eye-level. One must go closer to them and stretch to see what is displayed on the monitors. The motivation to do so may well be strengthened by the information that porno films are being shown in all nine columns. However, the columns insidiously track the approach of visitors and turn themselves off when someone comes too close. Many attempts are made to outwit the sensors, but very few succeed. In an ideal case, some unsuccessful attempts may lead the visitors to become more clearly conscious, if only for a moment, of their own behavior and their role as "on-lookers".

The counterpart to this work that refuses to reveal its secrets is Gerda Lampalzer's installation "Blaue Schachtel" ("Blue Box"): it wants to be opened, to reveal its interior and to reward the curious with the sight to be seen inside.

The aspect of playfulness is especially highlighted in "Video-Jojo" by David Moises, the youngest participant in this exhibition. In this work, a camera is mounted in the center of a yo-yo made of hubcaps. When you play with the yo-yo, the filmed surroundings spin accordingly.

The exhibition concludes with three works, in which the character of the object is largely dissolved. Actual objects are still found in "Tavoli" by Studio Azzurro, which are related to projected events that are triggered by the visitors through sensors. Christian Möller and Sven Thöne retrieved images from the body of the murderer Joseph Paul Jernigan from the Internet menu and used them to create "The Virtual Backbone" as a journey from the head to the toes. Finally, "Lovers" by Teiji Furuhashi is a room without objects, where figures move along the walls. These figures react to visitors either by opening their arms to them or running away. The figure of the artist, who died last year, is also present: the figure falls back, "dies", when someone approaches it.

Considering how often it has been maintained that "video art" has long since become obsolete, these sculptures, objects and installations exhibit an astonishingly fresh vitality. This is true not only for the "classic" pieces that are already well known and are found in museum collections, but also for the works by young artists, who provide continuity and continuously restate the categories of artistic thinking. A classification or even a measure for evaluation that is based

und sich strecken. Die Bemühung wird eventuell gefördert, nachdem bekannt ist, daß in allen neun Säulen Pornofilme laufen. Perfiderweise registrieren die Säulen das Näherkommen von Personen und schalten sich aus, wenn jemand zu nahekommt. Vielfach wird der Versuch unternommen, die Sensoren zu überlisten, was allerdings selten gelingt. Einige mißratene Versuche führen im Idealfall zum Moment, wo die eigene Verhaltensweise und das Rollenverhalten deutlich ins Bewußtsein dringt.

Als Gegenstück zu dieser Arbeit, die ihr Geheimnis nicht preisgibt, installiert Gerda Lampalzer ihre „Blaue Schachtel", die geöffnet werden will, um ihr Inneres herzuzeigen und die Neugierigen mit ihrem Anblick zu belohnen.

Der spielerische Aspekt kommt im „Video-Jojo" des jüngsten Teilnehmers an der Ausstellung, David Moises, zur Geltung. Im Mittelpunkt des aus Radkappen gebauten Jojospiels ist eine Kamera montiert, wodurch bei der spielerischen Betätigung die erfaßte Umgebung rotiert.

Den Abschluß bilden drei Installationen, bei denen sich der Objektcharakter weitgehend aufgelöst hat. Wirkliche Gegenstände finden sich noch bei den „Tavoli" von Studio Azzurro, Objekte, die in Beziehung stehen zu projizierten Geschehnissen, die wiederum via Sensoren von den Besuchern ausgelöst werden. Christian Möller und Sven Thöne holten die Bilder aus dem Körper des Mörders Joseph Paul Jernigan aus dem Internet-Menü und gestalteten damit „The Virtual Backbone" als eine Fahrt vom Kopf bis zu den Zehen. „Lovers" von Teiji Furuhashi ist nur noch ein objektloser Raum mit Figuren, die sich entland der Wände bewegen. Diese Figuren reagieren auf Besucher, in dem sie entweder die Arme öffnen oder weglaufen. Die Figur des im Vorjahr gestorbenen Künstlers fällt nach hinten, „stirbt", wenn man auf sie trifft.

Angesichts der vielfach gehörten Behauptung, daß die „Videokunst" längst obsolet sei, weisen die Skulpturen, Objekte und Installationen ein erstaunlich frisches Leben auf. Dies gilt nicht nur für die bereits bekannten „klassischen" Stücke, die sich in Museumssammlungen befinden, sondern auch für die Arbeiten der jungen Künstlerinnen und Künstler, die eine Kontinuität gewährleisten und die Kategorien künstlerischen Denkens immer wieder neu formulieren. Letztlich ist eine Klassifizierung oder gar eine Maßstabsetzung, die auf den Einsatz eines bestimmten Materials oder technischen Mittels beruht, völlig belanglos. Viele ausgerechnet jener Werke, die aufgrund technischer Avanciertheit eine Saison lang auf allen Festivals herumgereicht werden, sind in der nächsten Saison bereits verblaßt. Wenn sich nämlich hinter der Form und hinter der respektablen Rechnerleistung partout kein künstlerischer Geist finden läßt. Jede technische Innovation ist bloße Etappe zum nächsten Schritt, sie ist es, die alle Augenblicke obsolet wird. Künstlerische Innovationen hingegen gehören zu unserem spirituellen Leben und sind unabhängig von den Erfindungen der Ingenieure. Das ist beruhigend.

on the use of a particular material or certain technical means is ultimately irrelevant.
Many of the works that are passed around for a whole season from one festival to the next because of their technical sophistication, fade away again by the very next season. This happens when there is no artistic mind to be found anywhere behind the form and behind the impressive computational achievements.
Any technical innovation is merely a stepping stone to the next phase, thus that is what may become obsolete at any moment. Artistic innovations, on the other hand, are part of our spiritual life and do not depend on the inventions of engineers. That is reassuring.

Spiegel reflektiert Spiegel

KEIKO SEI

[In 1989, the author started taking orders from people to write short stories. She was living in Budapest at the time, and the people of the city had staged a mass demonstration for freedom of media before Hungarian TV. The change had begun.
She had been constantly searching for traces of video, walking all through Eastern Europe. Since she had to earn her own way in order to do this, she came up with the idea of taking orders from individual people for personal short stories. All her customers came from the West and wanted to have their own personal story with their own chosen subject. The customers would give the author a subject, she took the order and finished the story in a month or so; when she delivered the story, she was paid in cash and subsequently set out again to search for videos in another Eastern European town. Thus the story published here is on loan from the private collection of one of the author's customers, S.L.
Because of the particular circumstances surrounding the author's life, the readers/audience may sense her longing for video in the stories written at that time. Times have changed since then, both for video and for Eastern Europe. Yet she still takes an order occasionally, depending on the media landscape of the time and a customer's own vision in that landscape.]

[1989 begann die Autorin, Kurzgeschichten auf Bestellung für andere Leute zu schreiben. Zu diesem Zeitpunkt wohnte sie in Budapest, und die BewohnerInnen der Stadt hatten gerade vor dem ungarischen Fernsehen für Medienfreiheit demonstriert. Der Wandel hatte begonnen.
Jeden Tag suchte sie nach Spuren für Videos und ging dabei zu Fuß überall hin in Osteuropa. Um diese Suche fortzusetzen, mußte sie ihren Lebensunterhalt verdienen, so kam sie auf die Idee, persönliche Kurzgeschichten auf Bestellung zu schreiben. Ihre Kunden kamen alle aus dem Westen und wollten eine eigene Kurzgeschichte mit einem eigenen persönlichen Thema haben. Die Kunden gaben der Autorin ein Thema vor, sie nahm die Bestellung auf und lieferte die fertige Geschichte nach ca. einem Monat. Dafür wurde sie in bar bezahlt und zog dann wieder los, um ein anderes Video in einer anderen osteuropäischen Stadt zu suchen. Aus diesem Grund ist die Geschichte, die hier veröffentlicht wird, eine Leihgabe aus der Privatsammlung eines Kunden, S.L.
Auf Grund der besonderen Bedingungen unter denen die Autorin lebte, spürt man vielleicht in den Geschichten, die in dieser Zeit geschrieben wurden, ihre Sehnsucht nach dem Video. Die Zeiten haben sich inzwischen geändert, sowohl für Video wie auch für Osteuropa. Doch ab und zu nimmt sie immer noch eine Bestellung auf, je nach der jeweiligen Medienlandschaft und der eigenen Vision einer Kunde in dieser Landschaft.]

MIRROR REFLECTING MIRROR

1 I was coming down with a cold, and must have tossed and turned a good fourteen hours. I awoke realising I had somewhere to be and dashed out, umbrella in hand.

2 Out on the street, something's strange. Not an umbrella anywhere. Fourteen hours ago everyone was predicting rain. So there I was, conjuring up the thousand civil negotiations toward the downpour, charged with sheer helplessness against the impending storm, ready to be scattered like cut flowers before gale winds. Yet here the adults are strolling about now like nothing happened. What gives? Only the children seem to keep

1 Ich hatte mich verkühlt und mich sicher vierzehn Stunden lang im Bett gewälzt. Als ich wach wurde, fiel mir ein, daß ich einen Termin hatte und ich rannte mit dem Regenschirm in der Hand sofort los.

2 Auf der Straße stimmt etwas nicht. Nirgendwo ein Regenschirm in Sicht. Vor vierzehn Stunden sagten doch alle einen Regen voraus. Da stand ich also, beschwörte die Tausenden bürgerlichen Vorkehrungen in Hinblick auf den Regenguß, gewappnet gegen den anrückenden Sturm mit absoluter Hilflosigkeit; bereit, mich wie Schnittblumen im Wirbelwind zerstreuen zu lassen. Und da spazieren die Erwachsenen sorglos herum, als ob gar nichts gewesen wäre.

Was soll das? Bloß die Kinder haben die von mir vor gerade vierzehn Stunden vorgestellte Szene fest im Griff. Surrend noch schicken sie sich gegenseitig Signale mit ihren Regenschirmen; Ameisen, die mit den Antennen zucken. Unversehens haben die Kinder mit ihren Aktionen meine Aufmerksamkeit auf sich gezogen.

3 Für mich ist alles eine „Niedrigwinkelkomposition". Das sagt man mir unentwegt. Erstens ist mein Blickwinkel immer auf Fußebene. So funktioniert einfach meine Sicht. Eigentlich sollte ich an dieser Stelle wahrscheinlich die verschiedenen Fußarten beschreiben. Vielleicht hinzufügen <SEHEN SIE WIE DIESE FÜSSE INNERHALB MEINES BILDERRAHMENS VORBEIGEHEN, WIE SIE DIE VIELFÄLTIGKEIT DES LEBENS DER MENSCHEN ZUM AUSDRUCK BRINGEN>. Doch wie weit sollte man solchen Gedankengängen folgen? Schauen Sie doch selbst. Nur um zu sehen. Weil es wahr ist, <FÜSSE TRAGEN UND DRUCKEN DAS LEBEN DER MENSCHEN AUS...> (Übrigens, wußten Sie schon, daß manche Leute nicht einmal die Füße auseinanderhalten können?)

4 Selbst in diesem Moment, während ich darüber nachdenke, sind Menschenfüße unterwegs. Weiter, weiter, weiter. Sie entfernen sich, wie es scheint, immer weiter von mir weg. Und kehren niemals wieder zurück. Verfolgen tue ich sie auch nicht. Das liegt an meinem kompositionellen Einschlag.

5 Kunstlehrer. Schreiblehrer. Berater. Strenge Erzieher. Einweisende in alle Fächern (Bei dieser Gelegenheit möchte ich sie als meine „Lehrer des Lebens" bezeichnen). Mit vereinten Kräften bemühten sie sich alle, mich durch meine Kompositionen hindurch zu analysieren. Einige der mir eher Wohlgesinnten boten mir den angeblich freundlichen Ratschlag, daß es mir zukünftig eher besser, wenn auch nur geringfügig besser, ergehen würde, wenn ich mich unter die

any grips on the scene I envisioned just fourteen hours ago. Still buzzing, they signal to one another with their umbrellas, ants twitching their antennae. Before I know it, the kids and their antics have captured my attention.

3 Everything's a "low-angle composition" to me. People are foever telling me this. In the first place, my viewpoint is always at foot level. That's just how my vision works. Actually, I guess I ought to describe different kinds of feet here. Maybe add, <SEE THESE FEET CROSS WITHIN MY PICTURE FRAME, EXPRESSING THE DIVERSITY OF PEOPLE'S LIVES>. But how far do you have to take this sort of thing? Why don't you look for yourself? Just to see. Because it's true, <FEET SUPPORT AND EXPRESS PEOPLE'S LIVES...> (Incidentally, did you also know that some people can't even keep their feet straight?)

4 Even now, this very moment as I think these things, people's feet are on the march. Onward, onward, onward. Moving, it would seem, further and further away from me. Never to return. And neither do I give pursuit. That's because of my compositional bias.

5 Art teacher. Writing teacher. Advisors. Disciplinarians. Instructors in all subjects (Let me take this opportunity to call them my "Teachers in Living"). All of them pitched in to analyse me through my compositions. The more kindly among them offered ostensible guidance as how placing myself below others should work in my favour, however slightly, in the future. Which was all well and good, I suppose, if not for the fact that in the very same instant they killed any artistic value to my compositions. That's because they wove them into some little episodes.

6 The favourable future my art teacher painted had me becoming an artist. A renown "Painter of Feet". Or so went his clumsy

scenario, a pastiche progression up to an abrupt "Return to Basics -- Back to Oils." Though not before exhibitions on museum display, discovering aesthetic meaning in the very act of mounting the works, validating the efforts of the leading exhibition designers, masters in everything from lighting to layout, even their taste in picture frames (I can see it now: the guy who slaps a mirror into a frame with the unabashed title, <THE SUPREME WORK OF ART – YOU> Those were the days...) Then there'd be other causes, other banners to wave. Shows like <THE ARTIST CHOOSES HIS VIEWERS>. Or <DRAWINGS: ART BY LOTTERY – FIRST COME, FIRST CHANCE!> All the while priding myself on not selling out, on standing independent of the times, on remainig ever infathomable. I'd show them, swimming dry amist the currents of the mainstream!

7 There, does that make me a writer? If you've read this far, you no doubt see it coming, the predictable next bit about what my writing teacher made out of my compostiions. So let me say just this: <BETTER TO SWEEP UP STORIES FALLEN AT OTHER'S FEET, THAN TO COMPOSE FROM SCRATCH>. What say, for starters, I pick up a few lines I myself threw away?

8 *Hot water poured over the head / Runs cold by the time it reaches the feet.* A little something from a poem I once wrote. <HEAT GOES TO WAIST>, right? Well, the girlfriend who read it simply bubbled, "Surrealism, eh?" At the time I was dumbfounded by her presumptuousness, but that just goes to say that the poem only served for a girl to try out her very first "Surrealism" and for all that goes with that tender age. Of no use now, except to call up those memories.

9 Once again, to pull socks over my words: I have no recollection of ever writing a "Surrealist" poem.

anderen stelle. Das war ja alles gut und recht, nehme ich an, außer, daß sie jeden künstlerischen Wert in meinen Kompositionen damit abtöteten. Das kam von daher, daß sie sie in irgendwelche kleinen Episoden hineinwebten.

6 In der vorteilhaften Zukunft, die mir mein Kunstlehrer ausmalte, sollte ich Künstler werden. Ein berühmter „Füßemaler". Ungefähr so war sein stümperhaftes Szenario, ein pastiche Verlauf bis zu einer abrupten „Besinnung auf das Grundsätzliche – Zurück zum Öl". Doch vorher waren die Ausstellungen, die im Museum gezeigt wurden, die Entdeckung der ästhetische Bedeutung selbst in der Handlung des Aufhängens der Werke, die Bestätigung der Bemühungen führender Ausstellungsgestaltern, der Meistern des Ganzen von der Beleuchtung bis zum Layout, Experten selbst bei der Auswahl der Bilderrahmen (Ich sehe es schon vor mir: der Typ, der einen Spiegel in einen Rahmen klatscht, das Bild ganz unverschämt betitelt <DAS HERVORRAGENDSTE KUNSTWERK – DU!> Das waren ja Zeiten...). Dann gab es auch andere Ziele, andere Fahnen zu schwenken. Veranstaltungen wie <DER K\'dcNSTLER W\'c4HLT SEINE ZUSCHAUER>. Oder <ZEICHNUNGEN - ZIEHUNGEN: KUNST ALS LOTTERIE – DIE ERSTEN HABEN DIE BESTEN CHANCEN!>. Und die ganze Zeit war ich stolz darauf, mich nicht verkauft zu haben, meine Unabhängigkeit von den Zeiten zu bewahren, stets unergründlich zu bleiben. Ich würde es ihnen zeigen, ich würde trocken zwischen den Strömungen des Mainstreams schwimmen!

7 Also bin ich jetzt ein Schriftsteller oder nicht? Wenn Sie schon so weit gelesen haben, sehen Sie es sicher schon kommen, der nächste, vorhersehbare Teil, wo es darum geht, was mein Schreiblehrer aus meinen Kompositionen machte. Lassen Sie mich nur eines sagen: <ES IST BESSER, DIE GESCHICHTEN ZUSAMMENZUKEHREN, DIE DEN ANDEREN ZU FÜSSEN FALLEN, ALS AUS DEM NICHTS ZU KOMPO-

NIEREN>. Was halten Sie davon, wenn ich für den Anfang ein paar Zeilen zusammenkehre, die ich selber wegwarf?

8 *Heißes Wasser über den Kopf gegossen/Wird kalt, bis es die Füße erreicht.* Eine kleine Kostprobe aus einem Gedicht, das ich einmal schrieb. <HITZE SAMMELT SICH BEI DER TAILLE>, stimmt's? Nun, die Freundin, die das Gedicht damals las, sprudelte einfach, „Surrealismus, oder?" Damals hat ihre Vermessenheit mich vor den Kopf gestoßen, aber im Grunde hat das Gedicht mal dazu gereicht, daß ein Mädchen ihr erstes „Surrealismus" ausprobieren konnte, mit allem was in jenem zarten Alter dazugehört. Jetzt ist es natürlich nutzlos, außer um solche Erinnerungen wachzurufen.

9 Noch einmal, um meine Worte mit Socken zu bekleiden: Ich erinnere mich überhaupt nicht, jemals ein „surrealistisches" Gedicht geschrieben zu haben.

10 Im meines Bettes Rom
Der heißeste römische Sommer seit einem Jahrzehnt--
Ich sehe mich Rom fliehen
sehe mich, ein Blatt aus Stein zurücklassen
ein Blatt aus Stein mit Wasser befleckt
mit Wassertropfen groß und glänzend
Und wenn ich sie so sein lassen wollt' --
Die Steinblatttropfen zischen und werden Luft
... etc.

Ich bin überhaupt nie in Rom gewesen. Warum sollte ich ein „Römisches Gedicht" schreiben? Rom ist ungefähr das Entfernteste von unseren derzeitigen Zuständen. „Und Rom steht noch", würde man sagen, als ob gleichzeitig die ganze Welt zu jedem Jetzt oder Nie in x-Millionen Sekunden zufällig an die Ewige Stadt denkt. Wahrscheinlich war es bloß so ein momentanes Gefühl. Genauso wie ich von den Füßen der Welt immer wieder mitgerissen werde.

10 *In the Rome of my bed*
The hottest Roman summer in a decade--

I see myself fleeing Rome
see myself leaving behind a blade of stone
a blade of stone flecked with water
with water droplets large and shining

And though I'd wished to let them be--
The stone blade droplets sizzle into the air
...etc.

I've never even been to Rome. Why should I write a "Roman poem"? Rome's about the furthest thing imaginable from our present circumstances. "And still Rome stands," they'd say, as if every now or never in how many million seconds the whole world all at once happens to think about the Eternal City. It must have been one of those fleeting moments. Just as surely as I get swept along by the world's feet.

11 My thanks to the person (and the strength) that had me write this piece. So many poems get tossed by the wayside -- for want of episodes in which to incorporate them, more than anything -- actually, if the truth be known, I was hard up for something to do with them. Forget about getting them into print (prose is always preferable), I'd even thought of going straight to a gallery and scribbling them all over the walls. At least would have made for some easy small talk.

„Seen that exhibition?"

„You go to read the writing, not to look at pictures!"

„But wait, didn't somebody already do that?"

„Don't know, but I'm sure somebody'd thought of doing it."

12 If people feel like analysing, please be my guest and place each of these paragraphs in an analytical expostion.

13 Take, for instance, Paragraph N° 8. Picture my unseemly words and there, looking on with no real sense of the word, some dreamy-eyed kid working up to pronounce "Surrealism" as if she were spitting out a butterfly.

14 Whereas with Paragraph N° 11, you could set your mind immediately to work and imagine, hypothetically, the person who had me write the piece as <A MAN WHO SAYS THE WORLD DOESN'T NEED HIS CHILD>, taking what's in brackets for my image. Likewise you could picture me, pen in hand, insinuating how it seemed perfectly okay not to bear offspring, no?

15 Paragraph N° 2. My initial <RAINSCAPE> framed in the *paysage* outside. The umbrella kids, predictably, with more than just umbrellas. They're all done up in plastic rainboots, yellow slickers and hats. The children come coloured. The umbrella-less adults, in black and white. Somebody ought to seal the whole scene into a picture plane, myself the viewer included, and hang it up on a wall.

16 C'mon, go ahead.

On loan through the gracious permission of the Collection of Stephen Linfield.

11 Ich danke der Person (und der Stärke), die mich dazu veranlaßten, dieses Stück zu schreiben. So viele Gedichte werden achtlos unterwegs verworfen – eher weil eine Episode fehlt, in der sie eingebaut werden könnte, als sonst was – und um die Wahrheit zu sagen, brauchte ich doch dringend irgendeine Verwendung dafür. Die Gedichte gedruckt zu haben, ist irrelevant (Prosa wird immer vorgezogen), ich hatte mir bereits überlegt, ich könnte in eine Galerie gehen und sie an die Wände kritzeln. Zumindest gäbe das Anlaß für Small-Talk.

„Hast du die Ausstellung schon gesehen?"

„Du gehst hin, um die Gedichte zu lesen, nicht um die Bilder anzuschauen!"

„Warte mal, hat nicht schon irgend jemand das gemacht?"

„Weiß nicht, aber sicher hat jemand bereits die gleiche Idee gehabt."

12 Wenn jemand auf Analyse steht, dann bitte, gerne; stellen Sie jeden dieser Absätzen in eine analytische Darstellung.

13 Nehmen Sie, zum Beispiel, Absatz Nr. 8. Machen Sie sich ein Bild von meinen unpassenden Wörtern und von dem träumerischen Mädchen, das gänzlich ohne Welterfahrung sich darauf vorbereitet, das Wort „Surrealismus" so auszusprechen, als ob es einen Schmetterling ausspuckt.

14 Mit Absatz Nr. 11 dagegen, könnten Sie sofort Ihre Gedankenarbeit aufnehmen und sich, rein theoretisch, die Person vorstellen, die mich dazu veranlaßte, das Stück <DER MANN, DER SAGT, DASS DIE WELT SEIN KIND NICHT BRAUCHEN KANN> zu schreiben, und nehmen Sie dabei das, was in den Klammern steht, als mein Bild. In gleicher Weise könnten Sie sich mich vorstellen, wie ich mit Stift in der Hand andeute, es scheine mir ganz in Ordnung zu sein, keinen Nachwuchs zu gebären, nicht?

15 Absatz Nr. 2. Mein ursprüngliches <RAINSCAPE> mit dem ganzen Drumherum umrahmt. Die Regenschirmkinder haben erfahrungsgemäß natürlich mehr als nur Regenschirme bei sich. Sie sind alle mit Plastikgummistiefeln, gelben Regenschutz und Hut ausgestattet. Die Kinder treten in Farbe auf, die regenschirmlosen Erwachsenen in Schwarzweiß. Jemand sollte die ganze Szene, natürlich auch mit mir als Beobachter, auf einer Bildfläche festmachen und diese an die Wand hängen.

16 Geh, mach' schon.

Eine Leihgabe aus der Sammlung von Stephen Linfield, mit freundlicher Genehmigung zur Verfügung gestellt.

Katalog

Studio Azzurro (I)

Gundi Berghold (A)

Gudrun Bielz / Ruth Schnell (A)

Birgit Brenner (D)

David Cerny / Milan Gustar (CZ)

Susan Alexis Collins (GB)

Teiji Furuhashi (J)

Gusztáv Hámos (H)

Kirsten Johannsen (D)

Jaap de Jonge (NL)

Dieter Kiessling (D)

Richard Kriesche (A)

Gerda Lampalzer (A)

Helmut Mark (A)

Paul McCarthy (USA)

David Moises (A)

Christian Möller / Sven Thöne (D)

Friederike Pezold (A)

Ulrike Rosenbach (D)

Leo Schatzl (A)

Lydia Schouten (NL)

Paul Sermon (UK)

Servaas (NL)

Andrea van der Straeten (D)

Bill Viola (USA)

VA Wölfl (D)

Studio Azzurro

TAVOLI

„Dann ist es doch kein Traum. Endlich! Nicht einmal eine Vision, die Visionen sind stumm und ich verstumme vor ihnen. (Tritt vor, bleibt stehen, schaut in die Schüssel. Ohne Emotionen.) Armer Teufel. (Bewegt Hand vor den Augen. Wie oben.) Armer Teufel. (Pause) Jetzt kann ich wieder reingehen; das Geheimnis ist gelöst worden."

Sechs Bilder, die auf Tischen liegen, sind spürbar schwer. Still, unbeweglich oder leicht vibrierend, doch sie schütteln sich, wenn sie „berührt" werden. Dann finden sie wieder ihre Leichtigkeit, den Eindruck des Fließenden. So beteiligen sie sich an diesem Spiel. Indem sie von einem Tisch zum anderen wechseln. Von einem Übergang zum anderen. Sechs wesentliche Bilder, die in einem einfachen und absurden Raum leben. Sechs schwierige Gegenwarte, die vor allem „berührt" werden. Weil sie „arm" sind.

Von allen ist der Tastsinn wahrscheinlich der ärmste Sinn. Man muß sich ausstrecken, etwas wagen, schmutzig werden. Er hinterläßt keine Spuren, sondern empfängt sie nur, erduldet sie – sichtbar – wie keiner der anderen Sinne. Doch im Geiste ist er vielleicht der reichste. Durch ihn wird von der Geburt an die intensivste Information gefiltert. Auf ihn werden die intensivsten Andeutungen gedruckt. „Giotto, Masaccio ... Nie sehe ich sie ohne die gewaltigste Beteiligung des Bewußtseins meines Tastsinnes. Es kommt mir so vor, als ob ich jede Figur berühren könnte; ich

„Then it's not a dream. Finally! Not even a vision, the visions are mute and I'm mute before them. (Comes forward, stops, looks in the bowl. Without emotion). Poor devil. (Moves hand in front of eyes. As above). Poor devil. (Pause) Now I can go back in; the mystery has been solved."

Six images lying on some tables make all of their weight felt. Still, unmovable or slightly vibrating, they shake when they are "touched". Then they regain their lightness, their sense of flowing. They thus participate in this play. By going from one table to another. Between one pass and another. Six essential images that live in one simple and absurd space. Six difficult presences, above all to be "touched". Because they are "poor".

Probably, out of everything, touch is the poorest sense. You must extend, dare, get dirty. It doesn't only leave traces but it receives them, suffers them, visibly, as no other of the senses. But, perhaps, it is also the richest of the spirit. From it, the most intense information is filtered from the first day of birth. On it, the most intense suggestions are impressed. "Giotto, Masaccio ... I never see them again without the most violent participation of my tactile consciousness. I feel as if I could touch each figure; I evaluate the resistance that it would put up to my touch, the effort that I would

Studio Azzurro

Tavoli

1994 (Detail)
Interaktive Videoinstallation
3 Tische,
3 Videoprojektoren,
3 CDI-Diskplayer,
Audio-Verstärker,
Monitore, Computer,
Sensoren

schätze den Widerstand ein, mit dem meine Berührung erwidert werden würde, wie sehr ich mich bemühen müßte, um sie zu bewegen; es kommt mir so vor, als ob ich rund um sie herumgehen könnte" (Bernard Berenson). Ohne Berührung spüren auf den Handflächen, den Fingern, der Haut. Berührung schafft Beziehungen mit anderen Körpern, anderen Materien. In dem die eigene Fantasie leicht berührt wird. Wie wichtig das ist in einer Welt, in der die Materie immer weniger greifbar und die Fantasie immer sichtbarer wird, wodurch die Intimität der beiden verarmt wird.

Wie ein Pfahlbau tragen sechs Tische diese erschöpften Bilder. Doch grundsätzlich sind sie noch süß, ironisch, „sie können noch". Berühren wir sie.

„Eine Welt ohne Monster, kannst du dir das vorstellen? (hält inne, um sich vorzustellen)"

Die Zitate in Anführungszeichen stammen aus: Fragmente von Theater und Radio, „Pochade" von Samuel Beckett.

have to make to move it; I feel as I could walk all around them" (Bernard Berenson).
To feel on the palms, the fingers, the skin without touching. Touch creates relationships even without contact with other bodies, other materials. By lightly touching one's own imagination. How important it is in a world where matter is more and more impalpable and the imagination more and more visible, impoverishing both of their own intimacy.

Six tables support, like pile-works, these exhausted images. But, basically, they are still sweet, ironic, "they still can". Let's touch them.

"A world without monsters, can you imagine it? (pauses to imagine)"

The quotes in inverted commas are taken from: Fragments from the Theatre and Radio Poschade by Samuel Beckett.

Studio Azzurro
Tavoli

1994 (Detail)
Interaktive Videoinstallation
3 Tische, 3 Videoprojektoren, 3 CDI-Diskplayer, Audio-Verstärker, Monitore, Computer, Sensoren

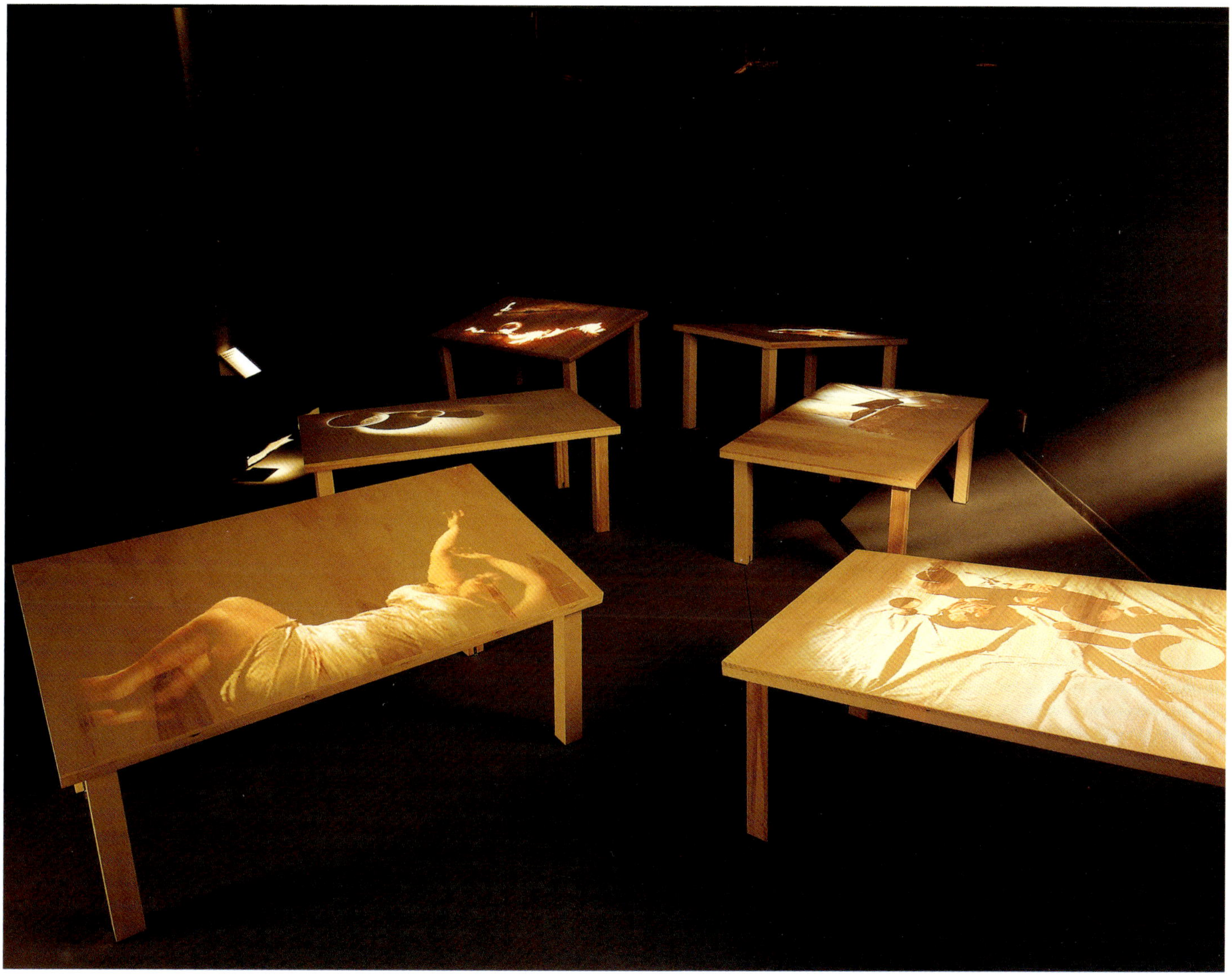

Gundi Berghold

>CUT 1/2<

In den Arbeiten Gundi Bergholds ist es signifikanterweise das Zeichen des offenen Kreises, das sie immer wieder als Code zur strukturellen Erweiterung des Apparates einsetzt. Schon als simples Piktogramm birgt der offene Kreis energetische Potentiale. Er suggeriert virtuelle Kraft, magnetische Spannung, ein Gerade-Noch, einen Riß, ein Zuschnappen. Anderseits regelt er etwa in Form der Sperrscheibe einer Filmkamera die regelmäßige Rotation der Bilder, ist also auch ein Zeichen von rhythmischer Bewegung und zyklischer Stops. Übertragen auf Gundi Bergholds Videoinstallationen ergibt sich aus dem Zeichen des offenen Kreises die orbitale Erweiterung des Monitorbildes in den Raum. Es läßt sich wie ein Dressurakt beschreiben, in dem der gezähmte elektronische Impuls kurzfristig aus seinem Käfig entlassen und zu einer zeitlich-räumlichen Exkursion veranlaßt wird. Der zirkulierende Kreis ist nicht nur das visuelle Motiv, er ist auch das energetische Grundmuster von Gundi Bergholds Installationen. In >cut 1/2< schreibt sie die Choreographie zudem in die skulpturale Form des offenen Kreises ein. Das Videobild verläßt den Monitor, mutiert zur Bewegungsform, zum imaginären Flugobjekt, zur exzentrischen Schleife, um sich im anderen Monitor wieder einzufinden. Der kreisförmige Körper fungiert als Umlaufbahn, als Gedächtnisstütze des Bildschirmsignales auf seinem virtuellen Flug durch den Raum.

Christian Rapp, Auszug aus einem Text im Katalog Gundi Berghold, Blau-Gelbe Galerie, 1993

In Gundi Berghold's work, it is typically the sign of the open circle that she keeps using as a code for structural expansion of the device. Even as a simple pictogram, the open circle holds some energetic potential. It implies virtual force, magnetic tension, a sense of on-the-brink, rupture and snapping shut. On the other hand, it can act – like the rotary disk shutter of the motion picture camera for instance – as a regulating element to govern the consistent sequence of images and thus it is also a sign for rhythmic movement and cyclical stops. In the context of Gundi Berghold's video installations, the sign of the open circle yields the orbital extension of the monitor image into space. It can be described like a training trick, in which the tamed electronic impulse is briefly let out of its cage and made to undertake a time/ space excursion. The circulating circle is not only the visual motif but also the basic energetic pattern of Gundi Berghold's installations. In >cut 1/2<, she inscribes even her choreography into the sculptural shape of the open circle. The video image leaves the monitor, mutates to become a moving form, an imaginary flying object, an eccentric loop, to reappear on the other monitor. The circular body acts as an orbital path, as a mnemonic aid of the TV image on its virtual flight through space.

Christian Rapp

Gundi Berghold
>cut 1/2<

Videoskulptur, 1992

Courtesy:
Blau-Gelbe Galerie, Wien

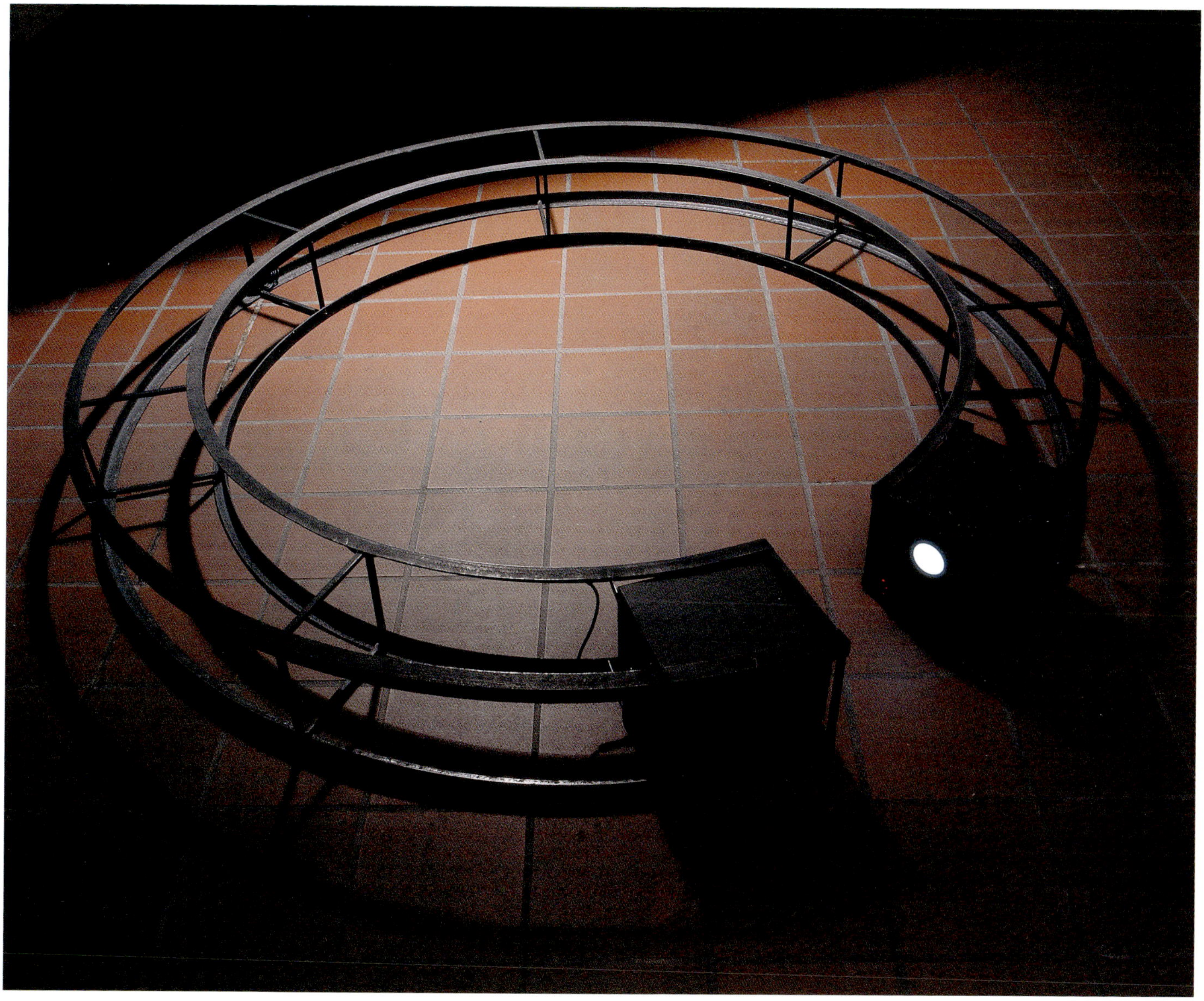

Gudrun Bielz / Ruth Schnell

VIDEOSCHWELLE

Diese Arbeit wurde 1988 für den öffentlichen Raum, Dorotheergasse in der Wiener Innenstadt, und ein Geschäftslokal konzipiert. Die vier Schwellen auf der Straße waren in Anlehnung an die Stuttgarter Schwellen als Markierung und Hindernis für Fahrzeuge gedacht. Dieser Teil wurde auch immer wieder ge- bzw. zerstört (das Sicherheitsglas mit Hämmern eingeschlagen, die Betonschwelle mit Reifenprofilen versehen etc.). Im Galeriebereich fortgesetzt waren die Schwellen bloß Ausstellungsstück im geschützten Raum.

„Woher uns heute die Bilder und Zeichen ansehen, spielt eigentlich keine Rolle mehr, denn sie sind allgegenwärtig, und wir sind mittlerweile gewohnt, daß sie wie die Natur (oder anstelle der Natur) wild wuchern. Er ist Sammelbecken aller für uns wichtigen Informationen, da sie ja erst die Realität, den Ausschnitt an Bedeutungen kanalisiert. So kann der Monitor auch eine Schwelle sein, welche auf der Straße zur Bewußtseinsbarriere wird, die den Fluß der Vehikel, den Drang nach der totalen Mobilität, stoppt. [...] Die „Videoschwellen" sind deshalb eine Videoskulptur im Außen- wie im Innenraum (der ja der Raum des Monitors ist, ein Unraum), an dem die Zeichen als Repräsentanten der Welt diejenige Realität definieren, die als unweigerlich Gegebene erscheint.

Gerhard Johann Lischka, in: „Der entfesselte Blick",
Seedamm-Kulturzentrum, 1992

This work was designed in 1988 for a public space, the Dorotheergasse, a small street in the central part of Vienna, and for a business location. The bumps on the street are reminiscent of the bumps in Stuttgart that serve as markers and impediments for vehicles. This part was also repeatedly disturbed and damaged (the safety glass was smashed with hammers, the cement bumps defaced with tire profiles, etc.) In the continuation in the space of the gallery, the bumps were merely exhibition pieces in a sheltered space.

"It does not really matter any more, from where the images and signs gaze at us, because they are omnipresent; we have become accustomed to them growing in wild profusion like nature (or instead of nature). [...] Thus the monitor can also be a bump, an obstacle, becoming a barrier to consciousness on the street that stops the flow of vehicles, that halts the urge towards total mobility. Like the monitor, the windows and rear view mirrors of the car are partial limitations and reverse the movement on the monitor during the drive – we are moved. [...] Therefore, the "Videoschwellen" (Video Bumps) are a video sculpture in external space and in internal space (which is the space of the monitor, a non-space), allowing the signs as representatives of the world to define that reality which appears to be an unconditional given.

Gerhard Johann Lischka

Gudrun Bielz
/ Ruth Schnell
Videoschwelle

8 Betonmodule,
8 integrierte s/w-Monitore,
2 computergenerierte Videotapes

Birgit Brenner

SELBSTVERSUCH III: ROUGE ESSENTIEL 52, LANCÔME

Bei dieser Arbeit handelt es sich um ein Wandtelefon mit einem eingebauten LCD-Bildschirm. Wird der Hörer von der Gabel genommen, erscheint auf dem sonst dunklen Bildschirm ein Videofilm. Dieser Film setzt sich aus drei hintereinander folgenden Szenen zusammen: Schminken der Lippen, Küssen des Kameraobjektivs, Abwischen der Lippen mit einem Papiertaschentuch. Abwischen und Küssen werden von den Sätzen „Bleib hier!" und „Geh weg!" aus dem Telefonhörer begeleitet. Diese Szenen wurden solange wiederholt, bis der ganze Lippenstift verbraucht war, was einer Zeit von 55 Minuten entsprach.

Bemalen der Lippen mit Lippenstift – Kuß – Abwischen der Lippen mit einem Papiertaschentuch – Bemalen der Lippen – Kuß – Abwischen der Lippen – Bemalen – Kuß – Abwischen der Lippen – Bemalen – Kuß – Abwischen – ...

The subject of this piece is a wall telephone with a fitted V.D.U. When the receiver is taken off the hook, a video film appears on the otherwise darkened screen. This film consists of three consecutive screens: painting of the lips, kissing of the lense of the camera, wiping of the lips with a paper handkerchief. Wiping and kissing are acompanied by the phrases „Stay here" and „go away" that can be heard from out of the telephone. These scenes were repeated until all the lipstick was used up, wich lasted 55 minutes.

painting of the lips with lipstick – kiss – wiping of the lips with a paper handkerchief – painting the lips – kiss – wiping – painting the lips – kiss – wiping – ...

Birgit Brenner
Selbstversuch III:
Rouge Essentiel 52,
Lancôme

Video-Objekt 1993,
Manipuliertes Wandtelefon mit eingebautem Schalter und LCD-TV, Videodisc, Tonverbindung TV - Telefonhörer.

Courtesy:
Galerie Eigen+Art, Berlin

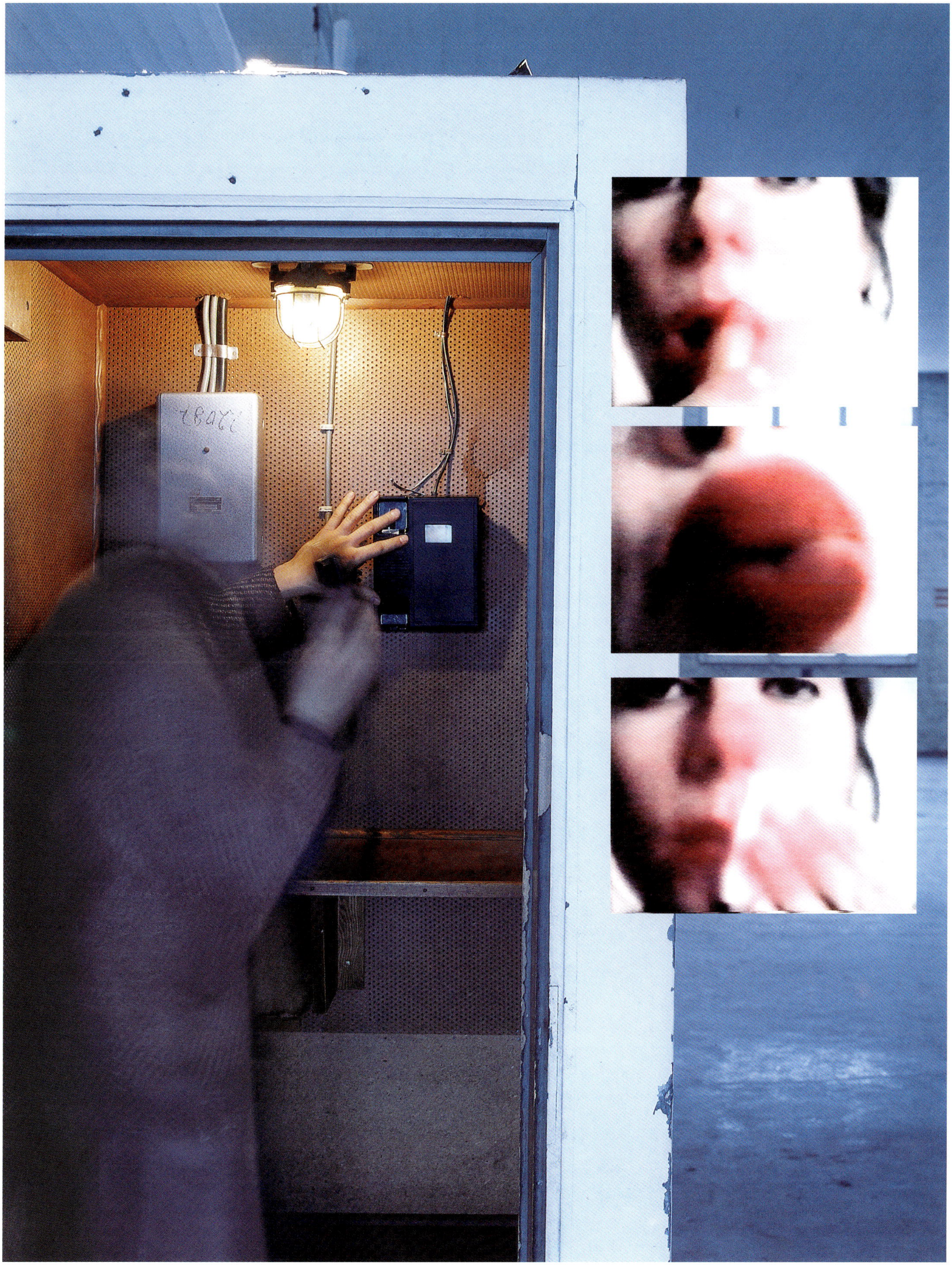

David Cerny / Milan Gustar

BEASTS

Sie sind im Vorteil, gar keine Frage, hier also ein kleines Heilmittel, um die Angewohnheit aufzugeben.

Oder ist es bloß ein Zusammenbruch?
Welche Kraft hat eigentlich visuelle Information, die bei den Angesprochenen gar nicht ankommt?

Oder hat sie ein eigenes autonomes Leben?

Ist es nicht etwas unpassend, wenn man heimgeht und eine Skulptur einschaltet?

Sie vermehren sich wie die Hasen.

The odds are in their favor, no doubt about that, so here is a little cure to drop the habit.

Or is it just a breakdown?
What is the real power of visual information that doesn't reach its addressee?

Or does it have its own autonomous life?

Isn't it a bit inappropriate to get home and turn on a sculpture?

They breed like rabbits.

David Cerny / Milan Gustar
Beasts

Video-Object, 8 Säulen, LCD-Monitore

Courtesy: Soros Center of Contemporary Arts, Prag

Susan Alexis Collins

TOUCHED

(**touch** *v.&n.* *-v.* **1** *tr.* come into or be in contact with (another thing) at one or more points. **2** *tr.* bring the hand etc. into contact with. **3a** *intr.* be in or come into contact with one another. **3b** *tr.* bring into mutual contact. **4** *tr.* rouse tender or painful feelings in. **6a** *tr.* disturb or harm. **6d** *tr.* affect. **7b** *tr.* concern. **8b** *tr.* approach. **10** *tr.* (as **touched** *adj.*) slightly mad. *-n.* **1** the act or an instance of touching, esp. with the body or hand. **2a** the faculty of perception through physical

Während die BesucherInnen den Gang entlanggehen, durchqueren sie ein immersives 3D Soundscape, das sich ständig im Raum herumbewegt. Unbeabsichtigt werden ihre Körper zum Wirt dem Werk gegenüber, da animierte Bilder auf sie projiziert werden. Die Klänge und Bilder sind von Natur aus intim und reagieren direkt auf die Anwesenheit und Bewegungen der BesucherInnen. Das Ergebnis ist eine mögliche (und manchmal auch zweideutige) persönliche Narration, die durch den Fortgang jedes Einzelnens durch den Raum choreographiert wird, wobei variable Erfahrungen alternative Lesemöglichkeiten des Werkes gestalten. *Touched*, das absichtlich „unsichtbar" ist, positioniert die Rolle der BetrachterInnen sowohl in der Verwirklichung, wie auch in der Wahrnehmung des Werkes neu.

As the viewer passes through the corridor, fragile, videoprojected images of hands are caught inadvertently on his/her body.....reaching out, touching, caressing, grasping. In each case the body of the viewer becomes host to, and therefore part of the image. Sensory audio provides an intimate and constantly moving soundscape, resulting in a suggested (and at times suggestive) narrative, choreographed by the individual's progress through the space, with variable experiences setting up alternative readings of the work. Deliberately ‚invisible', *Touched* repositions the role of the viewer within both the realisation and perception.

Susan Alexis Collins
Touched (Detail)

1996, Video/Audio Installation, 6 Videoprojektoren, Lautsprecher

(für Korridor in der oö. Landesgalerie)

Produziert im Rahmen des artist-in-residence-Programmes an der Kunsthochschule für Medien, Köln

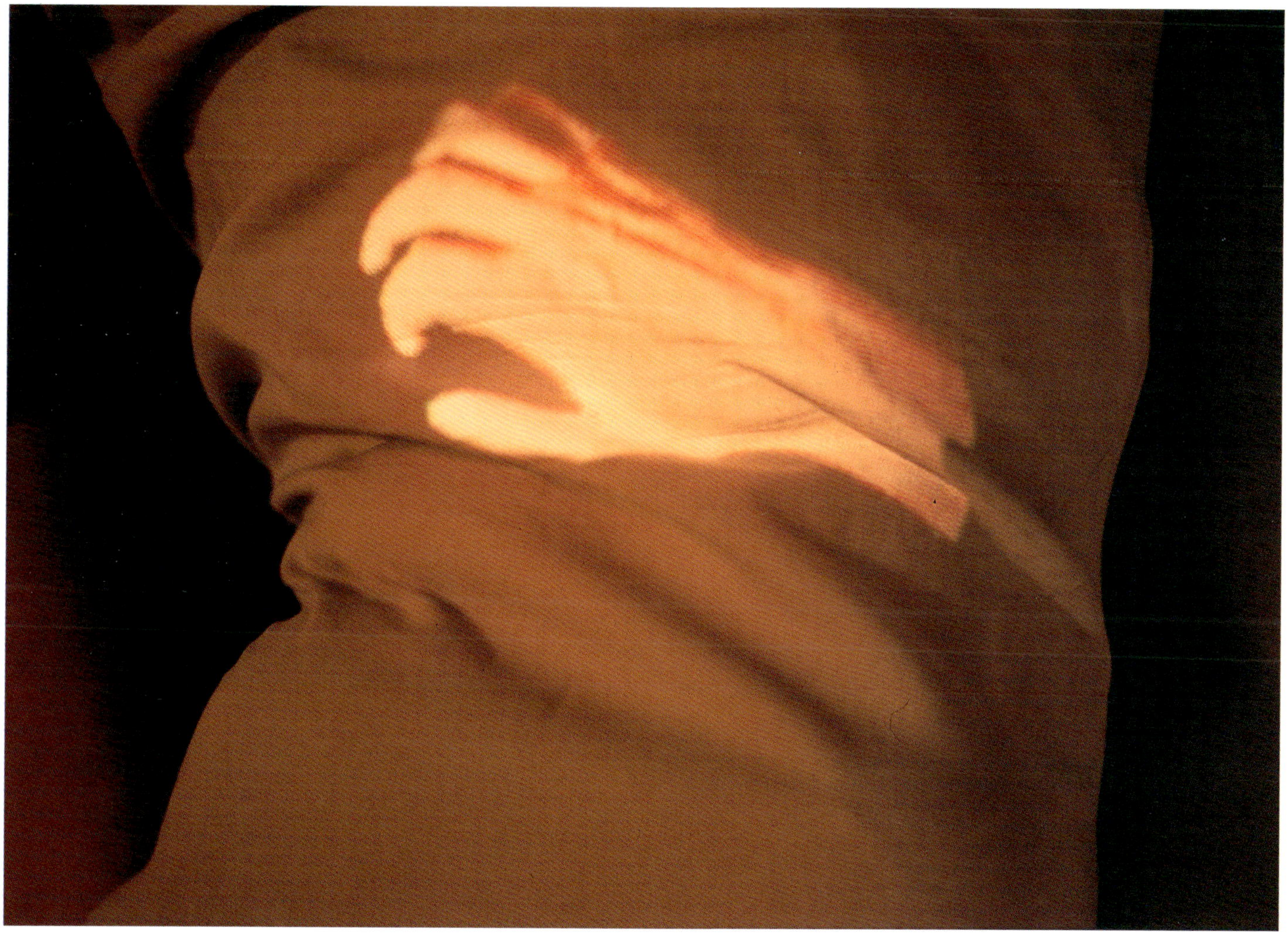

PEDESTRIAN GESTURES

Der Ausgangspunkt für Pedestrian Gestures, eine Installationsserie mit Computeranimationen, interaktiven Videoprojektionen und Klang an drei Orten, ist zwischenmenschliche Kommunikation (bzw. der Mangel davon) im öffentlichen Raum. Die Bilder und Klänge erforschen und stellen unseren oft unbewußten alltäglichen Umgang mit Unbekannten, wie auch mit unserer Umgebung, in Frage. Das Werk besteht aus verschiedenen Begegnungen, die der Natur wie auch der Größe nach intim sind. Animierte Augen, Münder, Hände und verbale Mitteilungen erforschen die Geste als eine Form der Kommunikation. BetrachterInnen begegnen kurzen photographischen und Audioausschnitten als unerwartete Momente in ihrem Tag; unbeabsichtigt choreographieren sie ihre eigene Erfahrung mit dem Werk mittels Sensoren, die verschiedene Bild- und Ton-Reaktionen auslösen. Umgekehrte Überwachung. Das Werk wird für verschiedene Orte immer wieder leicht modifiziert, um sich den jeweiligen Gegebenheiten anzupassen.

SCRATCHING

Ein videoprojiziertes Bild einer Hand, die am Boden der Stiege kratzt, während beschwörende Stimmen die BesucherInnen warnen „Treten Sie nicht auf diese Stelle, treten Sie nicht drauf". Scratching, das auf die verführerischen, vergänglichen Qualitäten der Videoprojektionen deutet, kann man gleichzeitig sowohl als selbstbefriedigende „Geste", wie auch als einen Versuch „an der Oberfläche zu kratzen" betrachten.

PEDESTRIAN GESTURES

A series of computer animated, interactive videoprojection and sound installations in three locations, Pedestrian Gestures is based on interpersonal communications in public spaces (and the lack of it), with the images and sounds seeking to question and explore aspects of our often unconscious daily exchanges with both strangers and our surroundings. The piece is made up of a number of encounters, intimate in both nature and scale. Animated eyes, mouths, hands and verbal utterances examine the gesture as a form of communication. Viewers encounter short photographic and audio snippets as unexpected moments in their day, inadvertently choreographing their own experience of the work with the sensors triggering a variety of audio and animated responses. Surveillance in reverse. As the work tours, the piece is adapted slightly according to each site and context.

SCRATCHING

A videoprojected image of a hand scratching the floor of the stairway, with persuasive voices discouraging the viewer "Don't step here, don't step on it". A play on the seductive, ephemeral qualities of videoprojections, Scratching can be seen simultaneously as both a masturbatory 'gesture' and an attempt to 'scratch beneath the surface'.

Susan Alexis Collins
Pedestrian Gestures

(Hauptbahnhof, Pfarrgasse, Galerie Hofkabinett)

Video/Audio Installation

Die Originalfassung ist ein Auftragswerk von Hull Time Based Arts für Paragon Train Station, Hull 1994

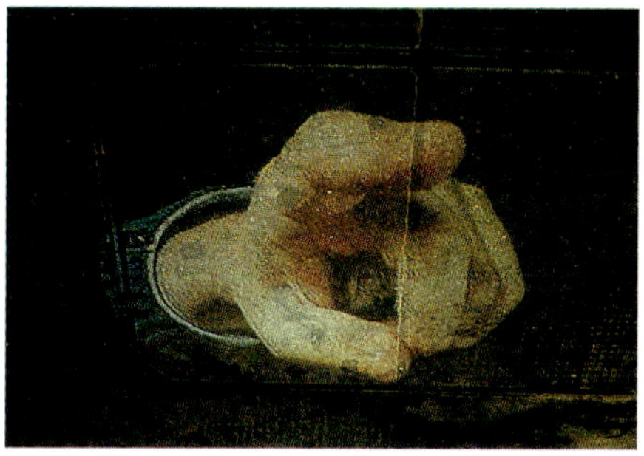

Susan Alexis Collins
Vitrine
(work in progress)

Video/Audio Installation

(für die Vitrine der oö. Landesgalerie am Linzer Hauptplatz)

INTRODUCTORY EXCHANGES II

Dieses Werk, das von menschlichen Verhaltensmustern in städtischen Nichtorten inspiriert wurde, zieht unvoreingenommene Passanten als aktive Bestandteile in die Verwirklichung des Werkes mit ein.

Das Werk besteht aus einer Reihe sensorengesteuerter Klanggeräte, die in bestimmten Abständen in der Unterführung aufgestellt werden. Die Klänge sind subtil, meistens sind es Klänge, die man an einem solchen Ort eigentlich erwarten könnte, wie Schritte, Wassertropfen oder hörbares Seufzen; andere sind absichtlich aus dem Zusammenhang gerissen dort (z. B. blökende Schafe). Die sensorgesteuerten Klänge vermischen sich mit der eigenen Klangumgebung des Raums; der Charakter und die Dichte des Werkes wird durch die Aktivität in diesem Raum zum jeweiligen Zeitpunkt in Zusammenhang mit den eigenen akustischen Qualitäten des Raums definiert.

INTRODUCTORY EXCHANGES II

(for the passageway underneath the platforms in the Train Station, based on Introductory Exchanges commissioned by Camerawork gallery for the Woolwich Foot Tunnel, 1993)

Inspired by human behavioural patterns in urban non-places, the piece involves unsuspecting passersby as active ingredients in the realisation of the work.

The piece consists of a series of sensor controlled sound devices placed at intervals along the passageway. The sounds are subtle, mostly the sounds that one might expect to be there such as footsteps, water dripping, and audible sighs; others are placed there delibarately out of context (for instance sheep baaing). The sensor driven sounds merge with the ambient sounds of the space itself; the character and density of the work defined by the activity in the space at any given time, combined with the acoustic qualities of the location itself.

VITRINE

(Vitrine des Landesmuseums am Hauptplatz)

Das Werk, im kleinen Maßstab und objektbezogen, setzt sich mit dem kombinierten Zusammenhang des traditionellen (vor der Erfindung des Fernsehens) Sammelplatzes auseinander – der Hauptplatz, die Stimme und das Herz der Stadt – und mit der Vitrine als Schaufenster, stellvertretend für etwas Anderes, das begehrenswert ist und sich woanders befindet.

VITRINE

A small scale, object based work responding to the combined context of the traditional (pre-television) meeting place, the town square, the voice and heart of the city; and the vitrine as showcase, representative of something other, desirable and elsewhere.

Teiji Furuhashi

LOVERS

Man tritt in einen leeren, quadratischen Raum ein. In der Dunkelheit erscheinen undeutliche Bilder an den Wänden rundherum. Einige nackte, fast lebensgroße Männer und Frauen gehen, bleiben stehen, umarmen sich. Ihre Bewegungen sind langsam und schwebend, wie in einem Traum. Nichts stört die Stille, außer dem leisen, fast unhörbaren Flüstern, das man ab und zu hört. Wenn man sich an die Dunkelheit etwas gewöhnt hat, geht man auf die Wände zu, um die Bilder besser sehen zu können; aber in dem Moment wird man von Sensoren erfaßt, und ein auf den Boden projizierten Ring aus Worten läßt einen erstarren. *„Berühren Sie die Linie nicht und springen Sie auch nicht daüber!* [1] Wenn man dann verwirrt auf die Wand schaut, als ob man Hilfe sucht, bemerkt man eine neue, ebenfalls nackte Figur, die sich langsam der/dem BesucherIn nähert. Diese Person, die der Künstler selbst ist, bleibt ganz nahe vor der/den BesucherIn stehen und öffnet seine Arme. Doch wenn man ihm die Hände entgegenstreckt, umarmt er sich und fällt langsam zurück und verschwindet. Eine Ästhetik des Verschwindens, die einen süßen – doch unvergleichlich kühlen – Narzißmus in sich birgt. Danach setzt sich die wortlose, traumähnliche Pantomime endlos fort. Auch wenn es aus Bildern lebensgroßer menschlicher Figuren besteht, ist dieses Werk mit dem Titel „Lovers" vom Konzept des lebenden Bildes, bzw. tableau vivant weit entfernt. Es ist speziell von der radikalsten Verwendung des Lebenden-Bild-Konzepts weit entfernt, mit der Pierre Klossowski die Gemälde von Balthus beschrieb, die auch auf die Zeichnungen Klossowskis zutreffen würde.

You enter an empty, a square room. In the darkness, indistinct images appear on the surrounding walls. Several nude, nearly life size men and women are walking, standing still, embracing one another. Their movements are slow and suspended, as if in a dream. Apart from the slight, almost inaudible whispers heard from time to time, there is nothing to break the silence. As your eyes adjust to the darkness you approach the walls in order to see the images better, but at that moment you are detected by sensors and a ring of words projected onto the floor around you transfixes you. *Do not cross the line or jump over!* [1]
When you look towards the wall in confusion as if to seek rescue, you will notice a new figure, also nude, moving slowly in your direction. This person, who is none other than the artist himself, stops close to you and spreads both arms. Yet when you reach your hands out to him, he embraces himself and slowly falls backwards, vanishing. An aesthetics of disappearance that contains a sweet – yet incomparably cool – narcissism. Afterwards, the wordless, dream-like pantomime continue ceaselessly. While its consits of images produced by life-size human figures, this work entitled „Lovers" is far removed from the concept of the living picture, or tableau vivant. It is especially removed from the most radical usage of the concept of living picture – the usage by which Pierre Klossowski described Balthus' paintings, and which could also be applied to Klossowski's own draw-

Teiji Furuhashi
Lovers

1995, interaktive Installation

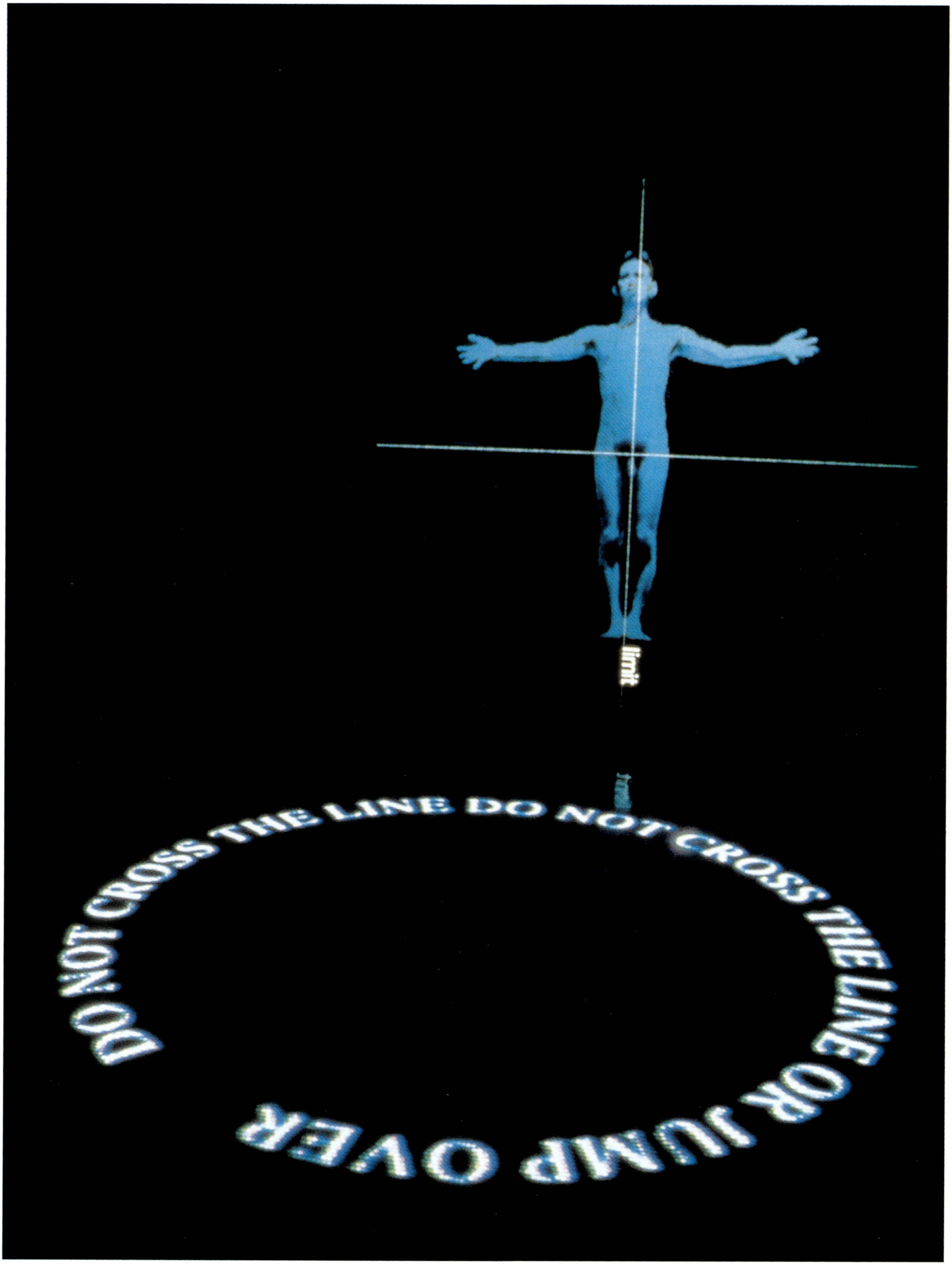
limit
DO NOT CROSS THE LINE DO NOT CROSS THE LINE OR JUMP OVER

Teiji Furuhashi
Lovers

1995, interaktive Installation

Im Gegensatz zum wörtlichen Sinn bezeichnet „lebendes Bild" in diesem Fall das Innehalten und die Erstarrung des lebendigen Dramas des Lebens, wobei die menschliche Figur vom Lebensfluß weggeführt und in eine Welt der unsterblichen, ewigen Existenz gesetzt wird. In einem solchen lebenden Bild werden die Figuren in stark überzogenen, steifen Haltungen fixiert, und die BetrachterInnen spüren eine Intensität, die in einem brodelnden Zustand festgehalten wird. „Lovers" stellt genau das Gegenteil dar. Hier werden menschlichen Figuren zu dünnen Schatten, die vorbeigleiten, schweben und schließlich lautlos verschwinden. Auch wenn die Szene aus lebensgroßen Figuren in Bewegung besteht, ist sie die genaue Umkehrung des lebenden Bildes; in diesem Sinn könnte sie als sterbendes Bild – tableau mourant – bezeichnet werden. Doch findet man hier keine Spur von Tragödie oder Verzweiflung, sondern nur eine stille Bestätigung der sich stets verändernden Welt, die eher an Epikur oder Lukrezius als an etwas Östliches erinnert. [...] Darf man „Lovers" dann als Ausdruck der „Ästhetik des Verschwindens", der dem Zeitalter der Informations- und biologischen Wissenschaften entspricht, betrachten – nicht aber im Sinne eines festen Ausdrucks der extremen Geschwindigkeit, wie Paul Virilio, der diesen Ausdruck prägte, meint, sondern als langsamen, sanften Ausdruck? Sollten wir in diesem schönen, fast zu schönem Werk eine Resignation und eine klare Vision in Bezug auf das Verschwinden und die Abwesenheit des Körpers – den Tod – unter den Bedingungen des Postmodernen sehen? *Akira Asada*

ings. In this case „living picture", in contrast to its lateral meaning, signifies the suspension and freezing of the vital drama of life in which the human figure is led away from life's flow and placed in a world of deathless, eternal existence. In this type of living picture, the human figures are fixed in boldly exaggerated, stiff poses, and the viewer senses an intensity that has been suspended in a boiling state. „Lovers" is completely the opposite. Here, human figures become thin shadows, sliding and floating by, eventually disappearing without a sound. While it is a scene consisting of moving, life-size figures, it is in fact the exact opposite of a living picture, and in this sense may perhaps be termed a dying picture – tableau mourant. Yet it contains not a trace of tragedy or dispair, but only a quiet affirmation of the constantly changing world, reminiscent of Epicurus or Lucretius more than anything Eastern. [...]
May „Lovers" then be considered an expression of the „aesthetics of disappearance" suited to the age of informational and biological science – not in this sense, however, of a hard expression of extreme speed as conceived by the creator of this phrase Paul Virilio, but rather as a slow, soft expresion? In this beautiful, almost too beautiful work should we perceive a resignation and clear vision regarding the disappearance and absence of the body – death – under the postmodern condition?
Akira Asada

(translated by Seiji Mizuta Lippit)

1 In der internationalen Version von „Lovers" werden die am Boden projizierten Worte ausgelassen.

1 In the international version of "Lovers", the projection of words onto the floor is omitted.

Gusztáv Hámos

THE HAMMER ON THE ANVIL

Die nicht eindeutige Position des Betrachters dem Fernsehen gegenüber ist das Thema des Werks „The Hammer on the Anvil". Es zeigt einen Hammer, der auf einem Amboß liegt, und einen Monitor, der daneben steht. Am Bildschirm fleht ein Mann den Zuschauer an, ihm zu helfen. Er will aus dem Fernsehrahmen befreit werden. Wenn aber der Besucher dann den Hammer aufnimmt, bettelt der Mann am Bildschirm, er solle den Hammer wieder hinlegen. Auf dieser Weise zeigt Hámos auf, wie die Beziehung zwischen dem Fernsehen und den ZuschauerInnen von gegenseitiger Abhängigkeit geprägt ist.

„In meiner Installation The Hammer on the Anvil *will der Zuschauer vom Fernsehen befreit werden. Eine echte Erleichterung ist aber nur möglich, wenn man das Bild zerstört, wodurch man auch den Zuschauer zerstört. Die Situation ist kompliziert: wir sind weniger vom Fernsehen als von unseren eigenen Grenzen gefangen. Darin spielt das Fernsehen seine eigene Rolle. Dadurch wird man sich der eigenen Grenzen bewußt." G.H.*

The ambigious position of the viewer in relation to the television is the subject of "The Hammer on the Anvil". In it, a hammer lies on an anvil with a monitor next to it. On screen, a man implores the spectator to help him. He wants to be released from the television framework. When the visitor picks up the hammer, however, the man begs for the hammer to be put down again. In this manner, Hámos put his finger on the relation of mutual dependency between television and viewer.

"In my installation 'The Hammer on the Anvil' *the viewer wants to be released from television. True relief is only possible when you destroy the image, which means you destroy the viewer. It is a complicated situation: we are not so much prisoners of television but of our own limitations. Television plays its own role in it. It makes you aware of your own limitations." G.H.*

Gusztáv Hámos
The Hammer on the Anvil

1995,
Interaktive Computer/Video-Skulptur

Monika Loster
Studencka 29 m10,
Warsaw, Poland

The artist completed "The Hammer on the Anvil" in Warsaw in 1995

Kirsten Johannsen

VIDEOPENDEL

Über einen kleinen Motor wird das Pendel, an dem ein LCD-Bildschirm befestigt ist, in unregelmäßigen Abständen angetrieben. Der maximale Ausschlag der Achse beträgt 40 cm.
Auf dem Bildschirm erscheint, je nach Position des Pendels und dem Standort des Betrachters, ein sich ständig änderndes Farbbild.
Das dem LCD-Schirm immanente Farbspektrum variiert von grün über rot zu leuchtend blau.
Um die durch die Farbwechsel und die Beweglichkeit des Objektes hervorgerufenen Irritationen zu verstärken, ist der Antriebsmotor des Pendels mit einem Zufallsgenerator gekoppelt. Somit bleiben der Bewegungs- und der Zeitverlauf nicht berechenbar.

The pendulum, which is attached to an LCD monitor, is driven at irregular intervals by a small motor. The maximum swing of the pendulum's axis is 40 cm.
An image is displayed in color on the monitor, which changes continuously depending on the position of the pendulum and the position of the viewer.
The color spectrum immanent to the LCD monitor varies from green to red to vibrant blue.
The motor that drives the pendulum is coupled with a random generator, which intensifies the irritation provoked by the changing colors and the mobility of the object. This makes the course of the movements and time periods unpredictable.

Kirsten Johannsen
Videopendel

1993, LCD Monitor,
Eisen, Gummi,
53 x 14 x 12 cm

Kirsten Johannsen
Glasen

1996, 2 Monitore, 2 Farb-Videokameras, Achsenkonstruktion mit modifiziertem Stundenglas

GLASEN

„Glasen" ist eine closed-circuit Videoinstallation. Zwei Bildschirme sind auf einer senkrechten Achse untereinander montiert. Ihre Bildflächen zeigen jeweils ein Häuflein Sand, das ‚scheinbar' vom oberen Monitor in den unteren herabrieselt. Ist die obere Bildebene ‚leer', dreht sich die Achsenkonstruktion mittels eines Elektromotors um 180° und der Sand fließt erneut von der oberen Hälfte in die untere.
Die Monitorachse ist an einer Wand installiert und über ein Drehmoment mit dem Aufnahmeobjekt an der Wandrückseite verbunden. Hier befindet sich, ebenfalls auf der Achse, ein modifiziertes Stundenglas, dessen Glaskörperhälften jeweils von einer Videokamera aufgezeichnet wird.
Die Monitore und die rückwärtigen Kameras sind über den gemeinsamen Drehmechanismus miteinander verbunden und entsprechend verkabelt, so daß das von der Kamera aufgezeichnete Bild simultan auf den Monitoren sichtbar wird.
Der ungestörte Durchlauf des Sandes beträgt 1/2 Stunde.

"Glasen" is a closed-circuit video installation.
Two screens are mounted one on top of the other along a vertical axis. Each of the screens displays a small pile of sand that "apparently" trickles down from the top monitor to the bottom one. When the upper image level is "empty", the axis construction rotates 180° using an electrical motor, and the sand begins to trickle down from the top into the bottom again.
The monitor axis is installed on a wall and connected by a pivot to the recorded object on the back side of the wall. Attached to the wall on the same axis on this side, there is a modified hourglass. The glass halves of the hour glass are each filmed by one of the video cameras.
The monitors and the cameras at the back are connected by a joint rotation mechanism and cables, so that the image recorded by the video camera simultaneously appears on the monitors.
If it is not disturbed, it takes half an hour for the sand to run through the hourglass.

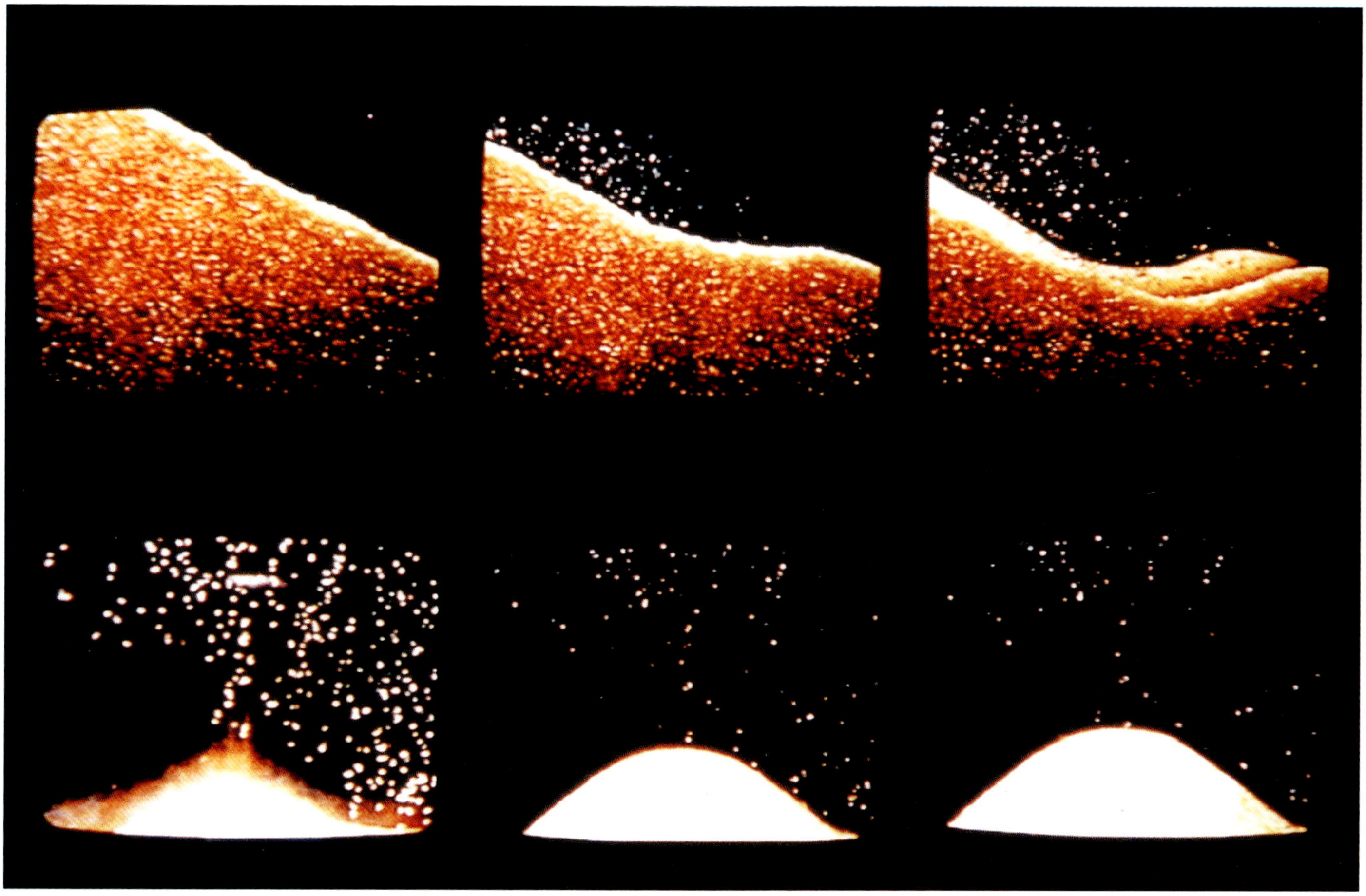

Jaap de Jonge

HORIZON

Ein abgeflachter kleiner Zug fährt hin und her. Nicht am Boden, sondern – als eine fast reduzierte Dreidimensionalität – waagerecht in Augenhöhe an der Wand entlang. Es stellt sich heraus, daß der Zug kein Zug ist. Es handelt sich um einen LCD-Monitor, der als Fenster fungiert. Durch das Fenster sieht man ein synthetisches, digitalisiertes Panorama. Wenn das Ende der Bahn erreicht wird, dreht sich der Motor um, und das kleine LCD fährt zurück. Die Bewegungen der Landschaft drehen sich ebenfalls um. Das Videosignal, der Monitor und der Motor werden von den Wischern getrieben. Das ganze erinnert an einen elektrischen Modelleisenbahnzug. Jaap de Jonge: „Es gibt etwas Jungenhaftes, etwas Schelmisches an diesem Konzept. ..." Die Landschaft ist leer. Es gibt digitalisierte Bilder vom Mars, die von Aufnahmen aus einem unbemannten Weltraumschiff erstellt wurden. Steine und Himmel, dazwischen wie eine gezeichnete Linie der Horizont.

De Jonge: *„Man könnte sich zwar die Leere der Landschaft als die Leere der Technologie vorstellen, doch ich finde das etwas weit hergeholt. Ich hoffe, daß das Werk für sich spricht und, daß das Publikum beim Betrachten lächeln muß. ..."*

A flattened little train runs back and forth. Not on the ground, but – as an almost reduced three dimensionality – vertically along the wall at eye-level. The train turns out not to be a train. It is an LCD monitor which functions as a window. Through the window can be seen a synthetic, digitalised panorama. Once at the end of the rails, the motor reverses and the little LCD runs back. The movement of the landscape is reversed as well. The video signal, the monitor and the motor are powered by wipers. It is reminiscent of a toy electric train. Jaap de Jonge: „The concept has something boyish about it, something schildism. ... The landscape is empty. There are digitalized images of shots made of Mars from unmanned spacecraft. Rocks and sky, in between as a drawing line the horizon. De Jonge: *"You could think of the emptiness of the landscape as the emptiness of technicque, but I find that a bit far fetched. I hope that the work speaks for itself and that the public finds themselves having to smile when they look at it."*

Jaap de Jonge
Horizon

Installation, 1991.
LCD-Monitor,
Spielzeug-
eisenbahnschienen,
Motor, Wischer.

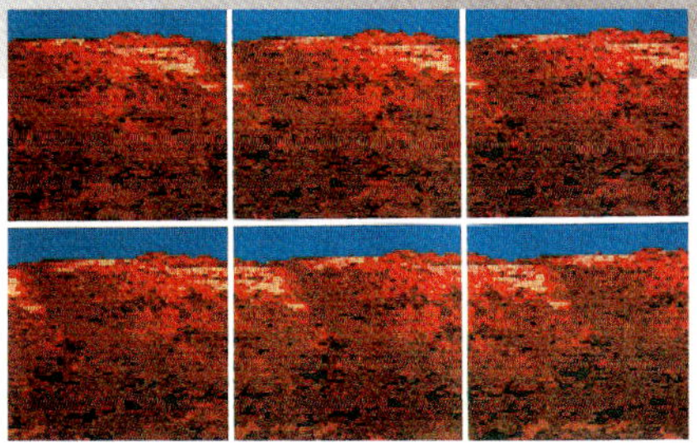

KRISTALLEN BOL

Eines der wichtigsten Kennzeichen der neuen Elektronik ist, daß es uns dadurch ermöglicht wird, nicht mehr ausdrücklich die Botschaft in den Mittelpunkt stellen zu müssen, sondern – kryptisch gesagt – die Bewegung der Bewegung. Die Botschaften, die übertragen werden und die wir jeden Tag in unseren Wohnzimmern empfangen, legen riesige Strecken innerhalb kurzer Zeit zurück. Netzwerke, die aus Satelliten, Antwortsendern und Empfängern bestehen, sorgen dafür, daß diese Botschaften rasch verbreitet werden. Es ist kaum verwunderlich, wenn wir uns fragen, was wir mit all den Botschaften tun sollten. ... Diese Botschaften kann man verändern und so manipulieren, daß sie etwas anderes als das, was sie sein wollen, werden. Das ist ungefähr das, was in der Installation von Jaap de Jonge geschieht. Hier werden jedoch die BetrachterInnen eingeladen, die Signale aus dem Äther selbst zu steuern. Man kann unter dem reichen Chaos der Fernsehsender über eine Satellitenverbindung wählen. Wenn man eine Kristallkugel dreht, verändert man gleichzeitig die Informationsquelle und die Klangquelle. Je schneller man die Kugel dreht, desto schneller verändern sich die Bilder und desto schneller folgen die Klänge aufeinander. Der Sound stammt von den verschiedenen Kanälen, die durch ein Mischpult gestapelt werden. Die Geschwindigkeit der Folge kann man bestimmen, indem man die Kugel dreht. Hier sind visuelles Wirrwarr und Klangkakophonie Geschwister. Bei De Jonge ist der „homo electronicus" ein Meister der sphärischen Denkweise und Performance.

One of the most important features of the new electronics is that they make it possible for us no longer to concentrate expressly on the „message" but, to put it cryptically, on the movement of the movement. The messages that are transmitted and that we receive every day in our living rooms, travel enormous distances in a short time. Networks of satellites, transponders and receivers ensure that those messages are also distributed at high speed. It seems obvious that we should wonder what we ought to do with all those messages. You can alter those messages and manipulate them to be something other than what they want to be. Something like that happens in Jaap de Jonge's installation. Except that the viewer himself is invited to direct the signals from the ether. You can choose from a rich chaos of television broadcasters via a satellite connection. By turning the crystal ball, you change the source of information and simultaneously, the source of sound. The faster you turn, the faster the images change and the faster the sounds follow each other. The sound comes from various channels stacked by a mixer. By turning the ball, you determine the speed of succession. Visual commotion and cacophony of sound are brother and sister here. With De Jonge, the „homo electronicus" is a virtuoso in spheric performance and thinking.

Jaap de Jonge
Kristallen Bol

Installation, 1996.
2 Satellitenschüsseln, Computer, Videomischpult, Monitor, Sensor, Glaskugel.

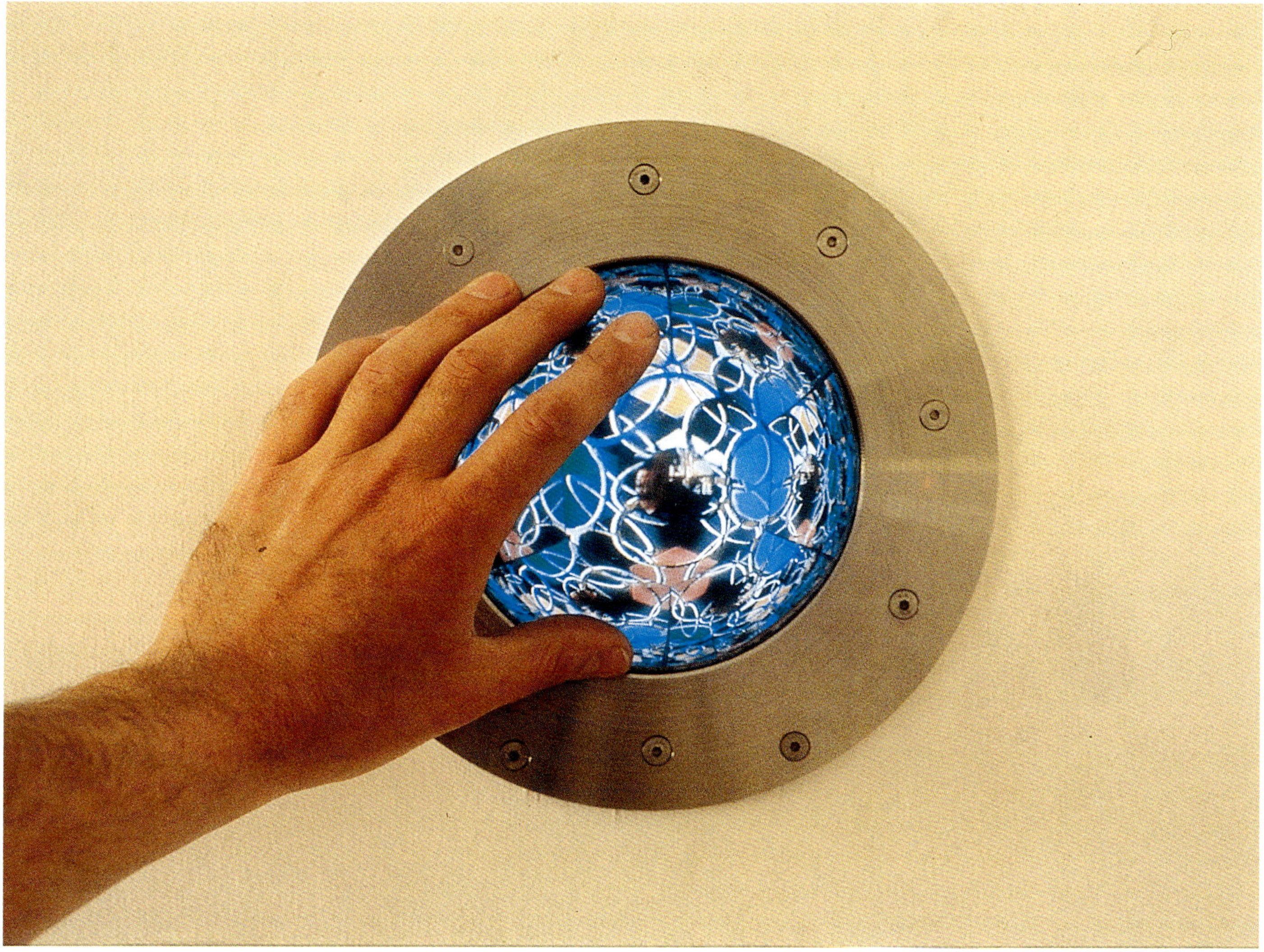

Dieter Kiessling

SCHLEUDERSTERN

In die Bildröhre des Fernsehers wurde ein Schleuderstern eingeschliffen.

A catapulted star is cut into a television picture tube.

Dieter Kiessling
Schleuderstern

1992,
Monitor, bearbeitet

SONY

O. T. (GLÜHBIRNE)

Die Videokamera nimmt die rote Glühbirne auf und überträgt ihr Abbild auf den Fernseher. Das Abbild erscheint direkt neben der Glühbirne und wird gleichzeitig aufgenommen und übertragen. Diese Reihe setzt sich fort, bis sechs Generationen von Abbildern der Glühbirne nebeneinander erscheinen. Durch das leicht blaue Licht des Fernsehers werden die Abbilder der Birne bei jeder Übertragung etwas stärker blau gefärbt.

The camera records a red light bulb and transmits the image to a television screen. The image appears next to the real light bulb, so that both are simultaneously recorded and transmitted. This process is continued until six generations of recorded light bulb images appear side by side. Due to the slightly blue light of the TV-set, the light bulb images turn a deeper shade of blue each time they are transmitted.

Dieter Kiessling
o. T. (Glühbirne)

Videoinstallation, 1994

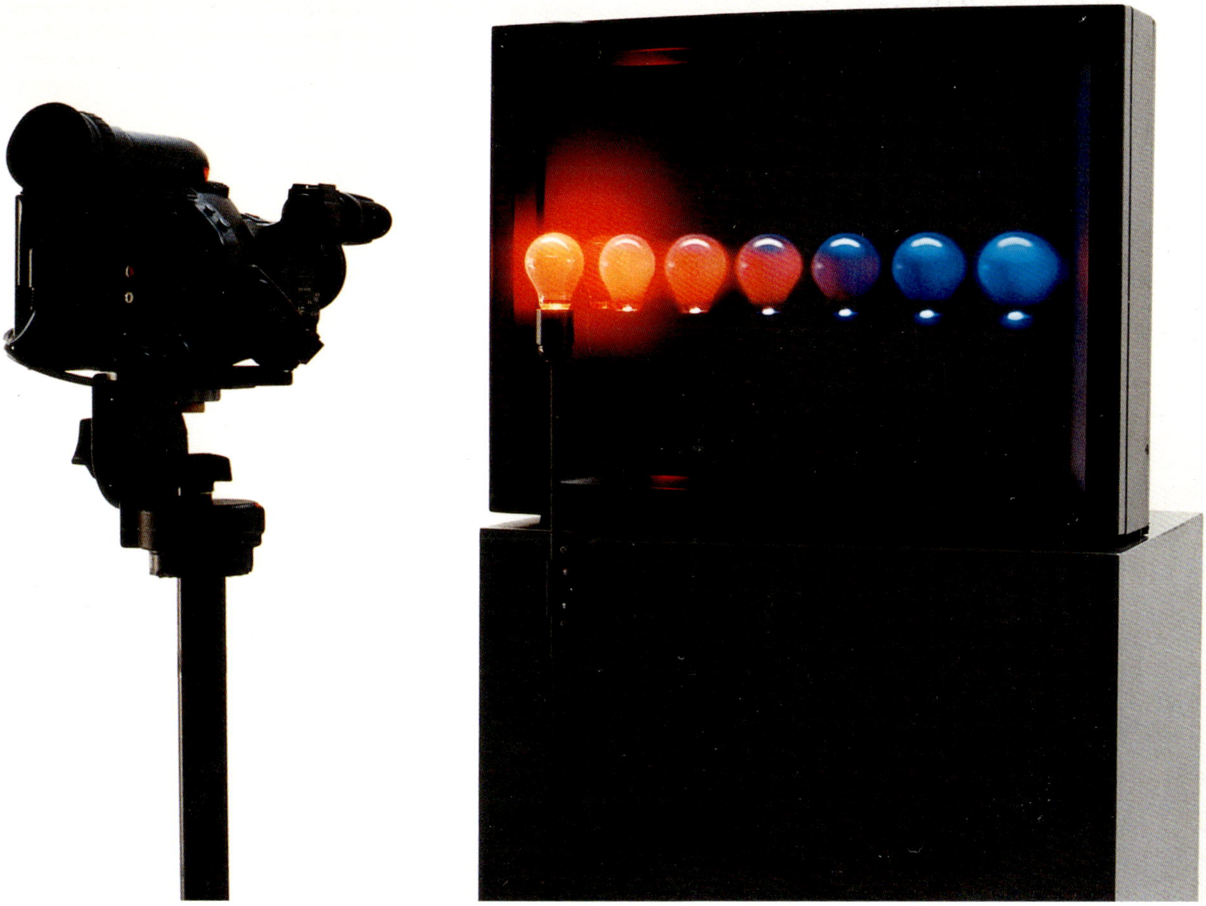

Richard Kriesche

TV-TOD 1+2

videodemonstration zur elektronischen wirklichkeit im fernsehen. in der installation von zwei videokameras und drei monitoren kommt es zu einer überlagerung bzw. verschränkung der zeitebenen, zur gleichzeitigkeit von produktion und reproduktion. der performende künstler wechselt zwischen den beiden ebenen, der realen und der medialen. als zuschauer beobachtet er sich selbst auf dem bildschirm, auf den letztlich von seinem assistenten geschossen wird. die zuschauer hingegen befinden sich in einem davon getrennten raum, dadurch ist ihre sichtweise eine ausschließlich mediale. ihr bildschirm reproduziert den durchschossenen bildschirm. die tonspur läuft weiter ... (r.k.)

a video demonstration of electronic reality on television. what takes place in this installation of two video cameras and three monitors is a superimposition or interlocking of time layers, a simultaneity of production and reproduction. the performing artist moves between the two planes of the real and the medial. as an observer, he views himself on the screen, at which his assistant then fires a shot. the audience, on the other hand, is in a separate room and thus has an entirely mediated perspective. their screen reproduces the screen that has been shot. the soundtrack continues ... (r.k.)

Richard Kriesche

tv-tod 1
stampa, Basel, 1975

tv-tod 2
Kölnischer Kunstverein, Köln 1975

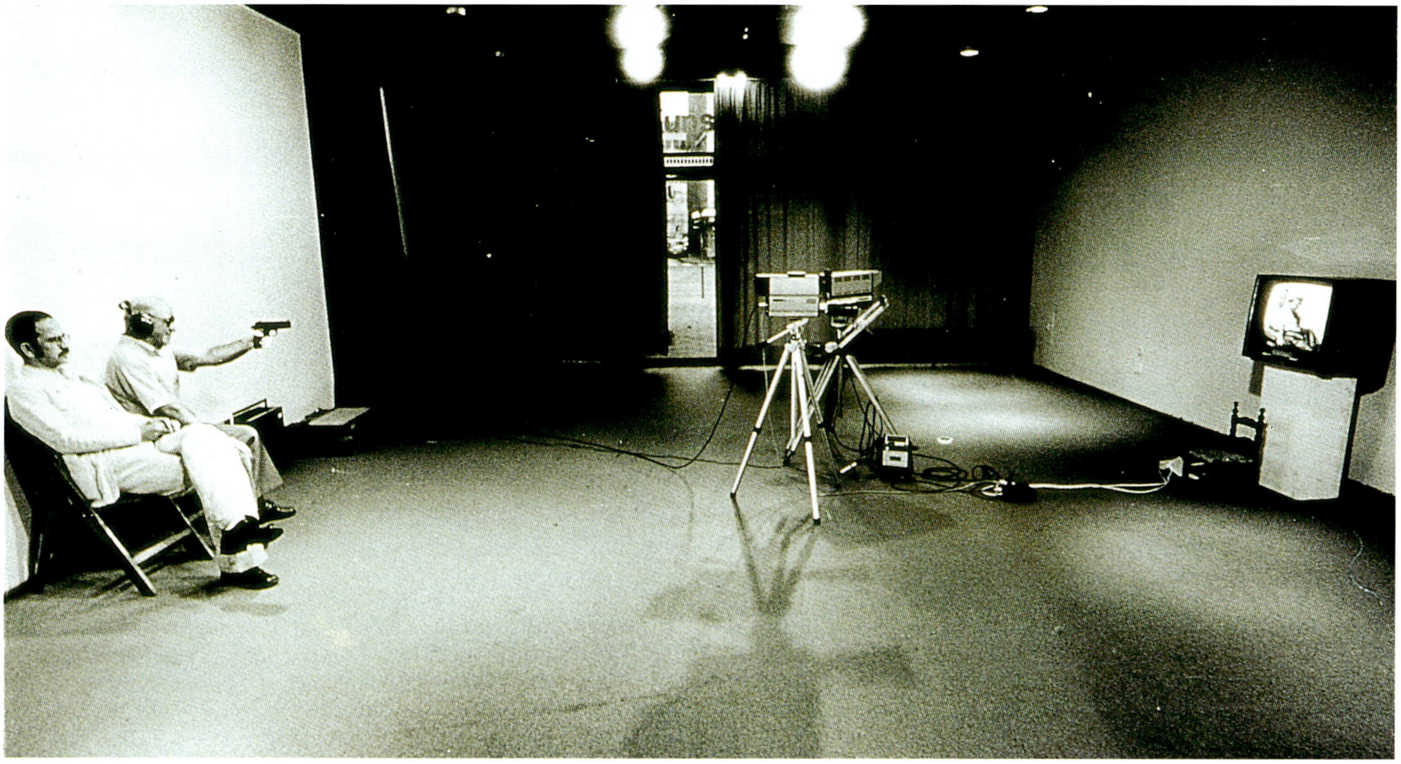

Gerda Lampalzer

BLAUE SCHACHTEL

Bei der blauen Schachtel geht es um das Geheimnis, eventuell auch um ein Geschenk. Da ein Kabel zur Schachtel führt, ist die Wahrscheinlichkeit groß, daß es drinnen etwas zu sehen gibt. Die Neugierde, den Deckel aufzumachen und hineinzuschauen, ist entfacht. Gibt man ihr nach, sind zu sehen: Rückkoppelungen, die wie kleine, bunte Explosionen dem Betrachter entgegenglühen. Sie sind von Begriffen aus der Magie und dem Schamanismus unterbrochen. Da man weiß, daß einige Leute über Rückkoppelungen mit Geistwesen kommunizieren, kann man nicht einmal sicher sein, ob sich in der blauen Schachtel nicht auch Geister aufhalten.

The blue box involves a secret, maybe even a present. Since there is a cable going into the box, it is very likely that there is something to see inside it. Curiosity urges you to open the lid and look inside. If you give in to your curiosity, you can see: back couplings that glow at the observer like colorful little explosions. They are interrupted by terms taken from magic and shamanism. Since you know that there are people who communicate with spirits by means of back couplings, you cannot be quite sure whether or not there might even be ghosts in the blue box.

Gerda Lampalzer
Blaue Schachtel

1995,
Karton, Papier, LCD-Monitor, Lautsprecher
12 x 12 x 110 cm

MAGIE

ESESS

Helmut Mark

O.T.

Den Monitor als Material zu verwenden, ihn analog zu anderen Kunst-Materialien (wie etwa Beton) als Element einer Skulptur zu setzen, kann als Form der klassischen Montage gelesen werden, als eine (postmoderne) Re-Synthetisierung von disparaten Systemen bzw. Zeichensystemen – es kann aber auch als spezifische Modifikation des Begriffs der Skulptur gedeutet werden, die sozusagen in ihr mediales Stadium eintritt. Skulptur als Medien-Skulptur besitzt nicht mehr nur eine Form, sie beinhaltet die Möglichkeit zu verschiedenen Formen – Medien-Skulpturen formen auch die Zeit ihrer Erscheinung, verfügen über eine Zeitform.
(Reinhard Braun)

Using the monitor as a material, placing it as an element in a sculpture in analogy to other artistic material (such as cement), may be read as a form of classic montage, as a (postmodern) resynthesizing of disparate systems or sign systems – but it may also be interpreted as a specific modification of the term sculpture which, in a way, is entering its media stadium. Sculpture as media sculpture no longer has just one form, but rather includes the possibility of various forms – media sculptures also form the temporality of their being, may also include a temporal form.
(Reinhard Braun)

Helmut Mark
O.T.
(Vorder- und Rückseite)

1989, Holz, Bildröhre, Videoband, Videoplayer

RED HEAT

Der (elektronische) Bildschirm, lange Zeit als „Fenster zur Welt" gefeiert, ist nicht zuletzt ein Produkt hochtechnisierter industrieller Produktion auf der Grundlage intensivierter Forschung und Produktoptimierung. Nicht nur aufgrund der visuellen Diskurse, die er repräsentiert, ist er ein paradigmatisches Objekt der Nachkriegskultur und damit der Nachmoderne. Seine Verbreitung im Zuge der Etablierung des Fernsehens als Massenmedium (an dessen Entwicklung Video anschließt) macht ihn im Anschluß an das Automobil und das Telefon zu einer jener (vergegenständlichten) Schnittstellen, auf denen sich eine Reihe von kulturellen Mustern quasi wie eine Tektonik der Gesellschaft spiegeln (etwa das Phänomen der Beschleunigung, der Implosion von Kontexten und kulturellen Differenzen, aber auch der Massenkommunikation, der Ökonomisierung der Privatsphäre, der Umformung des öffentlichen wie des privaten Raumes etc.). Der Bildschirm, als Fernsehgerät wie als Videomonitor, ist (war?) Sinnbild dafür, wie sich gesellschaftliche Mechanismen in einem komplexen Verhältnis zu bestimmten Oberflächen (und bestimmten Objekten) befinden, auf denen sie erscheinen, durch die sie (scheinbar) repräsentiert werden oder sich sogar darauf ereignen (sollen) – und die dadurch auch zum Austragungsort von kulturellen Konflikten werden, auf denen sich das Ringen um das Bewußtsein der Massen ablesen läßt. *(Reinhard Braun)*

The (electronic) screen, which has long been celebrated as a "window to the world", is indeed a product of highly technical industrial production based on intensified research and product optimization. It is a paradigmatic object of post-war culture and thus of the postmodern, but not only due to the visual discourses it represents. The dissemination of the screen in the course of the establishment of television as a mass media (with the ensuing development of video) places it alongside the automobile and the telephone as one of the (objectified) interfaces reflecting a series of cultural patterns that work like the tectonics of society (for instance, the phenomenon of acceleration, the implosion of contexts and cultural differences, but also mass communication, the economization of the private sphere, the restructuring of both public and private space, etc.). As a television set or video monitor, the screen is (was?) a symbol for the complex relationship between social mechanisms and certain surfaces (and certain objects), on which they appear, through which they are (apparently) represented, or in which they may even (be intended to) take place – and which thus become a theater for cultural conflicts indicating the state of the struggle for the mind of the masses.
(Reinhard Braun)

Helmut Mark
Red Heat

1990,
157,2 x 113,3 x 56,3 cm,
Holz, Acrylglas,
Monitor, Computer,
Diskette

Courtesy: Ing. Andreas
Unterpertinger

Panasonic

Paul McCarthy

PINOCCHIO PIPENOSE HOUSEHOLDDILEMMA

Das Video „Pinocchio Pipenose Householddilemma“ spielt in einem mannshohen Häuschen aus rohen Sperrholzplatten, in die unterschiedlich große runde Löcher gesägt worden sind. Es hat ein Giebeldach und ist mit einem kleinen Regal, einer Lampe, einem Tisch und einem Hocker spärlich möbliert. Für die ca. 10 Szenen, die gezeigt werden, wurden diverse Haushaltswaren, wie Kannen, Spaghettisieb, Löffel, Schüssel und Trichter sowie Substanzen wie Ketchup, Mayonnaise, Milch und Schokoguß verwendet. Als das Video in der Galerie Air de Paris im Oktober 1994 uraufgeführt wurde, betrat man einen Raum mit einem Kleiderständer voller Pinocchiokostüme, einem Korb voll Pinocchiomasken, weißen Handschuhen, weißen Socken und roten Clownschuhen. Jeder Besucher, der das Video sehen wollte, mußte sich ein Kostüm ausleihen und sich in einer bereitstehenden Umkleidekabine umziehen. Nur als Pinocchio verkleidet durfte man den kleinen Raum betreten, in dem das Videoband abgespielt wurde. Eine Zuschauerschaft aus lauter Pinocchios saß dort vor dem Bildschirm und schaute dem Treiben Pinocchios in dem Häuschen zu. Abgesehen von dem komischen Anblick, den Ausstellungsbesucher bieten, wenn sie in einer identischen Verkleidung herumtappen, während sie sich an die Maskierung gewöhnen, ist es eine kostbare Erfahrung zu erleben, wie sich die Wahrnehmung unter einer Vollmaske verändert. Unter der Maske schaut man nicht nur als Pinocchio einem Pinocchio zu, sondern sieht die aufgezeichnete Performance McCarthys als Pinocchio durch eine Folge unter-

The video "Pinocchio Pipenose Householddilemma" takes place in a little house about the height of an adult, that is made of plywood boards and has different sized round holes cut into it. It has a gabled roof and is scantily furnished with a small shelf, a lamp, a table and a stool. Various household goods, such as pitchers, a spaghetti strainer, spoons, bowls and a funnel were used for the approximately ten scenes that are shown, as well as substances such as ketchup, mayonnaise, milk and chocolate icing. When the video was presented for the first time at the gallery Air de Paris in October 1994, visitors entered a room with a clothes rack full of Pinocchio costumes, a basket full of Pinocchio masks, white gloves, white socks and red clown shoes. Every visitor who wanted to see the video had to borrow a costume and go into one of the changing rooms provided to put it on. People were only allowed to enter the room where the video tape was played, if they were dressed as Pinocchio. An entire audience of Pinocchios sat there in front of the screen watching Pinocchio's activities in the little house. Not only are exhibition visitors stumbling around in identical costumes a very funny sight as they try to become accustomed to the disguise, it is also a fascinating experience to see how perception is altered by a full costume. From behind the mask, you are not just Pinocchio watching Pinocchio, you also see McCarthy's taped performance as Pinocchio through a series of different holes. First it was the

Paul McCarthy:
Pinocchio Pipenose Householddilemma

1994, Performance Ansicht. Aufgeführt und mit Video aufgenommen in Villa Arson, Nizza, Sommer 1994. Video 43:50 Minuten, produziert von Air de Paris. Edition mit Einzel-, Paaren- und Party-Packs.

Courtesy: Air de Paris, Paris

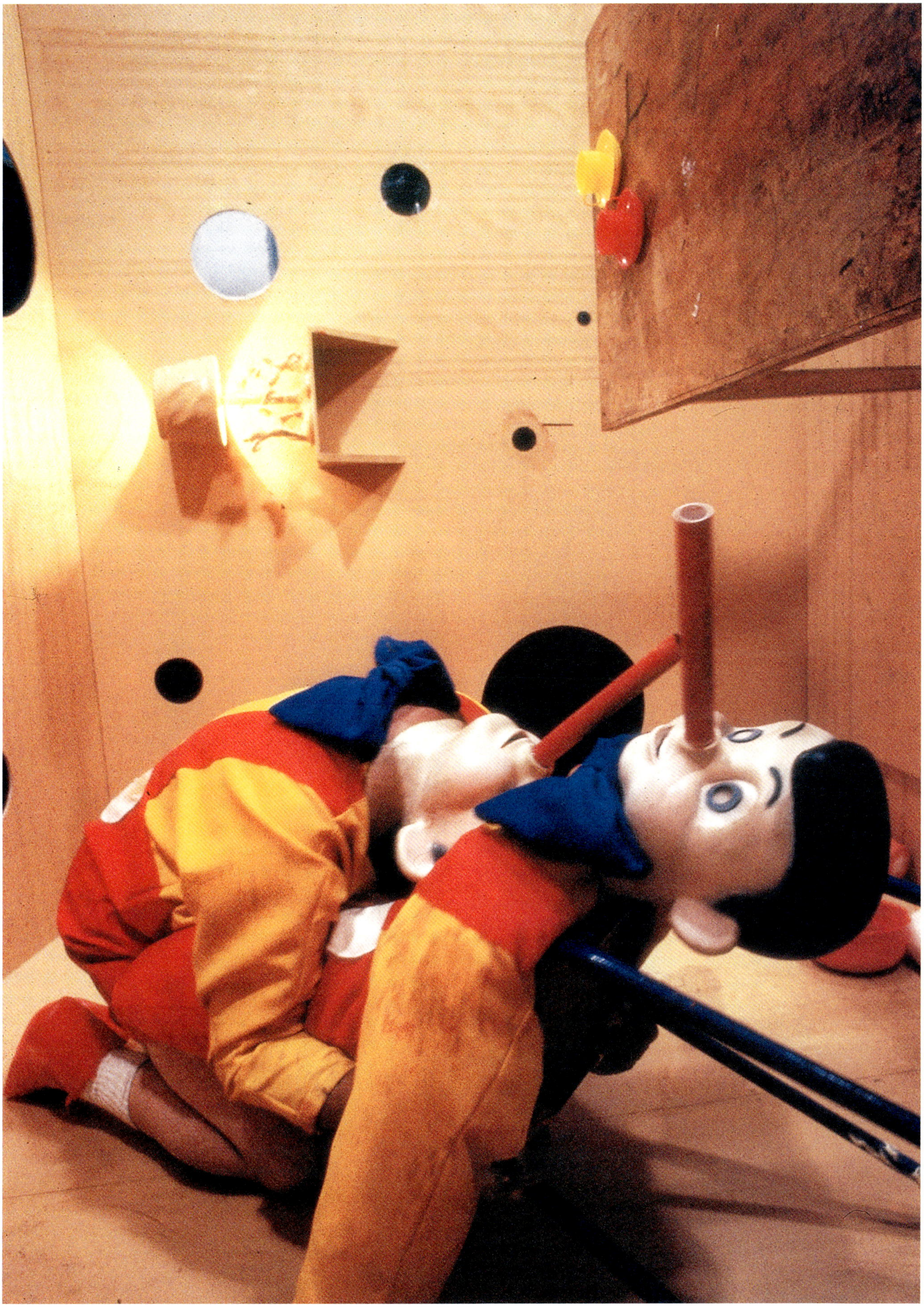

schiedlicher Löcher. Zunächst war es das Objektiv und die Blende der Kamera, die Pinocchio durch verschiedene Löcher im Häuschen beobachtete. Beim Betrachten des Videos blickt man durch die „Maske" des TV-Gerätes vor der Mattscheibe, die den Bildschirm verkleidet und zum Möbel macht. Davor sitzt man schließlich selbst und schaut durch die Augenlöcher der Maske auf die Mattscheibe. laut hört man seinen eigenen Atem und das Zischen der Luft, die durch die Augenlöcher, die lange, rohrartige, hohle Nase und den Hals in die Maske strömt. Konzentriert man sich so auf den Videoton, hört man mehrfach gebrochene und verzerrte Geräusche, die den gleichen verschlungenen Weg zu den Ohren finden, wie die Atemluft zum Mund. Außerdem wurde der Schall schon bei der Aufzeichnung in dem kleinen Holzhaus gebrochen. Dieser Effekt wiederholt sich im Vorführraum. Dadurch sind sehr laute, dumpfe und quietschende Geräusche entstanden, die das Blubbern von Ketchup, das Klatschen von Mayonnaise, das Tappen der Clownschuhe und das Rücken von Tisch und Hocker unwirklich, traumhaft und fern erscheinen lassen.

Aus: Johannes Lothar Schröder: „Paul McCarthy, Alpträume Alpräume", in: Kunstforum international, Bd.129, Januar-April 1995. Abdruck mit freundlicher Genehmigung des Verlages.

objective and the lens of the camera observing Pinocchio through different holes in the little house. Then when watching the video, you look through the television's "mask" in front of the screen, which disguises the television as a piece of furniture. Finally, you sit in front of this, watching the screen through the eye-holes in the mask, hearing your own breath as the air hisses in and out of the eye-holes, the long, pipe-like nose and the neck of the mask. If you concentrate like this on the sound of the video, you hear multiple, broken and distorted sounds that follow the same circuitous path to the ears as the air follows to the mouth. In addition, the sound was already broken as the scene in the little wooden house was filmed. The effect is echoed in the viewing room. This results in very loud, dull and squeaking sounds that make the gurgling of the ketchup, the splashing of the mayonnaise, the tapping of the clown shoes and the scraping of the table and stool appear unreal, dream-like and distant.

From: Johannes Lothar Schröder: "Paul McCarthy, Alpträume Alpräume", in: Kunstforum international, Vol. 129, January-April 1995.

Paul McCarthy
Pinocchio Pipenose Householddilemma (Party Pack),

1994,
Installation/ Vorführraum in der Galerie Air de Paris, Paris.
10 Pinocchio Kostüme (Kleider, Masken, Schuhe, Socken, Handschuhe), verschiedenes Display Material, Videodeck und Monitor. Besucher kostümieren sich im Ankleideraum, bevor sie in den Vorführraum eintreten.

Courtesy: Air de Paris, Paris

David Moises

VIDEO-JOJO

Es geht um Maschinen und Spielzeug und Maschinen, die spielen. Es ist der spielerische Zugang zu Geräten, zu sehen was sie können, wie sie funktionieren (oder nicht), ihnen neue Aufgaben zuzuteilen. In Spiele wird eine Ernsthaftigkeit gelegt und ernste Dinge erfahren eine spielerische Auseinandersetzung. Kombiniert man Maschinen, entsteht einfach neues, das es in dieser Form vorher nicht gab. Maschinen führen Handlungen aus, haben einen Benutzer/Operator/Steuermann, mit dem sie eine Einheit bilden, funktionieren sollten. Z.B. Jojo (Spielzeug oder auch einfache Maschine) und Videokamera ist eine Kombinationsmöglichkeit. Beim Jojo kann der Benutzer/Spieler mittels Video die Bewegung nachvollziehen, er sieht die grundlegende Stuktur dieser Maschine. Der Spieler spielt, und das Jojo antwortet in seiner speziellen mechanischen Jojosprache. Diese Sprache ist die Maschine selbst.

This is about machines and toys and machines that play. It is a playful approach to devices, in order to see what they can do, how they work (or don't work), to assign new tasks to them. Playing is considered seriously and serious things are addressed playfully. If you combine machines, something new is created, something that has never existed before in this form. Machines perform actions, have a user/operator/controller with whom they form a unit, with whom they are intended to function. For example, one possibility of combination consists of a yo-yo (a toy or a simple machine) and a video camera. With a yo-yo, a user/player may use the video to follow the motion, to understand the basic structure of this machine. The player plays and the yo-yo responds in its special mechanical yo-yo language. This language is the machine itself.

David Moises
Video-Jojo

1996, Radkappen, Videokamera, Monitor

Courtesy: Archimedia, Linz

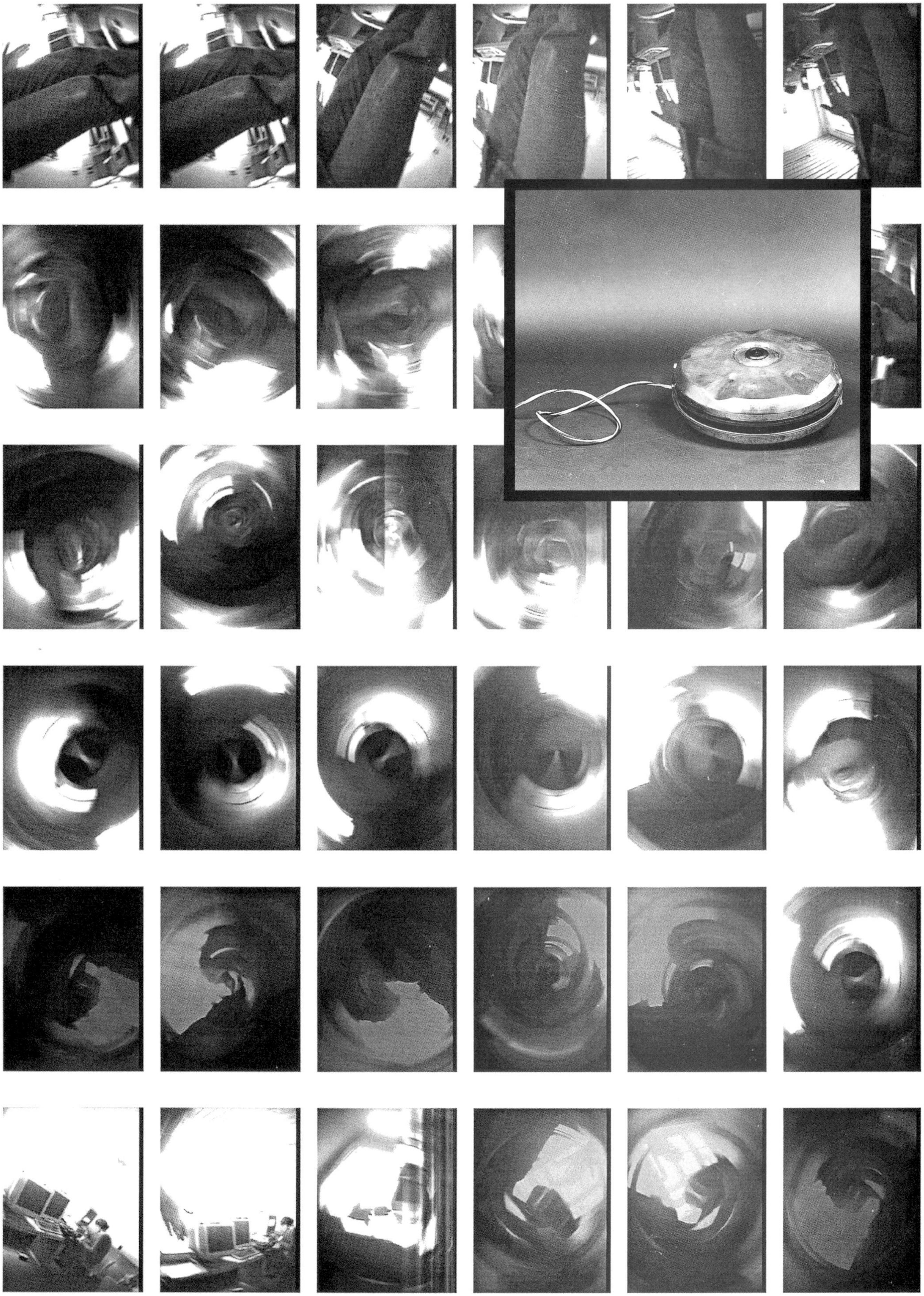

Christian Möller / Sven Thöne

THE VIRTUAL BACKBONE

Die Installation basiert auf den Bilddaten des Körpers des 39 Jahre alt gewordenen Joseph Paul Jernigan. Er wurde für schuldig befunden, einen Mann in Dawson, Texas ausgeraubt und erschossen zu haben, und wurde vom Gericht zum Tode verurteilt. Er starb am 5. August 1993 um 12:31 durch die Injektion eines schnellwirkenden und in hoher Dosierung atemlähmend wirkenden Schlafmittels im Gefängnis Huntsville, Texas. Sofort anschließend wurde seine Leiche in das Health and Science Center der University of Colerado nach Denver geflogen. Die Leiche wurde in Trockeneis gepackt, mit blauer Gelatine umhüllt und bei minus 70° Celsius eingefroren. Dem Körper wurden dann, beginnend bei den Füßen, mit einem lasergesteuerten Kältemakrotom, je ein Millimeter dicke Scheiben abgeschnitten. Nach jedem Schneidevorgang wurden vom verbleibenden Block Farbaufnahmen gemacht.

In der Installation „The Virtual Backbone" werden die über 1800 Schnittbilder auf einer Längsachse von ca. 7 m Länge *virtuell* ausgestellt. Die Abbildungsebene fährt durch den scheinbar im Raum liegenden und um Faktor 3,5 vergrößerten Körper Paul Jernigans und zeigt entsprechend der aktuellen Position den jeweiligen Körperschnitt auf einer 2,5 x 1,4 m großen Projektionsfläche.

The installation is based on image data from the body of Joseph Paul Jarnigan, who lived to be 39 years old. He had been tried in court and found guilty of having robbed and shot a man in Dawson, Texas and was sentenced to death. He died on August 5, 1993 in the Huntsville, Texas prison after being injected with a high dosage of a quickly effective sleeping medication that lames respiration. His corpse was then immediately flown to the Health and Science Center at the University of Colorado in Denver. The cadaver was packed in dry ice, embedded in blue gelatin and frozen at minus 70° Celsius. Then, beginning at the feet, the body was cut into slices of one millimeter each using a laser-controlled cryomacrotome. Color photographs were made of the remaining cadaver as each slice was removed.
In the installation "The Virtual Backbone", the more than 1800 slice images are exhibited *virtually* along a longitudinal axis about 7 meters long. The image plane leads through the body of Paul Jernigan, that seems to be lying in the room and is magnified by a factor of 3.5. According to the momentarily current position of each slice of the body, an image is displayed on a 2.5 x 1.4 meters projection surface.

Christian Möller / Sven Thöne
The Virtual Backbone

Installation, 1996
Bildsequenzen:
Ohren, Genital, Knie

Realisierung:
Sven Thöne
Technik:
Hermann Gruber
Produktion:
Archimedia Institute for Arts and Technology der Hochschule für künstlerische und industrielle Gestaltung in Linz.

Courtesy:
oö. Landesgalerie, Linz

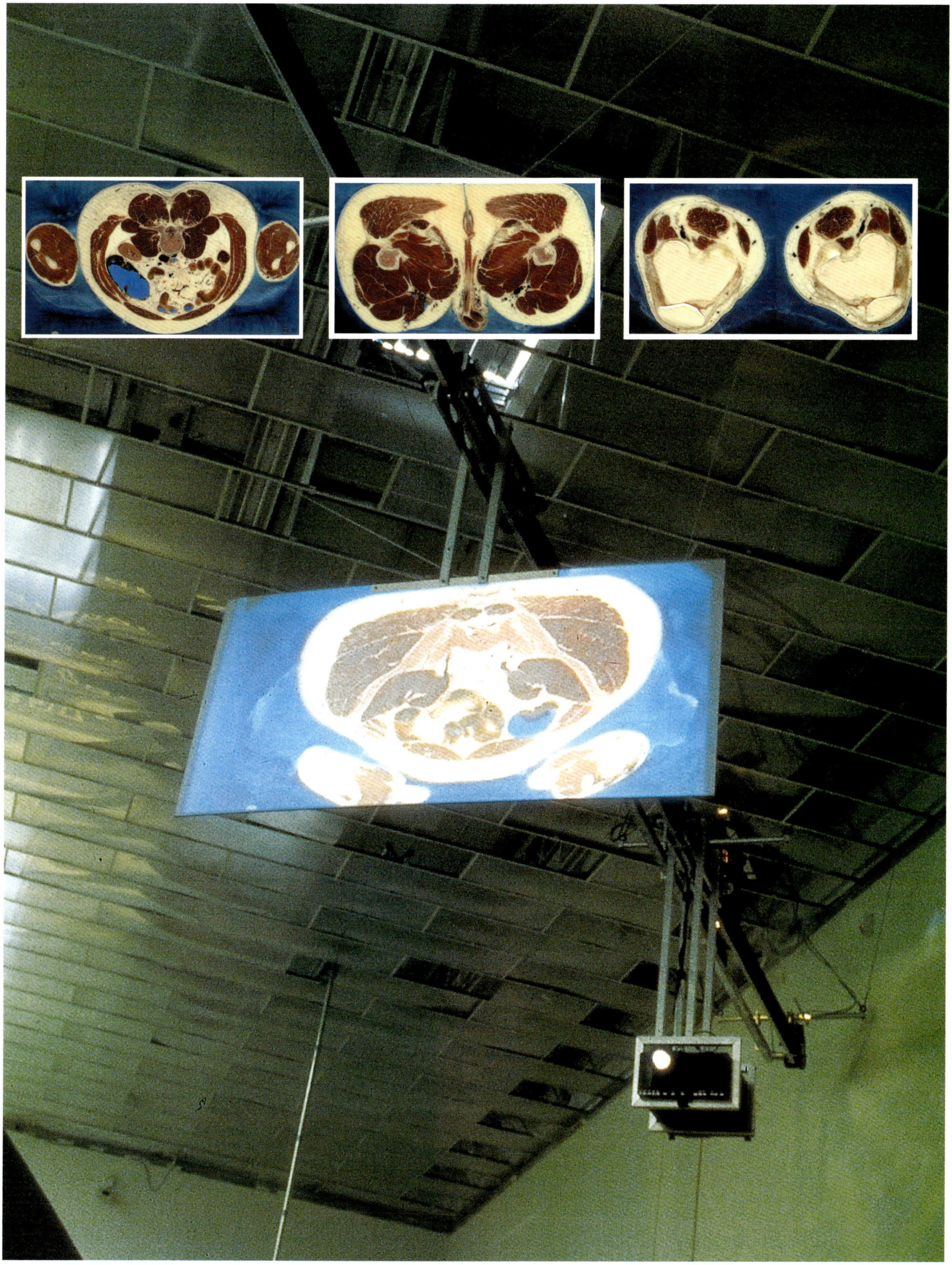

Pezoldo alias Friederike Pezold

DIE ERSTEN ELEKTRONISCH LANGSAM BEWEGTEN FRAUEN AUS TIBET, GUATEMALA UND AFRIKA

Die *Tibeterin* ist Teil einer gerade im Entstehen begriffenen Serie, die Frauen verschiedener Völker (insbesondere der ausgebeuteten und unterdrückten Völker Afrikas und Südamerikas) auf ungewöhnliche Weise präsentiert. Dieser multikulturelle Beitrag ist eine Stellungnahme gegen Rassismus, Xenophobie und Diskriminierung. Der oberste Monitor zeigt die Augenpartie der Tibeterin; was man auf den unteren drei Monitoren sieht, ist nicht auf den ersten Blick zu entschlüsseln. Man meint, unendlich langsam bewegte, abstrakte Bilder zu betrachten, bis man nach einer Weile erkennt, daß es sich um Ausschnitte des Gewandes der Frau handelt. Durch die Anordnung der Monitore übereinander auf einem Holzsockel und die Bildinhalte (oben Gesicht, unten verschiedene Musterungen) erinnert diese Skulptur an einen indianischen Totempfahl, der von einem Gesicht bekrönt ist und im unteren Teil mit Schnitzereien verziert ist. Den Betrachter zu fesseln und möglichst lange im Bann der langsam bewegten Bilder zu halten, das ist ein Aspekt, der sich durch Friederike Pezolds gesamtes Werk zieht; sie nennt es „Tai-chi für die Augen", und meint damit die Wirkung, die die Langsamkeit der Bewegung der Bilder am Monitor auf den Betrachter hat. Diese Langsamkeit und Ruhe der Bilder zwingen den Betrachter, sich Zeit zum Schauen zu nehmen, den Blick zu vertiefen. [...] Formal entsteht die Spannung in der Skulptur zum einen dadurch, daß sich die Bilder auf den vier Ebenen unterschiedlich langsam und in verschiedene Richtungen bewegen; zum anderen durch die verschiedenartige Musterung der Stoffe, die somit einen reizvollen Kontrast bilden. Ein Monitor zeigt

The *Tibetan woman* is part of a series currently being developed, which presents women from various peoples (particularly the exploited and oppressed peoples of Africa and South America) in an unusual way. This multicultural contribution is a statement against racism, xenophobia and discrimination. The monitor on top shows the eyes of the Tibetan woman; what you see on the three lower monitors is not to be recognized at first glance. First you have an impression of very slowly moving abstract images, but after some time, you realize that you are looking a sections of the woman's dress. In the way the monitors are stacked on top of one another and with the contents of the images (the face on top with various types of patterns below), this sculpture is reminiscent of an Indian totem pole, which has a face at the top and is decorated with carvings in the lower part. Capturing the viewer's attention and holding it through the fascination of the slowly moving images is an aspect that is found throughout Friederike Pezold's work; she calls it "Tai-chi for the eyes", referring to the effect that the slowness of the movements of the images in the monitor has on the viewers. The slowness and calmness of the images force the viewer to take time to look, to gaze deeper. [...] The tension in the form of the sculpture emerges in part from the way the images on the four levels move with varying slowness and in different directions; in addition, the different types of patterns in the cloth provide a provocative contrast. One monitor

Pezoldo alias Friederike Pezold

Die erste elektronisch langsam bewegte Frau aus Tibet

Gesamtkunstwerk in Farbe.
4 schwarze Monitore auf schwarzem Holzsockel übereinander angeordnet (1996)

Courtesy:
1. Wiener Museum für Bodyart & Videoart, Wien

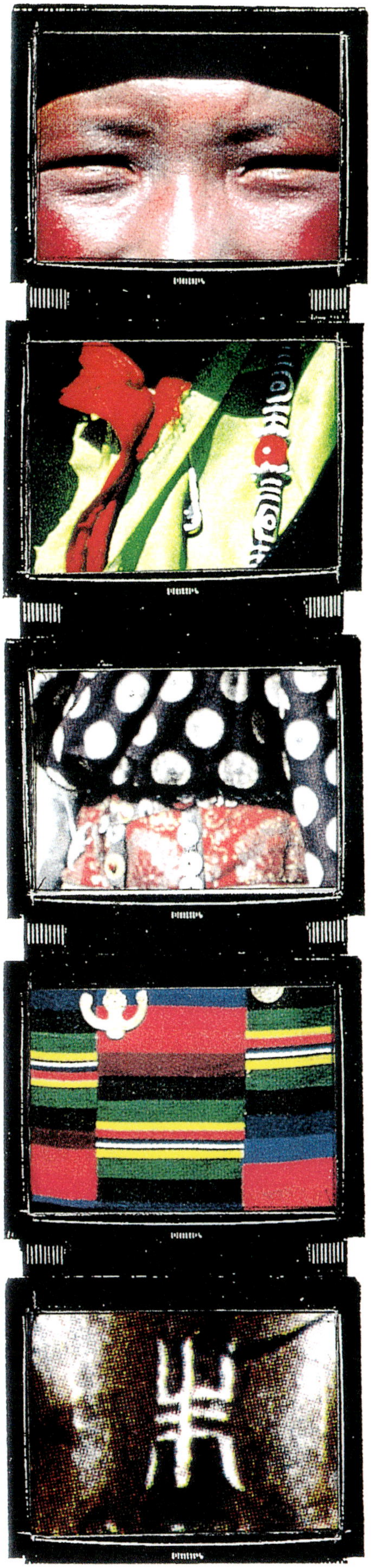

einen blauen Stoff, der weiß gepunktet ist; der nächste eine bunt gestreifte Gewandpartie; am untersten Monitor sieht man einen Teil eines schwarzen Stoffes, der ein weißes Zeichen trägt, das an ein japanisches Schriftzeichen erinnert. Die Skulptur wirkt sehr poetisch, sie könnte als Liebesgedicht der Künstlerin an ihre geistige Heimat Tibet verstanden werden. [...]

Auch bei der *Südamerikanerin* zeigt der oberste Monitor einen Ausschnitt des Gesichts der Frau. Das Bild bewegt sich ganz langsam zur Seite und nach einiger Zeit sieht man statt der Augenpartie einen Teil der traditionellen Kopfbedeckung. Die unteren drei Monitore zeigen Partien der Kleidung der Frau. Die Stoffe der Tracht wirken durch ihre sehr einfache, geometrische Musterung: Kreise, Dreiecke, Rauten und Linienblöcke. Wie bei der Tibeterin bewegen sich die Bilder extrem langsam und faszinieren durch ein harmonisches und zugleich spannungsvolles Zusammenspiel von Farben und Formen. Ein wichtiger Aspekt der Kleidung der Südamerikanerin ist ihre Symbolik: Spinnen und Weben sind wesentliche Handlungen zur Darstellung des mythischen Universums der Maya. Jede Weberin betätigt sich als „Weltschöpferin" (vgl.: Friederike Pezold ist die Erschafferin eines neuen Frauentyps: Sie kreiiert die elektronische Göttin.) Jedes Gewebe stellt einen Mikrokosmos dar, dessen Elemente aus der Mythologie entlehnt sind. Komposition und Muster des Stoffes lassen sich folglich wie ein Text lesen. Das Gewebe der Brustpartie symbolisiert Fruchtbarkeit; die doppelköpfigen Tiere am Stoff des dritten Monitors verbildlichen die den mesoamerikanischen Kul-

displays blue cloth with white dots, the next a colorfully striped portion of the dress; on the monitor at the bottom, you see part of a black cloth with white symbols on it, reminiscent of Japanese written characters. The sculpture has a very poetic effect; it may also be interpreted as the artist's love poem for her spiritual home, Tibet. [...]

In the *South American Woman*, the top monitor also shows a section of the woman's face. The image slowly moves to the side, and eventually you see a part of the woman's traditional head covering rather than the eyes. The lower three monitors display parts of the woman's dress. The textiles of the traditional dress are emphasized by their very simple, geometric patterns: circles, triangles, diamond shapes and blocks of lines. Like the Tibetan woman, here the images move extremely slowly, and their fascination is based on a harmonious, yet exciting interplay of colors and forms. One important aspect of the South American woman's clothing is its symbolism: spinning and weaving are essential elements of the Mayan representation of the mythic universe. Every weaving woman takes part in the „creation of the world" (in comparison: Friederike Pezold is the creatrix of a new type of woman: she creates the electronic goddess.) Each woven cloth represents a microcosm using elements from mythology. As a result, the composition and patterns of the cloth may be read like a text. The cloth from the area of the breast symbolizes fertility; the

Pezoldo alias Friederike Pezold

Die erste elektronisch langsam bewegte Frau aus Guatemala

Gesamtkunstwerk in Farbe. 4 schwarze Monitore auf schwarzem Holzsockel übereinander angeordnet (1996)

Courtesy: 1. Wiener Museum für Bodyart & Videoart, Wien

turen gemeinsame dualistische Weltanschauung. Das Webmuster, das am untersten Monitor zu sehen ist, stellt menschen- und tiergestaltige Symbole dar, die auf die Naturgewalten hinweisen.

Die *Afrikanerin* unterscheidet sich ganz wesentlich von der Tibeterin und der Südamerikanerin: am obersten Monitor sieht man statt dem Auge der Frau ihren Mund, einen großen, lächelnden Mund mit blitzenden, weißen Zähnen. Die unteren Monitore zeigen wieder Ausschnitte der traditionellen Kleidung. Da hier der Mund die Stelle des Auges einnimmt, verteilt sich die Aufmerksamkeit des Betrachters gleichmäßig auf alle vier Monitore, während bei den beiden anderen Frauen jeweils das Auge der „Blickfang" ist: Das Auge hat die Fähigkeit, mit dem Betrachter zu kommunizieren, und ihn in die Arbeit miteinzubeziehen; der Mund tut das nicht mit dieser Stärke. Auch hier bewegen sich die Bilder mit spannender Langsamkeit, durch die pezoldo eine Gegenwelt in einem Zeitalter der Beschleunigung und einer gehetzten Gesellschaft erschaffen möchte. So ist die Afrikanerin an sich ein scharfer Kontrast zur hektischen Europäerin: Nach den Maßstäben der Afrikaner leben wir falsch, indem wir unere Körper wie Maschinen behandlen und uns nach einer Maschine – der Uhr – richten und die Beschleunigung zum Maß aller Dinge erheben. Friederike Pezold gibt dem Körper und somit dem Menschen seine Eigenrhythmik zurück und damit das rechte Maß der Bewegung.

Eva Ebersberger

double-headed animals in the cloth of the third monitor depict the dualistic world view that is common to the Mesoamerican cultures. The weaving pattern that is seen on the lowest monitor represents symbols in the form of humans and animals that indicate the forces of nature.
The *African Woman* is quite different from the Tibetan woman and the South American woman: rather than the woman's eyes, you see her mouth in the top monitor, a large, laughing mouth with dazzling white teeth. The lower monitors display sections of traditional clothing again. Since the mouth takes the place of the eyes in this case, the viewer's attention is equally attracted to all four monitors, whereas with the other women, the eyes "catch the eye" of the observer: eyes are able to communicate with the viewers and draw them into the work; the mouth does not have this effect with the same intensity.
But here again, the images move with the same captivating slowness that pezoldo uses to create an alternative world in our age of acceleration and hurried society. In this way, the African woman provides a sharp contrast to the hectic European woman: according to the attitudes of the Africans, the way we live is wrong when we treat our bodies like machines and pace ourselves according to a machine – the clock – and raise acceleration to the measure of all things. Friederike Pezold returns a sense of internal rhythm to the body and thus to people and with this rhythm the right measure of motion.
Eva Ebersberger

Pezoldo alias Friederike Pezold

Die erste elektronisch langsam bewegte Frau aus Afrika

Gesamtkunstwerk in Farbe.
4 schwarze Monitore auf schwarzem Holzsockel übereinander angeordnet (1996)

Courtesy:
1. Wiener Museum für Bodyart & Videoart, Wien

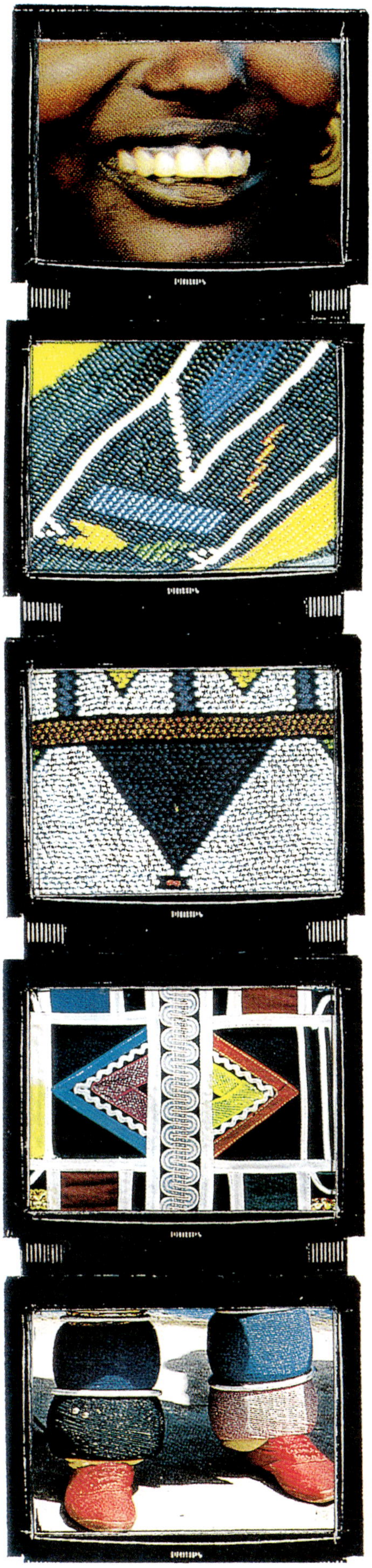

Ulrike Rosenbach

REQUIEM FÜR EINE EICHE

„Requiem für eine Eiche" besteht aus leichten Stahlgerüsten, die etwas über Augenhöhe Monitore tragen. Auf den Videobändern dieser Monitore flackern Fackeln im Dunkel eines nicht näher zu definierenden Hintergrunds. Unter den Monitoren wächst das Wurzelwerk der Eiche. Monitor und Wurzelwerk werden betrachtet durch große Seidenpapierbahnen hindurch, die mit Öl getränkt und damit auf den Mattscheiben zur Haftung gebracht worden sind. Durch das so erzeugte Schattenspiel erscheinen die Wurzeln optisch vergrößert, als geheimnisvolles Gewirr, das sich mal zu einem Torbogen, mal zu einer chinesischen Tuschezeichnung zu formen scheint.
Die Eiche, der diese Wurzeln entstammen, ist wie kein anderer Baum Symbol für Kraft, Mut, Schutz, Beständigkeit, aber auch für den Menschen selber. In der chinesischen Tradition ist sie die männliche Stärke, auch die schwache Seite der Kraft, die sich widersetzt und im Sturme bricht, im Gegensatz zur Kraft der Schwäche in der Weide, die sich biegt und am Leben bleibt.
Die Eiche ist aber auch Symbol für den Naturmythos des ewigen Werdens und Vergehens, der Synthese von Himmel, Erde und Wasser, verwurzelt in der Tiefe der Erde, wachsend in der Welt der Zeit, sich ständig neu reproduzierend und gen Himmel strebend.

Renate Petzinger

aus: Ulrike Rosenbach: „Über den Tod", Katalog St. Petri Kirche, Dortmund, 1995

"Requiem für eine Eiche" ("Requiem for an Oak") consists of light steel frames supporting monitors just above eye level. There are torches flickering against the darkness of a background, which is not otherwise specified, on the video tapes of these monitors. The roots of the oak grow under the monitors. The monitor and the roots are seen through tissue paper that has been soaked in oil and fixed this way to the screen of the monitor. The shadow play thus created makes the roots appear optically enlarged, like a mysterious tangle that seems to form an archway sometimes, or sometimes a Chinese ink drawing.
Like no other tree, the oak from which these roots are taken is a symbol of strength, courage, protection, consistency, but also for human beings themselves. In Chinese tradition, it represents male strength, which is also the weak aspect of strength that resists and breaks in a storm; the counterpart to this is the strength of the weakness of the willow that bends and thus remains alive.
Yet the oak is also a symbol of the nature myth of eternal growth and decay, the synthesis of heaven, earth and water rooted in the depths of the earth, growing into the temporal world, continuously reproducing itself anew and reaching for the sky.

Renate Petzinger
Excerpt from: Ulrike Rosenbach: "Über den Tod", Catalog from St. Petri Church, Dortmund, 1995

Ulrike Rosenbach
Requiem für eine Eiche

Videoskulptur in 4 Elementen (Originalversion 6 Elemente), 4 Stahlsockel mit Zweigeinbindungen, Seidenpapiere, 4 Monitore, 1993

Leo Schatzl

OXO (OXO WONDER VISION)

OXO besteht aus zwei Elektrokochplatten mit großen Kochtöpfen, die mit Spezialsuppe gefüllt sind (X). Dazwischen befindet sich ein Farbfernseher (O) mit einer Spezialantenne (zwei Rohre, an deren Ende jeweils ein nach unten gerichteter Trichter befestigt ist). Die Suppe wird erhitzt, bis Dampf aufsteigt und von den Trichterantennen aufgesaugt wird. Auf dem Bildschirm zeigt sich – je mehr Dampf desto deutlicher – langsam das Bild der brodelnden Suppe. Die Dauer der AV-Übertragung entspricht der Verdampfungszeit der Suppe. Der Ausstellungsraum ist vom Duft der Suppe erfüllt, sie ist auch genießbar und – je nach Kochdauer und Betreuung – mehr oder weniger schmackhaft.

OXO consists of two electric hot plates with large pots filled with a special soup (X). In between, there is a color television (O) with a special antenna (two tubes that each have a funnel attached to the end). The soup is warmed until it is steaming, then the steam is sucked in by the funnel antennas. Slowly, an image of the boiling soup emerges on the screen – the more steam there is, the clearer the image becomes. The length of the AV transmission corresponds to the time it takes the soup to evaporate. The smell of the soup pervades the exhibition room, and depending on how long it is cooked and how well it is attended, the soup is also more or less tasty.

Leo Schatzl
OXO
(oxo wonder vision)

1 Videomonitor, Antenne mit Ansaugtrichtern, 2 Kochplatten, Kochtöpfe, Suppe, 1990/96

Lydia Schouten

A VIRUS OF SADNESS

Im Laufe eines Jahres verfolgte und photographierte ich die Sechs-Uhr-Nachrichten in New York, die über die Morde des Tages berichten und gewaltsame Festnahmen und Interviews mit den Familien des Mörders und des Opfers zeigen. Daraus entstanden sechs Photographien. Wenn die im Photo abgebildeten Einzelheiten uns auch nichts lehren, wird in der Ganzheit die Einsamkeit offenbart. Es ist die Einsamkeit des Einzelnen, der mit der beeinflussenden Kraft der Medien nicht zurechtkommt. Es geht nicht um das romantische Gefühl der Verlassenheit oder das Gefühl, in einer gleichgültig gewordenen Welt verloren zu sein; vielmehr geht es um die radikale und moderne Einsamkeit, die aus einem Zuviel an Kontakt, aus einer Überdosis an Kanälen und Verbindungen entsteht. Das Paradox, das sich vor uns aufbaut ist dies: der Drang zur Kommunikation produziert Einsamkeit.

Dieses Thema wiederholt sich in allen Elementen der Installation: in den Videokontaktanzeigen, die in den hellgrünen, durchsichtigen Lehnstühlen gefunden werden, in den tragikomischen „Köpfen" der Clowns, in dem Bauchredner, der alle 2 Minuten die Jacke aufmacht und bittet „Bitte berühren", und natürlich im Raum selbst, der türkisblau angemalt ist.

Er ist scheinbar ein Zimmer aus dem Film „Secret Beyond the Door" von Fritz Lang ähnlich, eins der sieben geheimnisvollen Zimmer, die schließlich als Nachbildungen von Zimmern, in denen einst ein Verbrechen begangen wurde, erkannt werden.

During a year I watched and photographed the six o'clock news in New York, which reports on the murders of the day, and shows the forcible arrests and interviews with the murderers' and victim's families. Six photographs came out of this. If the individual items on the photo hardly make us any the wiser, the totality reveals loneliness. The loneliness of the individual that cannot cope with the influencing forces of the media. It has nothing to do with the romantic feeling of abandonment and of feeling lost in a world that has become indifferent, but it's the radical and modern loneliness created by too much contact, by an overdose of channels and connections. This reoccurs in all elements of the installation: in the video-personal-adds to be found in the light green, transparent armchairs, in the tragi-comic clowns'heads, in the ventriloquist that opens it's jacket every 2 minutes and asks ,Please Touch', and of course in the room itself, painted turquoise blue. It would seem to resemble one of the rooms from Fritz Lang's film ,Secret Beyond the Door', one of those seven mysterious rooms that eventually turn out to be reconstructions of rooms in which a crime was once committed. Each element of the installation can be judged on its own merits, as each of them carries the virus of loneliness. And at the same time, each element shows the symptoms of brute violence that can break loose at any moment in the turquoise murder room.

Lydia Schouten

Lydia Schouten
A Virus of Sadness

Installation, 1990,
6 x 8 m
Video, Fotos, Masken, Sofa, Puppe

Technik: Monte Video, Amsterdam

Courtesy: Rijkdienst Beeldende Kunst, Den Haag

Lydia Schouten
A Virus of Sadness

Installation, 1990,
6 x 8 m
Video, Fotos, Masken,
Sofa, Puppe

Courtesy: Rijkdienst Beeldende Kunst, Den Haag

Technik:
Monte Video, Amsterdam

Jedes Element der Installation kann unabhängig von den anderen beurteilt werden, da jedes davon den Virus der Einsamkeit trägt. Gleichzeitig zeigt auch jedes einzelne Element die Symptome der nackten Gewalt, die jeden Moment im türkisen Mordraum ausbrechen kann.

Lydia Schouten

Paul Sermon

TELEMATIC DREAMING

„Telematic Dreaming" ist eine Installation, die innerhalb des digitalen Telefonnetzwerkes existiert. Es gibt zwei getrennte Schnittstellen an verschiedenen Orten, die gleichfalls dynamische Installationen sind, die als eigene Videoconferencing-Systeme fungieren. An jedem Ort steht ein Doppelbett, wobei der eine Ort verdunkelt und der andere beleuchtet ist. Direkt über dem Bett am beleuchteten Ort ist eine Kamera montiert, die live Videoaufnahmen des Betts, sowie einer Person („A") auf dem Bett an einen Videoprojektor über dem Bett am verdunkelten Ort sendet. Das Live- Videobild wird auf das Bett, wo eine zweite Person („B") liegt, projiziert. Eine zweite Kamera neben dem Videoprojektor sendet ein Live- Videobild der projizierten Person „A" mit der Person „B" an eine Reihe von das Bett und die Person „A" umgebende Monitore am beleuchteten Ort zurück. Das Telepräsenzbild wirkt wie ein Spiegel, der eine Person innerhalb der Widerspiegelung einer anderen Person reflektiert. Die psychologische Komplexität des Objekts löst die geographische Entfernung und die mit der gesamten ISDN-Installation verbundene Technologie auf. Die Möglichkeit, außerhalb des eigenen Raumes und der eigenen Zeit des Anwenders zu existieren, entsteht durch eine bestürzend echte Wahrnehmung des Tastsinnes, die durch den Zusammenhang mit dem Bett verstärkt und durch eine gesteigerte Verschiebung der Sinneswahrnehmungen in diesem telematischen Raum verursacht wird. Innerhalb des Telepräsenzkörpers wird das Bewußtsein des Benützers durch einen Voyeurismus des Selbst gesteuert.

Telematic Dreaming is an installation that exists within the ISDN digital telephone network. Two separate interfaces are located in separate locations, these interfaces in themselves are dynamic installations that function as customized videoconferencing systems. A double bed is located within both locations, one location is blacked out, the other is lighted. The bed in the light location has a camera situated directly above it, sending a live video image of the bed, and a person ("A") on it, to a video projector located above the other bed in the blacked out location. The live video image is projected down on to the bed with another person ("B") on it. A second camera, next to the video projector, sends a live video image of the projection of person "A" with person "B" back to a series of monitors that surround the bed and person "A" in the lighted location. The telepresence image functions like a mirror that reflects one person within another person's reflection. *Telematic Dreaming* delibarately plays with the ambigous connotations of a bed as a telepresent projection surface. The psychological complexity of the object dissolves the geographical distance and technology involved in the complete ISDN installation. The ability to exist outside of the users own space and time is created by an alarmingly real sense of touch that is enhanced by the context of the bed and caused by an acute shift of senses in this telematic space. The user's consciousness is within the telepresent body controlled by a voyeurism of itself.

Paul Sermon
Telematic Dreaming

1995, Installation

In Zusammenarbeit mit Oö. Kulturvermerke, Gmunden, und Ars Electronica Center, Linz

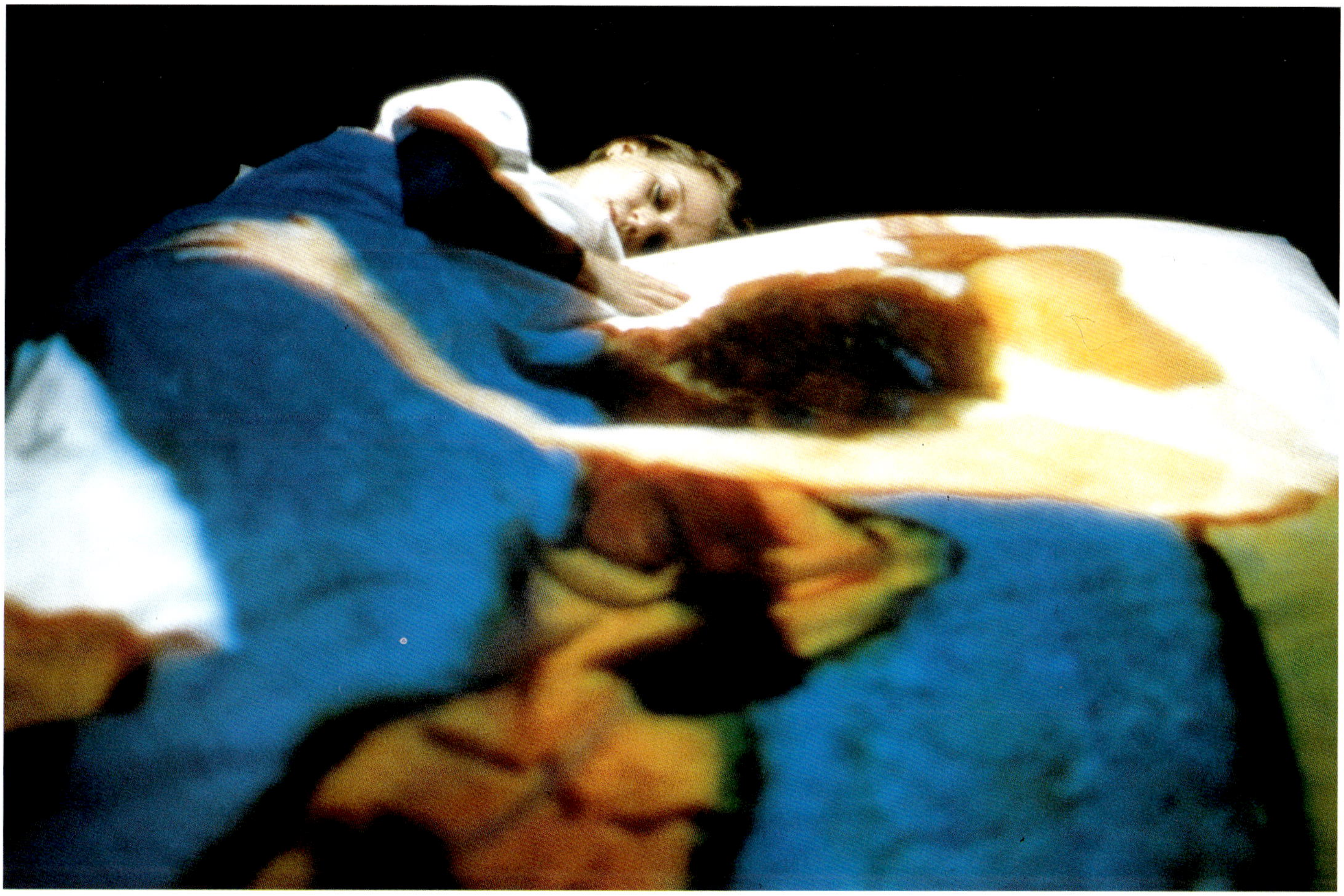

Servaas

PFFT... / ARE YOU AFRAID OF VIDEO?

1979 begann Servaas seine Arbeit im Bereich der bildenden Kunst. 1980 atmete er sozusagen Leben in seine „Malerei", indem er pneumatische Auslösevorrichtungen in Verbindung mit Audio auf vielfältige Weise einsetzte, wodurch schließlich fünfzehn Videoproduktionen entstanden. Servaas' weiterführende Arbeit mit pneumatischen Installationen gipfelte 1981 mit der Gestaltung autonomer Kunstwerke, u.a. der Videoskulptur mit dem wunderbaren Namen „Pfft ...".
Vor einem kleinen Schwarzweißmonitor wird eine weiße Feder befestigt. Am Bildschirm sehen wir eine Nahaufnahme von Servaas' Mund; es sieht so aus, also ob der Mund durch das Glas des Videomonitors pustet, um die Feder zu bewegen. Illusion und Wirklichkeit werden in seinem Werk auf plastische Weise miteinander verbunden, wobei sich die Frage stellt: Wer manipuliert wen?
Einige der pneumatischen Videoinstallationen von Servaas wurden bereits international ausgestellt, z.B. bei der Video-Sculptur Exhibition (eine Retrospektive zur Videokunst von 1963 bis 1989 in Köln).
Zweifellos ist die treibende Kraft hinter seinen so entstehenden Bildern jene der Medien. Bei Interviews 1994 behauptete Servaas, daß das Fernsehen ein sehr gefährliches Medium sei; außerdem hatte er dieser Vorstellung in seinen Installationen, u.a. „Pfft..." und „Are You Afraid of Video?", Gestalt verliehen.
Nach Servaas wird die gesamte durch Fernsehen vermittelte Information viel zu oft als Fiktion betrachtet! Demnach werden wir in der

Servaas began his work in the field of the fine arts in 1979. In 1980 he breathed life into his 'paintings' as it were, by his versatile use of pneumatic triggering devices combined with audio sounds, which eventually gave rise to fifteen video productions. Servaas's continued work on his pneumatic installations culminated in 1981 with the creation of autonomous art works, including, a.o., the video sculpture, rejoicing in the name of „Pfft...".
A white feather is secured in front of a small black and white monitor. On the screen we see a close-up image of Servaas's mouth, which appears to be blowing right through the glass of the video monitor screen and causing the feather to flutter. Illusion and reality are graphically brought together in his work, which begs the question: who is manipulating who?
A number of Servaas's pneumatic video installations have been exhibited at venues thruout the world, such as the Video-Sculptur Exhibition (a retrospective of video art from 1963 to 1989, held in Cologne).
The motivating force behind his resulting imagery is undoubtedly that of the media. During interviews in 1994, Servaas expressed the view that TV is a very dangerous medium; moreover, he had given this concept material form in his installations, "Pfft..." and „Are You Afraid of Video?" among others.
According to Servaas, all information on TV is far too often viewed as fiction! Consequently, in the installation "Are You Afraid of Video", we are also confronted with the question:

Servaas
Pfft...

1982, Videoskulptur, Monitor, Videoband, Feder, pneumatische Vorrichtung

Courtesy: Collection Rijksdienst/The Hague

Installation „Are You Afraid of Video?" mit der Frage konfrontiert: „Worin besteht der Unterschied zwischen einer Unterhaltungsserie wie z. B. Miami Vice und den auf Tatsachen beruhenden, lebensechten Bildern, die in den Nachrichtensendungen eingeblendet werden? Verwunderte ZuseherInnen, die ziellos durch den Senderdschungel mit der Fernbedienung herumschalten, erkennen überhaupt keinen Unterschied mehr." Um den Unterschied zwischen Fiktion und Wirklichkeit neu zu definieren, arbeitet Servaas an dem sogenannten „The Screen Seal of Approval Project for TV pictures".
Links unten am Bildschirm sehen wir ein oranges Symbol, das für die ZuseherInnen Bilder einer tatsächlichen Nachrichtensendung kennzeichnet; dadurch kann man klar zwischen Wirklichkeit und Fiktion unterscheiden. Über dieses Projekt wurde Mai 1996 in den Nachrichten in St. Louis (USA) im Rahmen einer Würdigung des „People Communications Charter" berichtet.

S. Steal, 1996

"What's the difference between, for instance, a fictional series such as Miami Vice and the factual, real-life pictures that accompany the news? Channel-hopping with the remote across the grab-bag of stations, the bemused viewer just doesn't know the difference anymore.
In order to define, once more, the difference between fiction and reality, Servaas has been working on the so-called „The Screen Seal of Approval Project for TV pictures."
On the left, under the monitor screen we shall see an orange symbol, which indicates that the viewer is watching actual news pictures; so that he/she will now clearly be in a position to distinguish between what is reality or fiction.
This project made news in St.Louis (USA) in May 1996 during an appraisal of ‚The People Communications Charter'.
(S. Steal, 1996)

Servaas
Are You Afraid of Video?

1994, Videoskultptur, 4 Monitore, Videoband, Kunststoffseil, pneumatische Vorrichtung

Courtesy: Collection Stedelijk Museum Amsterdam

Andrea van der Straeten

MEIN VIDEO IST MEIN HEMD

an den
2. marler video-kunstpreis
skulpturenmuseum glaskasten
postfach 1120
4370 marl

hamburg, 27. 4. 86

liebes organisationskomitee – liebe jury !

zum diesjährigen marler video-kunst-preis sende ich ihnen meinen beitrag
MEIN VIDEO IST MEIN HEMD .
soweit ich das ihren wettbewerbsbedingungen entnehmen kann erfüllt mein beitrag die dort formulierten punkte:
er ist eine medienspezifische umsetzung
keine einfache dokumentararbeit
entstand von februar bis april 1986
aus 1/2 zoll
länge 35 minuten
die frage nach der technischen bearbeitung und künstlerischen qualität obliegt der jury.
ich möchte sie bitten, meinem beitrag die gleiche wertschätzung wie allen anderen eingereichten arbeiten zuteil werden zu lassen und ihn – bei einer eventuellen nicht-auswahl – sorgfältig verpackt und versichert an mich zurückzusenden.

mit lieben grüßen & besten wünschen für eine angenehme & humorvolle festivalarbeit

andrea van der straeten

dear organizational committee –
dear jury:
for this year's marler video prize,
i am submitting my entry
MY VIDEO IS MY SHIRT
as far as i can tell from your competition regulations my entry meets the specifications stated there:
it is a media-specific realization
not simply a documentary work
created between february and april 1986
from 1/2 inch
length 35 minutes
it is up to the jury to evaluate the technical craft and artistic quality
i request that you grant my submission the same esteemed consideration as all the other submitted works and – should it not be selected – return it to me carefully packed and insured

with warmest regards & best wishes for pleasant & amusing festival work
andrea van der straeten

Andrea van der Straeten
Mein Video ist mein Hemd

1986, Videobänder, Kleiderbügel

Courtesy: Martin Fritz und Franco Kappl, Wien

Bill Viola

HEAVEN AND EARTH

Eine kleine Nische beherbergt ein säulenähnliches Gebilde aus Holz, das sich vom Boden bis zur Decke streckt. Ein Lücke von nur wenigen Zentimetern in Augenhöhe teilt die Säule in zwei Teile auf. Dazwischen sind zwei nackte Bildröhren von Schwarzweißmonitoren eng zueinander, ohne sich jedoch zu berühren, montiert. Der obere Monitor zeigt eine Nahaufnahme einer sterbenden alten Frau, der untere Monitor zeigt Nahaufnahmen eines Neugeborenen, das nur ein paar Tage alt ist. Die Bilder sind tonlos. Da die Oberfläche der Monitorbildschirme aus Glas besteht, sieht man durch die Oberfläche jedes Bildes die Spiegelung des anderen Bildes, so wie das Leben und der Tod sich gegenseitig spiegeln und bedingen.

Das Werk ist der 1991 verstorbenen Mutter des Künstlers, sowie seinem zweiten, neun Monate später geborenen Sohn gewidmet.

A column-like structure is enclosed in a small alcove. It is made of wood and extends from floor to ceiling. There is a gap of several inches at eye level in the column, dividing the structure in two. At this gap, positioned facing each other and not touching, are the exposed tubes of two black and white video monitors. The upper monitor shows a close-up image of an old woman on the verge of death, and the lower monitor shows a close-up image of a new baby only days old. The images are silent. Since the surface of each monitor screen is glass, a reflected image of the screen opposite to it can be seen through the surface of each image, as life and death reflect and contain each other.

The work is dedicated to the artist's mother who passed away in 1991 and his second son who was born nine months later.

Bill Viola
Heaven and Earth

1992,
Video Installation

Courtesy:
Ydessa Hendeles Art Foundation, Toronto

Bill Viola
Heaven and Earth

1992,
Video Installation
(Detail)

Courtesy:
Ydessa Hendeles Art
Foundation, Toronto

VA Wölfl

FLAGGE

Die Installation *Flagge* zeigt in der nicht mehr vorhandenen Originalversion für das 'Worldwide Video Festival' Den Haag die Farben der Niederlande in drei übereinander angeordneten Fernsehapparaten. Die Bildschirme sind gegen die Wand gerichtet, man nimmt also nur deren Widerschein wahr. Obwohl die Monitore nicht direkt sichtbar sind, entsteht ein Wiedererkennungseffekt als 'Fahne'. Letztendlich wurden in der Installation jedoch nur die drei Apparate in den Farben Rot, Weiß und Blau eingestellt, erst die Reflektion an der Wand ergibt die „Flaggen"-Wirkung.

Für die Linzer Ausstellung wird die *Flagge* von VA Wölfl als österreichische Variante in den Farben Rot-Weiß-Rot rekonstruiert.

In the no longer existant original version for the "Worldwide Video Festival" in The Hague, the installation "Flagge" showed the colors of the Dutch flag in three televisions stacked one above the other. The screens are placed facing the wall, so that only the reflection of the colors is perceived. Although the screens are not viewed directly, the reflection of their light on the wall creates the effect of a "flag". Thus, the three apparatuses in the installation were set to the colors red, white and blue, resulting in a "flag" effect. For the exhibition in Linz, V. A. Wölfl's "Flagge" is reconstructed in a special Austrian variation with the colors red-white-red.

VA Wölfl
Niederländische Fernsehflagge

1984,
Videoinstallation,
3 Tv-Geräte auf Rot-Weiß-Blau eingestellt

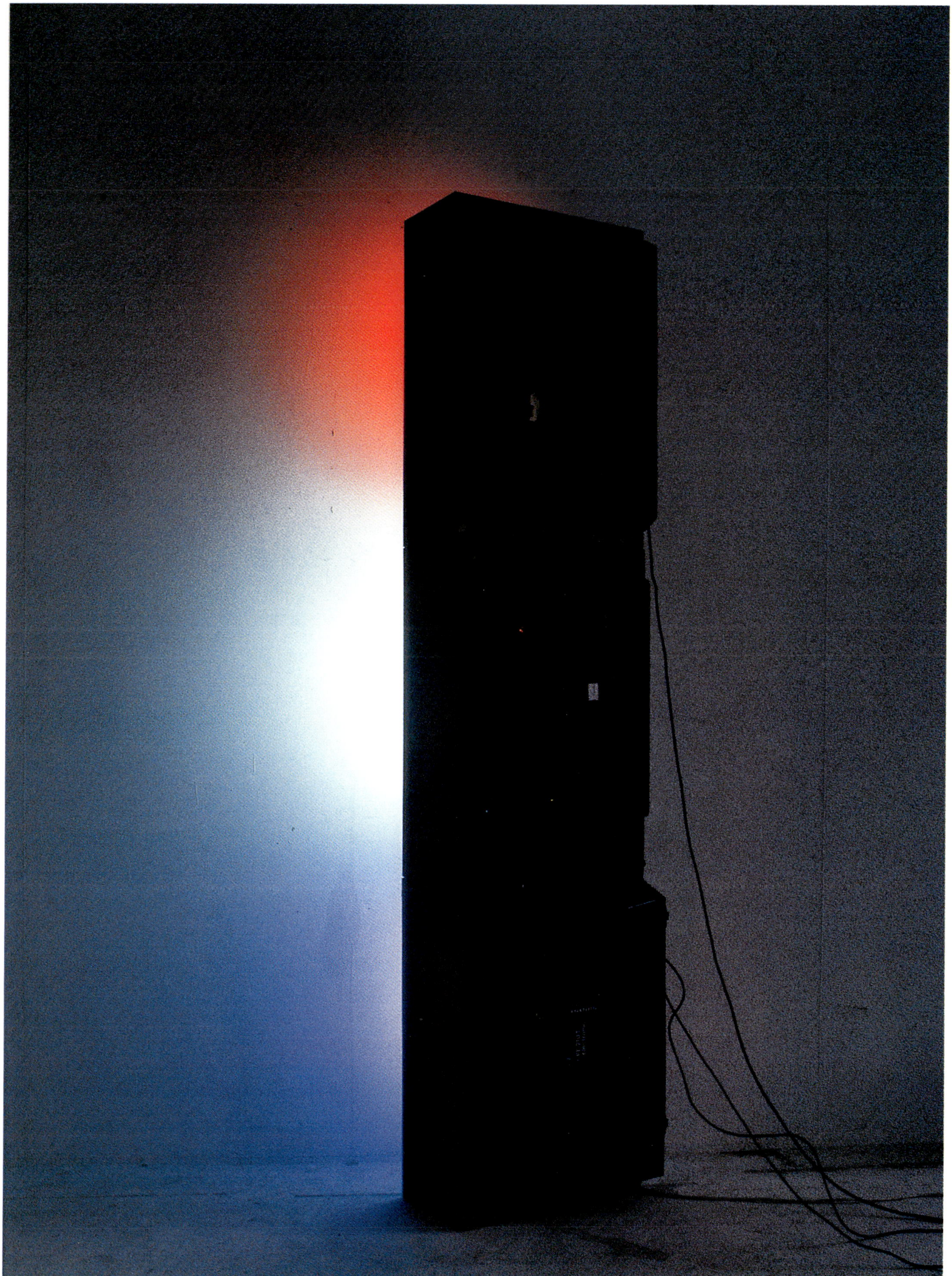

Autoren:

CHRISTINE VAN ASSCHE
ist Kustodin für Videokunst und Film am Centre Georges Pompidou, Paris.

PETER ASSMANN
1963 geboren, Mag.phil., Dr.phil., Studium der Kunstgeschichte, Geschichte und Germanistik, mehrjährige Forschungsaufenthalte in Italien und Frankreich, seit 1992 Leiter der oö. Landesgalerie, Lehrbeauftragter der Hochschule für Gestaltung in Linz, der Universität Innsbruck, der Kath. Theolog. Hochschule Linz. Div. Ausstellungen, Symposien und Fachpublikationen zur österreichischen und internationalen Kunst des 20. Jahrhunderts, z. B. „Kubin-Projekt 1995", „Ars Electronica", „Werkzeuge – Design des Elementaren", „Hans Fronius", „ObjektTextilBild", „Kopigrafie", „Arnulf Rainer" bzw. zur italienische Kunst des 16. Jahrhunderts.

DIETER DANIELS
1957 in Bonn geboren. Studium der Kunstgeschichte, Philosophie und Kunst. Mitbegründer der Videonale Bonn, internationales Festival für Kunstvideo seit 1984; seit 1991 Aufbau der Videosammlung am Zentrum für Kunst und Medientechnologie Karlsruhe; seit 1993 Professur für Kunstgeschichte und Medientheorie an der Hochschule für Grafik und Buchkunst Leipzig; 1994 Konzept und Leitung von „Minima Media", Medienbiennale Leipzig 94. Kurator mehrerer Ausstellungen, u.a.: „Übrigens sterben immer die anderen, Marcel Duchamp und die Avantgarde seit 1950, Museum Ludwig Köln, 1988; „Neues Video aus der BRD", Museum für Gegenwartskunst Basel, Kunsthaus Aarau, Kunstmuseum Luzern, 1987; „Zeitzeichen Kunst" (Videoprogramm), Museum der Bildenden Künste Leipzig, Lehmbruck Museum Duisburg, 1989; „Moving Image – Electronic Art" (Mitarbeit), Fundació Miró Barcelona und ZKM Karlsruhe, 1992; „kryptisch" (Videoinstallationen), ZKM Karlsruhe, 1993; „Europa – Europa" (Videoprogramm), Kunst- und Ausstellungshalle der Bundesrepublik Deutschland Bonn, 1994; Kurator der bundesdeutschen Video-Sektion auf mehreren internationalen Festivals (Locarno 1985, 1987, Bologna „L'Immagine Elettronica" 1985, Linz „Ars Electronica" 1987, Tokyo „Japan 92 Video Television Festival" 1992.
Zahlreiche Publikationen, u.a.: „Video heute – Kunst oder was sonst?", Themenheft „Kunstforum", Band 98, Jan. 1989; „Fluxus – ein Nachruf zu Lebzeiten", Themenheft „Kunstforum", Band 115, Sept. 1991; „Sammlung Cremer Bd. 1 & Bd. 2", Bestandskatalog, Museum am Ostwall & Edition Cantz, 1991; „George Brecht – notebooks, Vol. I-III", Verlag Walther König, Köln 1991; „Duchamp und die anderen. Der Modellfall einer künstlerischen Wirkungsgeschichte in der Moderne", DuMont, Köln 1992; „Art-intact", ZKM Karlsruhe & Cantz Verlag 1994.

VITTORIO FAGONE
1939 geboren, Kunsthistoriker und Kunstkritiker für zeitgenössische, lebt in Mailand. International bekannt für seine Untersuchungen zur modernen Kunst und als Kurator, u.a. für Biennale Venedig 1978 und 1980, documenta Kassel 1987. Er befaßt sich vorwiegend mit den Beziehungen zwischen Kunst und moderner Technologie. 1981-1985 war er Direktor des Videoart Festivals in Locarno, 1986-1988 leitete er das Festival Arte Elettronica in Camerino. Seit 1989 war er einer der Direktoren der Biennale ARTEC in Nagoya/Japan. Zusammen mit Dieter Ronte ist er verantwortlich für die Ausstellungen innerhalb des internationalen Projekts „Art in Nature". Während seiner Lehrtätigkeit als Professor an der Fakultät für Architektur an der Polytechnischen Universität Mailand hielt er Kurse und Seminare über Kunst und neue visuelle Technologien in Italien (Parma, Staatsuniversität Mailand, Turin, La Sapienza Rom, Palermo und Siena) und an internationalen Instituten (New York University, Montral, Tokyo, Osaka, Liège, Belgrad Buenos Aires). Seit 1993 ist er Direktor der Galleria D'Arte Moderna e Contemporanea, Accademia Carrara, Bergamo. Er ist Autor zahlreicher Studien und Monographien über zeitgenössische Kunst, Architektur und Design. Eine Auswahl seiner Essays erschien in Buchform „L'immagine video – Arti visuali e nuovi media elettronice" bei Feltrinelli, Mailand 1990. Er ist Ehrenpräsident der Association International pour la Video dans les Arts et la Culture (AIVAC – UNESCO).

GOTTFRIED HATTINGER
1950 im Hausruckwald geboren. 1986-1991 künstlerischer Leiter des Festivals „Ars Electronica", arbeitet seitdem als freischaffender Kurator und als Buchgestalter in Linz.
Wichtigste Aktivitäten: 1991 „International Video Biennal", Fukui/Japan; 1992 „Zwei x Zwei", Posthof, Linz; „Survival Research Laboratories", steirischer herbst, Graz; 1993 „Synästhesie: Simulation und Stimulation", V2, s'Hertogenbosch, Holland; „Klangobjekt", Kunsthalle Krems; „Performance: Relikte und Sedimente", Offenes Kulturhaus, Linz; 1994 „Klingende Dinge", Ausstellung auf Schloß Ottenstein, Niederösterreich; „Maschinenklang", Marstall, Bayerisches Staatsschauspiel, München; 1994/96 „Reihe Video Kunst", oö. Landesgalerie, Linz; „Spiel.Art", Theaterbiennale, München. 1996 „Klangturm", Eröffnungsprogramm, St. Pölten; „Der Himmel ist blau: Philosophie und Schrott", Contained, Linz; Konsulent für „PhotoArts 2000", Huddersfield, Yorkshire.

KEIKO SEI
ist Autorin und Kuratorin, lebt in Prag. Derzeit arbeitet sie an einem Buch über Medien und Osteuropa, das 1997 in Japan erscheinen wird.
Kuratortätigkeit und Publikationsprojekte (Auswahl): „Infermental 8 – The Tokyo Edition", 1987/88; „Von der Bürokratie zur Telekratie", Merve Verlag, Berlin 1990; „The Media Are With Us! – The Role of Television in the

Romanian Revolution", Internationales Symposion, Budapest 1990; „The Age of Nikola Tesla", European Media Art Festival, Osnabrück 1991; „Extra Sense and Computer – Bulgaria, the Country of Future", European Media Art Festival, Osnabrück 1992; „Eastern Europe TV & Politics", Hallwalls Contemporary Art Center, Buffalo, NY 1993; „Ex-Oriente-Lux – Romanian Video Week", Soros Center for Contemporary Arts, Bukarest 1993; „Orbis Fictus – New Media in Contemporary Arts", Soros Center for Contemporary Arts, Prag 1995; „Semtex, Radar und V.R. – A Pardubice Model", European Media Art Festival, Osnabrück1996.

Künstlerlnnen:

STUDIO AZZURRO
ist eine Künstlergruppe, die sich auf Videoproduktion, künstlerische Experimente und High-Tech-Forschung spezialisiert. Gegründet wurde das Studio von drei Künstlern, die aus unterschiedlichen Bereichen stammen: FABIO CIRIFINO (Fotografie), PAOLO ROSA (Visuelle Kunst und Film), und LEONARDO SANGIORGI (Grafik und Animation).
Ausstellungen und Beteiligungen (Auswahl): 1983 Video D.C., Lubljana; World-Wide Festival Video, Olanda; Fortezza da Basso, Florenz; Palazzo Fortuny, Venedig. 1984 Palazzo del Senato, Mailand; Fortezza da Basso, Florenz; Centro Multivediale, Volterra; Palazzo Fortuny, Venedig; DuMont Kunsthalle, Köln; Berliner Festwochen; Musée d'Art Moderne et d'Art Contemporain, Nizza. 1985 Teatro Stabile, Turin; INTEL ,85, Mailand; Centro Multivediale, Volterra; Palazzo Fortuny, Venedig; Museo Communale Gambalunga, Rimini; Teatro La Piramide, Rom; Lantaren, Rotterdam; Inter. Teatre, Oslo. 1986 Giardini di Villa Medici, Rom; Time Base Art, Amsterdam; Festival dell'Arte Elettronica, Camerino; Palazzo Fortuny, Venedig. 1987 Santa Scolastica, Bari; documenta 8, Kassel; TIVZ, Leningrad; Wiener Festwochen; Laforet Akasaka, Tokyo. 1988 Rotondo di via Besana, Mailand; Festival Internationale Videoart, Locarno; XVII Triennale Milano; TTVV Festival, Riccione. 1989 Festival Tucano Artes, Rio de Janeiro; TTVV Festival, Riccione. 1990 Festival Teatro Due di Parma; ARTEL, Galleria Communale d'Arte Moderna, Cagliari; Biennale Internationale Francesco Speranza, Bitonto; Dentre Culturel de Cavaillon; Taormina Arte Festival, Taormina; Ars Electronica, Linz. 1991 Maggio Musicale Fiorentino, Florenz; Artec ,91, City Art Museum, Nagoya/Japan; Spazio Ansaldo, Mailand. 1992 XVIII Esposizione Internazionale Triennale di Milano, Mailand. 1993 Fondazione Mudima, Mailand. 1994 „Paint Show ,94", Tokyo; Laforet Museum Ikura, Tokyo; Teatro di Porta Romana, Mailand; Palazzo Reale, Mailand. 1995 Triennale di Milano, Mailand; Mole Anonelliana, Turin.

GUNDI BERGHOLD
1962 in Graz geboren. 1983-1990 Hochschule für Angewandte Kunst Wien (Freie Graphik / Visuelle Mediengestaltung); 1988-1989 Hochschule für Musik und Darstellende Kunst (Elektroakustik / Experimentelle Musik). 1995 Staatsstipendium; Artist in Residence UMAS, Durham Ontario, Kanada.
Ausstellungen: 1989 Planetarium Wien; 1. Österreichische Filmtage, Wels; „Musik und Technik", Technisches Museum, Wien. 1990 Galerie Arcade, Mödling; Neue Galerie, Graz. 1991 Video und Computerfestival, St.Veit/Glan; Blau-Gelbe Galerie, Wien. 1992 „Zeitschnitte 92", Wien. 1993 Galerie nächst St. Stephan, Wien; Studio Neue Galerie, Graz; „Das Fremde – Der Gast", Offenes Kulturhaus, Linz; „Diagonale 93", Österreichisches Filmfestival, Salzburg. 1994 Lokalzeit-Raum Strouhal, Wien; „Positionen", Hallein. 1995 UMAS, Durham, Ontario. 1996 Museum Abteiberg, Mönchengladbach.

GUDRUN BIELZ
1954 in Linz geboren. 1977-1980 Studium an der Hochschule für künstlerische und industrielle Gestaltung, Linz; 1980/81 Aufenthalt in London; 1981-1987 Studium an der Hochschule für angewandte Kunst in Wien; 1988-1994 Lehrauftrag an der Hochschule für künstlerische und industrielle Gestaltung, Meisterklasse für Visuelle Gestaltung, Linz; 1989/90 Postgraduate am Central St. Martins college of Art and Desingn, Dept. Film and Video, British Council Fellowship; 1992-1994 funktionelle Assistenz an der Hochschule für angewandte Kunst, Meisterklasse für Visuelle Mediengestaltung, Wien; 1995 Sommerkakademie Schloß Topolcianky, Leitung des Kurses „Projektion-Licht", Slowakei.
Mitglied der London Filmmakers' Co-op. Teilnahme an zahlreichen Film- und Videofestivals, u.a. London Filmmakers' Co-op, London; Cinema giovani, Torino; Mostra internazionale des cinema non professionale, Montcatini; Centre Pompidou, Paris; „Forum des jungen Films", Berlinale, Berlin; „Arte Austriaca", Bologna; Videofestival Sydney; Long Beach Museum of Arts, USA; Circulo de bellas artes, Madrid; Art Institute of Chicago, USA.
Ausstellungen und Beteiligungen: 1984 „Videowochen im Wenkenpark", Stipendium und Installation, Basel. 1985 Gesamtpräsentation, Universität Klagenfurt; „Scultura Video Berri Berri", Museum Moderner Kunst, Wien. 1987 „Grauer Raum mit Blau", Trigon, Steirischer Herbst, Graz. 1989 „You aren't a voyeur. Are you?", Central St. Martins College of Art and Design, Long Acre, London. 1990 „x44", Dionysos Gallery, Rotterdam. 1991 „The organs of sense", Lethaby Gallery, London. 1992 „Art d'Eco", Triennale Maribor, Slowenien; „Im Raum Schule", Offenes Kulturhaus, Linz. 1993 Biennale d'arte contemporanea, Marostica. 1994 „Lokalzeit – Wiener Material im Spiegel des Unbehagens", Forum aktueller Kunst – Raum Strohal, Wien und Museum of Modern Art, Ljubljana; „Diagonale 94", Galerie 5020, Salzburg. 1995 „Lokalzeit", Fondazione Querini, Venezia.

1996 „Rays 1“ Galerie im Stifterhaus, Linz.
Ausstellungen gemeinsam mit Ruth Schnell (Auswahl): 1984 "1984", Museum des 20. Jahrhunderts, Wien. 1986 „Terminal Art“, Ars Electronica, Linz. 1987 „Junge Szene Wien“, Secession, Wien. 1988 „Freizone Dorotheergasse“, Wiener Festwochen und Galerie Metropol, Wien; „Der pornographische Blick“, Künstlerhaus, Salzburg. 1989 „60 Tage Museum des 21. Jahrhunderts“, Wien; „Im Netz der Systeme“, Ars Electronica, Linz. 1990 „Aperto“, Biennale di Venezia; „Video IV“, Ferdinandeuzm, Innsbruck; „Im Licht des Monitors“, Kunstverein Horn, Künstlerhaus Graz und Haus zur Glocke Prag. 1991 „Take Over III“, Fabian Carlsson Gallery, London; „Außerhalb von Mittendrin“, TIK, NGBK, Berlin; „4. Internationale Videobiennale“, Fukui City, Japan; „Topographie II – Untergrund“, Wiener Festwochen. 1992 „Der entfesselte Blick“, Kulturzentrum Pfäffikon; „Identität:Differenz“, Tribüne Trigon 1940-1990, steirischer herbst, Graz. 1991/92/93 „Absolutismus und Ekzentrik“, Wanderausstellung in Italien (Bozen, Malo, Bari, Rimini. 1993 „Transparenz“, Palais Liechtenstein, Feldkirch. 1994 „Shape Your Body“, La Giarina, Verona; „Transparenz“, Kunstverein, Hallein. 1995 „Fiktion/non-fiction“, oö. Landesgalerie, Linz; „A New Europe – Supranational Art“, Le Zitelle, Biennale di Venizia.

BIRGIT BRENNER
1964 in Ulm geboren. 1985-1990 Studium Grafik-Design in Darmstadt; 1990-1995 Studium an der Hochschule der Künste Berlin bei Rebecca Horn; lebt und arbeitet in Paris.
Ausstellungen: 1991 Galerie ART ACKER, Berlin; 1992 „37 Räume“, Kunstwerke e.V., Berlin; 1993 Galerie EIGEN +ART, Berlin; Galerie Franz Mehring, Kunstamt Kreuzberg, Berlin; „Video-Skulptur in Deutschland seit 1963, Institut für Auslandsbeziehungen, Kunsthalle Rostock, Video Centre Den Haag, Centrum beeldende Kunst Groningen, Nationalgalerie Peking, Hongkong Arts Centre; Große Kunstausstellung NRW, Düsseldorf; Galerie EIGEN+ART, Independent Art Space, London; 1995 „Transit-Permanenz“, Künstlerbahnhof, Karl-Hofer-Gesellschaft Berlin; Dirty Window Galerie, Berlin; Lindenau-Museum, Altenburg; ART Chicago, Chicago; Biennale Venedig 1995, Club Berlin; 1996 Galerie EIGEN+ART, Berlin.

DAVID CERNY
1967 in Prag geboren. 1987-1993 Studium an der Akademie der Angewandten Kunst in Prag. Lebt und arbeitet in New York und Prag.
Ausstellungen und Beteiligungen: 1987 „The Neostunners“, Untergrund-Ausstellung, Prag. 1989 „Smile, Joke, and Grin“, Palast der Kultur, Prag. 1990 Club Delta, Prag (zusammen mit Tomas Pospiszil); „Totalitarian Zone“, ehemaliges Stalin-Monument in Prag; „Quo Vadis“, Open-Air-Ausstellung in der Altstadt von Prag; „Czech Alternative“, ULUV Galerie, Prag. 1991 Andy Warhol Museum of Modern Art, Medzilaborec; Staatsgalerie Znojmo; „Light Fesival“ Sargfabrik, Wien. 1992 Ruin Club, Center of Performing Arts, Prag (zusammen mit Markela Bankova); „Edge 92“, Madrid und London. 1993 Epalova Galerie, Prestige State Gallery, Prag; „Europe without Walls“, Manchester. 1994 Ronald Feldman Fine Arts, New York (zusammen mit Milena Dopilova); „Die jungen Künstler aus Prag“, Kunsthalle Düsseldorf; „7 artists from the Czech Republic“, The World financial Center, New York; 22. Internationale Biennale Sao Paulo; Seoul International Art Festival, Seoul/ Korea. 1995 „Artcircolo“, Prag; „Beyond Belief – Contemporary Art from East Central Europe“, Chicago; „Orbis Fictus – New Media in Contemporary Art“, SCCA Prag.
Performances und Aktionen: 1986 „Sounds“, Ostrava. 1987 „Bridge“, Prag. 1988 „The Posc“, Museum of Modern Art, Paris. 1989 „Secret Action“, Prag. 1991 „The Pink Tank“ (rosa Übermalung des Sowjetischen Kriegerdenkmals), Prag.

SUSAN ALEXIS COLLINS
1964 in London geboren. 1982-1983 Chelsea Scholl of Art, London. 1983-1987 Slade School of Fine Art, Univeristy College London. 1990-91 The School of the Art Institute of Chicago (postgraduate studies). 1992-1994 Research Fellow am West Surrey College of Design and Art. Seit 1993 Lehrtätigkeit an der Univerity of Reading, Deparment of Fine Art. Seit 1995 Leitung des Slade Centre for Electronic Media, Slade School of Fine Art, University College London.
Preise, Auszeichnungen und Förderungen: 1989 Greater London Arts, Artists Individual Production Grant; American Association of University Women International Fellowship. 1990 Fulbright Travel Award. 1991 Fulbright Professional Enhancement Grant. 1992 National Endowment of the Arts, Regional Artists Project Grant, Randolph Street Gallery, Chicago. 1994 Arts Council of Great Britain New Technologies Trainign Grant; London Arts Board „Go and See“ Grant nach Helsinki. 1995 Arts Council/Channel 4 Hi-Tech Fund Award. 1996 British Council Visual Arts Grant; European Artists Pepinière, Köln.
Ausstellungen und Beteiligungen (Auswahl): 1988-1990 „Art and Computers“, The Cleveland Gallery, Middlesborough; „First International Symposium of Electronic Art (FISEA); Artspace, Aberdeen; The Collins Gallery, Glasgow; Cartwright Hall, Bradford. 1990 „Words and Images“, Shire Hall, Reading; M.O.V.E, London. 1991 Gallery 2, Chicago; „Focus on Printmaking“, The Center for Contemporary Art, St. Louis, Missouri; „Brave New Pixels“, A.R.C. Gallery, Chicago; „4th International Holography Exhibition“, Durand Art Institute, Lake Forest, Illinois; „Luz Elasicá“, Museum of Modern Art, Rio de Janeiro. 1992 „Computer Art: Pushing The Boundaries“, State of Illinois Art Gallery, Chicago; „Wonne/Bliss“, Schöneberg, Berlin. 1993 „River Crossings: Projecting The Image“, Camerawork Gallery, London; „Handle With Care“, Museum of Science and Industry, Manchester. 1994 „On Location“, Blue Coat Gallery, Liverpool; „Pedestrian Gestures“, Hull Time-Based Arts; „V-Topia“, Tramway, Glasgow. 1995 „Every Dog Has

Its Day", Warrington Museum and Art Gallery. 1996 „Command, Shift, CTRL", NAME Gallery, Chigago.

TEIJI FURUHASHI
In Kyoto, Japan, geboren. 1984 Gründung der Gruppe „Dumb Type" während seines Studiums der Videokunst und konzeptuellen Kunst an der Kyoto University of Arts. 1995 in Kyoto gestorben.
1985 „7 Conversation Styles" (Video), Kyoto Municipal Museum of Arts; Museum of Modern Arts, New York; 1988 „Pleasure Live" (Performance), Quest Hall, New York; Theater im Pumpenhaus, Münster; ICA, London; Royal Museum of Arts, Copenhagen; Alti, Tokyo; 1989 „The Polygonal Journey #1" (Performance), Artspace Mumonkan, Kyoto; „Play Back" (Videoinstallation), San Francisco Museum of Modern Art; Akron Art Museum, Boston; Seattle Art Museum, Seattle; Contemporary Arts Center, Cincinnati; Grey Art Gallery, New York; Contemporary Arts Museum, Houston; ICA Nagoya; 1990 „The Polygonal Journey #2" (Performance), Northern Light Planetarium Trømso/Norwegen; „pH" (Performance), Spiral Hall, Tokyo; Artspace Mumonkan, Kyoto; 1991 „pH" (Performance), Kyoto Municipal Museum of Arts, Kyoto; ICA, Nagoya; Granada Festival; Art in the Anchorage, New York; Moda Hall, Osaka; Chapter, Cardiff; Tramway, Glasgow; „pH" (Video), Japan Satellite Broadcasting; 1992 „pH" (Performance), Wiener Festwochen, Wien; Centro de Arte Reina Sofia, Madrid; Theater im Pumpenhaus, Münster; Museum of Contemporary Art, Sydney; „pH" (Video) Preis „Sole d'Ora", TTVV Riccione; Preis „Best Stage Recording", Alte Oper, Frankfurt; „S/N #1" (Installation), Museum of Ixelles, Brüssel; Kunsthalle, Wien; „The Enigma of the late Afternoon" (Performance, Kooperation mit „Hotel Pro Forma), Glyptotek Museum, Copenhagen; „S/N #2" (Installation), ATM Contemporary Art Gallery, Milo; 1993 „pH" (Performance), Sprial Hall, Tokyo; Theaterhaus Gessnerallee, Zürich; 1994 „Love/Sex/Death/ Money/Live" (Installation), Spiral, Tokyo; „S/N #1" (Installation), Yokohama Art Museum; Gugenheim Soho, New York; „S/N" (Performance) Adelaide Festival; Musée d'Art Contemporain de Montréal; King Theatre, Seattle; Landmark Hall Yokohama; „Lovers" (Installation), Artlab 4 Hillside Plaza, Tokyo; 1995 „S/N" (Performance), Spiral, Tokyo; Festival MIT, Maubeuge; Esch Theater, Luxemburg; Cankarjev Dom, Ljubljana; Halle Münsterland/Theater im Puppenhaus, Münster; Festival Exit, Crétail; Kunsten Festival des ARts de Bruxelles, Brüssel; Zürcher Theater Spektakel, Zürich; Århus Festuge, Dänemark; Spiel.Art Theater Festival, München; International Festival of Performing Arts, Sao Paulo; „pH" (Performance), Harbourfront Center, Toronto; Festival MIT, Maubeuge; Festival EXIT, Créteil; „S/N #1" (Installation), Yerba Buena Center for the Arts, San Francisco; „Lovers" (Installation), Museum of Modern Art, New York; 1996 „S/N" (Performance) Tokyo Festival, Kyoto; Hong Kong Arts Festival, Hongkong; International New Zealand Festival of Arts, Wellington; Teatro Central, Sevilla; Festival Exit, Créteil; „Lovers" (Installation), Biennale de Lyon, Lyon; Festival VISAS, Maubeuge; Festival EXIT, Créteil; Sonar Festival, Barcelona.

MILAN GUSTAR
1963 in Kolín/CZ geboren. 1981-1986 Studium an der Tschechischen Technischen Universität, Prag. 1981-1990 Musik für Theater und Film.
Ausstellungsbeteiligungen: 1987 „Ugliness", Dejvická Galerie, Prag. 1988 „Golden Eyes", Delta Club, Prag. 1989 Infermental, Wien. 1994 „Hermit III – Transparent Messenger, Plasy; „Bell", Haus Stone Bell, Prag. 1995 „FAMU Exhibition", Archa club, Prag; „Test Run", Mánes Galerie, Prag; „Hermit IV", Plasy; „Orbis fictus", SCCA Prag.

GUSZTÁV HÁMOS
1955 in Budapest geboren. 1972-1978 erste Filme, Fotoausstellungen in Budapest, Ostberlin, Eindhoven. 1979 Emigration nach Westberlin, Studium an der Deutschen Film- und Fernsehakademie Berlin. 1982-1992 Mitarbeit an „Infermental 1" und Teilnahme mit Arbeiten an mehreren Infermentalausgaben. 1985 Abschluß an der DFFB mit dem Spielfilm „Der Unbesiegbare" (gezeigt in München, Cannes, Berlin). 1987 Stipendium am P.S.One, New York. 1988 Vortragsreihe in nordamerikanischen Goethe-Instituten; Artist in Residence in Vancouver. 1989 Gastdozentur an der School of Visual Arts in New York. 1990-1991 Vorträge an der Hochschule der Künste in Budapest; 1991 Workshop in der Black Box, Budapest. 1992 Nipkow Stipendium für die Rekonstruktion von Walter Ruttmanns Film „Berlin. Die Sinfonie der Großstadt". 1993 Workshop in der Filhochschule Lodz. 1994-1996 Vortragstätigkeit (Kunsthochschule für Medien, Köln; Center for Contemporary Art, Warschau; Hochschule der Künste, Dresden; Contemporary Art Gallery, Peking; Kunsthalle, Budapest. 1995/1996 Lehrauftrag an der Deutschen Film- und Fernsehakademie, Berlin. Auszeichnungen: 1980 Special Mention for a First Work, Video Roma; 1984 Sonderpreis des 1. Marler Video-Kunst-Preises; 1991 Decerne le prix Saint-Gervai 4e SIV, Genf; 1992 Hauptpreis DokumentART, Neubrandenburg; The Best Discovery Video Award, Nuovo Cinema de Montrèal; 1993 Special Mention, Prix Futura, Berlin; Golden Gate Award, Special Jury Award, SFilm Festival, San Francisco.
Ausstellungen: Seit 1980 in zahlreichen Ausstellungen mit Medienkunst vertreten, u.a. Museum of Modern Art, New York; Centre Georges Pompidou, Paris; Documenta 8, Kassel; Biennale Venedig; Centro de Arte Sofia, Madrid; Stedelijk Museum, Amsterdam; San Francisco Museum of Modern Art, San Francisco; Musée d'Art contemporain de Montrèal; Taormina Arte, Sizilien; Jeu de Paume, Paris; Artist Museum, Lodz; Mücsarnok, Budapest.
Installationen: Seit 1981 u.a. Kino Arsenal, Berlin; Biennale Venedig; Kölnischer Kunstverein; Künstlerhaus Dortmund; P.S.1, New York; Kijkhuis, Den Haag; Bauhaus, Dessau; Sztuki Warszawa, Warschau; Media Scape 3, Zagreb; Peking; Podewil, Berlin; Stiftung Starke, Berlin.

Festivals: Seit 1980 Teilnahme an internationalen Filmfestivals, u.a. Filmfestival Montrèal, Cannes Filmfestival, Internationales Forum des jungen Films Berlin, Westdeutsche Kurzfilmtage Oberhausen, DokumentART, Neubrandenburg, Locarno-Laggo Maggiore, Prix Futura Berlin, Festival Internacional de Cine San Sebastian, Duisburger Filmwoche.
Fernsehausstrahlungen: Seit 1984 Arbeiten für ZDF, Arte, Channel Four, London; Agent Orange, Kanada; CAT Fund/WGBH, USA; TVE/CNE, Spanien; La Sept, Frankreich; ORF, Österreich; RTBF, Belgien; WDR, Deutschland; FMS/MTV, Ungarn.

KIRSTEN JOHANNSEN
1957 in Bremen geboren, lebt und arbeitet seit 1982 in Berlin. Studien: Bühnenbild an der Akademie der bildenden Künste Stuttgart und an der Accademia di Belle Arti Florenz; Visuelle Kommunikation an der Hochschule der Künste Berlin. 1995 Projektstipendium am Institut für Bildmedien am Zentrum für Kunst und Medientechnologie Karlsruhe; Projektförderung durch die Stiftung Kulturfonds Berlin.
Videobänder in den Sammlungen Kijkhuis, Den Haag; Neuer Berliner Kunstverein, Berlin; Museum Ludwig, Köln; Mike Steiner Art Tapes, Berlin.
Ausstellungen und Festivals (Auswahl): 1983 World Wide Video Festival, Den Haag; Montbeliard. 1984 14. Forum des jungen Films, Berlin; XLI. Espositione Intern. d'Arte la Biennale di Venezia, Venedig; Festival Intern. de Cine de San Sebastian; Videonale, Bonn. 1985 „Kunst mit Eigensinn", Wien; European Media Festival, Osnabrück; Infermental. 1986 Student Film Festival, Tel Aviv; World Wide Video Festival, Den Haag; National Video Festival, Los Angeles. 1987 Festival Salsomaggiore; Intern. Kurzfilmtage, Oberhausen. 1988 Intern. Photoszene, Museum Ludwig, Köln. 1989 European Media Art Festival, Osnabrück. 1991 Nationalgalerie, Budapest; European Media Art Festival, Osnabrück; Ave, Arnheim; „Interferenzen", Riga und St. Petersburg. 1992 „Euro Aim", San Sebastian. 1994 Festival Intern. de Video, Vigo. 1995 Galerie Vorsetzen, Hamburg; „Cherchez la femme", Kunsthaus Hamburg. 1996 „female coalities", Städtische Galerie, Bremen; Première Biannale, Ars multimédiale, Metz.

JAAP DE JONGE
1956 in Amsterdam geboren. 1977-1983 Academie voor beeldende kunsten St. Joost, Breda; 1983 Jan van Eyck Academie Maastricht; 1991-1995 Dozent an der Rietvelt Academie Amsterdam; 1990-1992 Dozent für Videografik an der Academie St. Joost, Breda. Preise: 1992 Media Award des World Wide Video Festival, Den Haag; 1994 Gemeente aankopen Stedelijk Museum, Amsterdam; Videokunstpreis ZKM/SWF, Karlsruhe.
Ausstellungen und Beteiligungen (Auswahl): 1990 Museum De Prinsenhof, Delft; Paradiso 0+ Ball Video installatie, Amsterdam; Museum Fodor Gemeente aankopen 3D, Amsterdam; Medienfestival, Osnabrück; Video-objekt Table of Contents T.B.A., Amsterdam. 1991 Theater het Hoogt Ekko exp. kunst, Utrecht; Medienfestival, Osnabrück. 1992 Schau mir in die Augen, Documenta Archiv, Kassel; Verein für Viduelle Kommunikation, Hannover; Poetry and Images, Odense; World Wide Video Festival, Den Haag; Fotografie Biennale, Rotterdam; Kunstkanaal, Amsterdam; 7th Australian int. Videofestival, Sidney. 1993 Genesis local, Enkhuizen; Kijkhuis videocentre retrospective, Den Haag; Park TV, Amsterdam; Collective gallery, Edinburgh; park to the people paradiso, Amsterdam; TV TV vpro televisie, Amsterdam; electric cinema video presentatie, Amsterdam. 1994 Associacao cultural videobrasil, Sao Paulo; World Wide Video Festival, Den Haag; Gallerie Johan Jonker, Amsterdam; Video Art Plastique, St. Clair; Ferdinandeum; Innsbruck; Kunstkanaal, Amsterdam; OTS park televisie Filmmuseum, Amsterdam. 1995 CBK Ausstellung „Babbage Dream", Groningen; PARK/Riga/Amsterdam, Riga; Video Fest ,95, Berlin; Museum Het Domeim, Sittard; Staten Galerie, Den Haag; ART Cologne, Keulen; v2 organisatie, Rotterdam. 1996 Stedelijk Museum Copenhagen, Kopenhagen; Gemeente museum WWVF, Den Haag.

DIETER KIESSLING
1957 geboren in Münster. 1978-1986 Studium an der Kunstakademie Münster. 1986 Produktionspreis der Internationalen Videonale Bonn; 1990 Förderpreis des Kulturkreises im BDI; Karl Schmidt-Rottluff Stipendium; Caspar-von-Zumbusch-Preis; 1991 Förderpreis des Landes Nordrhein-Westfalen; 1992 Förderpreis zum ersten Deutschen Videopreis; 1993 Arbeitsstipendium des Kunstfonds Bonn e.V.
Ausstellungen und Beteiligungen: 1986 2. Internationale Videonale Bonn; „Elektronische Künste", Wissenschaftszentrum, Bonn. 1987 Galerie Hake, Münster; Ars Electronica, Linz; „Arbeit und Rhythmus", Kunsthalle Recklinghausen; „Neues Video aus der BRD", Museum für Gegenwartskunst, Basel. 1988 Galerie Hake, Wiesbaden; 3. Internationale Videonale, Bonn; IX Videoart Festival, Locarno; „Deutsche Videokunst 1986 bis 1988", Skulpturenmuseum Glaskasten, Marl; 2nd Fukui International Video Biennale, Fukui City, Japan. 1989 Städtisches Museum Abteiberg, Mönchengladbach; „Videoskulptur retrospektiv und aktuell 1963-1989", Kölnischer Kunstverein Köln, Kongresshalle Berlin, Kunsthaus Zürich; „Metissage et Croisement", Fonds Regional d'Art Conemporain, Marseille. 1990 „Videokunst der 80er Jahre in der BRD", Tiroler Landesmuseum Ferdinandeum, Innsbruck; 4. Internationale Videonale, Bonn; „Ars Viva 90/91", Heidelberger Kunstverein, Hochschule für Grafik und Buchkunst Leipzig, Nassauischer Kunstverein Wiesbaden. 1991 Thomas Backhauß Galerie, Düsseldorf; „Videoformes", Festival de la Creation Video, Clermon-Ferrand; „Multimediale 2", Zentrum für Kunst und Medientechnologie, Karlsruhe. 1992 „Tiefgang", Schloßbunker, Mannheim; „Fluxux-Virus", Aktionsforum Praterinsel, München; „Deutscher Videokunstpreis Südwestfunk Baden-Baden, Zentrum für Kunst und Medientechnologie,

Karlsruhe; „Avantgarde Reflex Ost-West", Altes Rathaus, Potsdam. 1993 „Gegenbilder", Kirchen in Münster; „Multimediale 3", Zentrum für Kunst und Medientechnologie, Karlsruhe; Ausstellung der Karl Schmidt-Rottluff Stipendiaten, Kunsthalle, Düsseldorf. 1994 Räume für neue Kunst, Rolf Hengesbach, Wuppertal; „Medienbiennale", Leipzig; „Videoskulptur in Deutschland seit 1963, Kunsthalle Rostock, Centrum Beeldende Kunst Groningen, World Wide Video Centre Den Haag, Museum van Hedendaagse Kunst Gent; „Videobrasil", Sesc Pompeji, Sao Paulo. 1995 Gesellschaft für Aktuelle Kunst, Bremen; „Art & Electronics", Pao Gallerys, Hong Kong Arts Centre; „Multimediale 4", Zentrum für Kunst und Medientechnologie, Karlsruhe; „Paradoxien", Galerie der Stadt Schwaz im Palais Enzenberg, Schwaz; Video-Forum der Art 26 ,95, Basel; European Media Art Festival, Osnabrück; ,95 Kwangju Biennale, Kwangju, Korea. 1996 Räume für neue Kunst, Rolf Hengesbach, Wuppertal.

RICHARD KRIESCHE
1940 geboren in Wien. 1958 Matura am Bundesrealgymnasium Fürstenfeld. 1963 Abschluß der Studien an der Akademie der bildenden Künste Wien (Graphik und Malerei) und an der Universität Wien (Kunstgeschichte); Beginn der Lehrtätigkeit an der höheren technischen Bundeslehranstalt Graz; 1973 Gründung und Aufbau der Versuchsabteilung „Audiovisuelle Medien". 1964 Diplom für Graphik und Malerei an der Akademie der bildenden Künste Wien. 1968 Assistent an der Hochschule für angewandte Kunst Wien. 1969 Gründung des Kunstvereins „pool"; Mitherausgeber der Zeitschrift „pfirsich"; Fortsetzung der Lehrtätigkeit an der Höheren technischen Bundeslehranstalt. 1970/71 Studienjahr am University College London. 1973 Gründung der „poolerie", einer Mediengalerie für Fotographik, Film und Video. 1977 Ernennung zum Leiter des Experimentalbereiches des AVZ-Graz (Audiovisuelles Zentrum). 1978 Gründung des „bvöst" (erster regionaler Interessensverband bildender Künstler). 1983/84 DAAD Einladung Künstlerprogramm Berlin. 1984 Gründung von „kulturd@ta", Labor für medien und Kommunikationsgestaltung, Video-, Computer, Kommunikationsexperimente. 1985/86 Forschungsaufenthalt am M.I.T. Cambridge, Albert and Vera List Visual Arts Centre am „Media Lab" des M.I.T. 1988-1991 Lehrauftrag an der Technischen Universität Wien über „Ästhetik wissenschaftlich-technischer Operationen". Seit 1991 Professor an der Hochschule für Gestaltung Offenbach/Main, „Theorie und Praxis der elektronischen Bilderzeugung". 1995/96 Gastprofessur an der „École supérieure des beaux arts" für Elektronische Kunst, Paris.
Ausstellungen (Kurzversion seit 1963): Einzelausstellungen im Museum of Modern Art, Los Angeles; Museum moderner Kunst, Wien; Massachusetts Institute of Technology, M.I.T.-Media Lab, Boston; Washington Project for the Arts, Washington; Kunsthaus Zürich; Kunsthalle Baden-Baden; Museum of Modern Art, Oxford. Ausstellungsbeteiligungen an: documenta 6, Kassel; documenta 8, Kassel; Ars Electronica 1989, 1994, Linz; ARTSAT – Weltraumstation MIR (erstes Kunstexperiment in der dreißigjährigen Geschichte Sowjetischer Raumfahrt, 1991); 34. Biennale di Venezia; 42. Biennale di Venezia; 46. Biennale di Venezia (Menzio d'onore / seit Bestehen der Biennale von Venedig ergeht erstmals ein Preis der Biennale an einen österreichischen Künstler).

GERDA LAMPALZER
1959 geboren. Seit 1979 Arbeit mit Video; seit 1980 Mitarbeit in der Medienwerkstatt Wien; seit 1987 Lehrauftrag an der Hochschule für angewandte Kunst in Wien (Lehrkanzel für Kommunikationstheorie). Kuratorin, Vorträge, Workshops und Publikationen zu Video; 1992 Österreichischer Förderungspreis für Videokunst. Arbeiten im Bereich Video, Super 8, Fotografie, Objekte. Zwischen 1983 und 1996 diverse Festivalteilnahmen und Vorführungen.
Aussellungen: 1989 „Cadavre exquisit" (Video + Polaroid), Blau-Gelbe Galerie Wien, die thede Hamburg; Teilahme an „Reverse Angle" Transcultprojekt Chicago-Wien. 1991 Teilnahme an „Kunst 91", Minoritenkirche Stein; „Transformator" Computer- und Videofestival St.Veit/Glan; „Kunststraße" Innsbruck; „Wasser und Stein", Kulturtage Ötz/Tirol; „außenräume innenräume", Museum moderner Kunst im Palais Liechtenstein Wien. 1987-1991 Beiträge zur „Kunst der Reise", Wien, Frankfurt, London, Athen. 1992 Teilnahme an „Zur Zukunft des Erinnerns in der Medienkultur", Palais Rasumowsky Wien; Videowall bei der HIT 92, Messegelände Wien; „Im Augenblick", Haus Wittgenstein Wien; „100x", Casa des Serralves Porto, Portugal. 1993 Teilnahme an „Im Augenblick", Thurn und Taxis Palais Bregenz; „Connect the universe", Frauenopening Börse Wien; „100 Umkleidekabinen", steirischer herbst Graz. 1995 „Mediale Objekte", „Fotostories" (mit Manfred Oppermann), Kunstraumgalerie Arcade Mödling; „Film- und Videobrunch", Filmbühne Mödling (mit Manfred Oppermann); Teilnahme an „Schaufenster Medienwerkstatt", Depot Wien; „Elektronische Galerie", Kunstlabor Wien; „Weitsicht", Schleiermacherhaus Halle, Deutschland; „Orakel", Galerie Bois Wien. 1996 Teilnahme an „Wunderkammer", Medienwerkstatt Wien; „Videopräsentation", Kunstraumgalerie Arcade Mödling.

HELMUT MARK
1958 geboren, lebt in Wien und Leipzig.
Ausstellungen und Beteiligungen (Auswahl): 1982 „Multivision 82", Wiener Festwochen, Wien. 1983 „Junge Künstler", Galerie Grita Insam, Wien; „Multivision 83", Wiener Festwochen, Wien. 1984 „Junge Szene", Secession, Wien; Museum des 20. Jahrhunderts (mit Robert Adrian); „Nuovi Media", Volterra; „Multivision 84", Wiener Festwochen, Karlsplatz Wien. 1985 Galerie Aufbau-Abbau, Berlin; steirischer herbst, Graz. 1986 Galerie Amer, Wien; „Kunst und Technologie", Wissenschaftszentrum, Bonn; Galerie Amer, Wien; „Kunst-Raumkunst", Schloß Buchberg; „Nuovi Geometrie", Rotunda, Mailand; „Aperto 86", Biennale Venedig, „Das Offene Auge", Wien; „Wien Signaal", Aorta,

Amsterdam. 1987 Galerie Maria Bonk, Köln; Galerie Winter, Wien; steirischer herbst, Graz; „Im Rahmen der Zeichnung", Secession, Wien; Galerie Uks, Oslo; „Geometrien", Schloß Buchberg. 1988 „Skulpturenrepublik", Messepalast, Wien; „Brennpunkt Wien", Kunstverein, Bonn; „Der Hund in mir", Galerie Hubert Winter, Wien; „Jugendwerke", Akademie der Bildenden Künste, Wien; „Beton", Galerie Grita Insam, Wien. 1989 Galerie Grita Insam, Wien; „60 Tage österreichisches Museum des 21. Jahrhunderts", Wien; „Moskau-Wien-New York", Messepalast, Wien; „Video", Tiroler Landesmuseum Ferdinandeum, Innsbruck; „Prospekt", Kunstverein, Frankfurt; „Raum annehmen II", Forum Alpbach; Kongreßhalle, Berlin; „Video Skulptur", Kunstverein, Köln; „Melencolia", Galerie Grita Insam, Wien; „Design Wien", Museum für Angewandte Kunst, Wien; „Skulpturenrepublik", John Hansard Gallery Southhampton, Thrid Eye Center Glasgow, Arnolfini Bristol, Mücsarnok Budapest; „Brennpunkt Wien", Kunstverein, Karlsruhe. 1990 Galerie Orms, Innsbruck; Galerie Arcade, Mödling; Insam-Gleicher-Gallery, Chicago (mit Robert Adrian); „Poliset", Padiglione d'Arte Contemporanea, Ferrara; „Texas", Station Rose, Wien (mit F.E. Rakuschan); Galerie Alberto Weber, Turin; „Multiples", Galerie Gawlik-Schorm, Wien; „Im Licht des Montiors", Kunstverein Horn, Künstlerhaus Graz, Künstlerhaus Prag; „Plastik Akut", Landesgalerie, Klagenfurt; „Ursprung und Moderne", Neue Galerie, Linz; „Wider-Schein", Tiroler Landesmuseum Ferdinandeum, Innsbruck; Biennale, Sidney; „Raum annehmen III", Forum Alpach. 1991 „Zeitsprünge", Neue Galerie Landesmuseum Joanneum, Graz; „Dissipative Inszenationen", Museum Moderner Kunst, Wien; „Die Augen der Minerva", Kunstverein, Salzburg; „Junge Kunst aus Österreich", Kunstverein Hamburg, Galerie Rähnitzgasse Dresden; „5 Skulpturen", Akademie der Bildenden Künste, Wien. 1992 „Transit eine mediative Skulptur", ORF-Fernsehen (mit Reinhard Braun); Gobelinsaal Wiener Staatsoper, Wien; „Identität:Differenz", steirischer herbst 92, Graz; „The New Editions", Galerie Waßermann, München; „Neue Medien", Kunsthaus, Horn; „Objekt versus Raum", Villa Merkel Stuttgart, The Nordic Arts Centre Helsinki, Tallinn Art Hall Tallinn; „Die Künstlerpostkarte", Altonaer Museum Hamburg, Deutsches Postmuseum Frankfurt; „Interferenzen IV", Radiokunst, Museum Moderner Kunst, Wien; „Neue Medien", Kulturpädagogisches Institut, Graz. 1993 Galerie Orms, Innsbruck; Galerie Waßermann, München; „Compkuenstlerg", Lothringer Str., München; Galerie Karin Sachs, Müchen; „Objekt versus Raum", Museum Moderner Kunst Bozen, Galerie Gerald Piltzer Paris, Centre Cultural Telca Sala Barcelona; „Multiples", Galerie Bob van Orsouw, Zürich. 1994 „Bad zur Sonne", steirischer herbst, Graz; „Positionen", Galerie Pohlhammer Steyr, Kunstforum beim Rathaus Hallein; Medienbiennale, Leipzig; „Zeitgleich", Salzmagazin Hall in Tirol; „Lokalzeit", Forum aktueller Kunst-Raum Strohal, Wien; „Translucent Writings", Neuberger Museum, New York. 1996 „Hybrid", Forum Stadtpark, Graz.

PAUL McCARTHY
1945 in Salt Lake City geboren. 1969 B.F.A. San Francisco Art Institute, 1973 M.F.A. – Intermedia, Film, Video, Kunstgeschichte, University of Southern California. Lebt in Altadena, CA.
Ausstellungen und Beteiligungen (Auswahl): 1973 Conceptual Art, Librta Gallery, Pomona, CA. 1974 Newspace Gallery, Los Angeles.1975 Southern California Video Anthology II, Long Beach Museum, CA. 1978 Video Tapes from L.A., DeAppel, Amsterdam. 1979 LAICA, Los Angeles. 1981 California Performance Now and Then, Museum of Contemporary Art, Chicago. 1982 LACE, Los Angeles; Video Tapes America, American Centre, Paris. 1983 Cirque Divers, Lüttich; Video by Performance Artists, Hallwalls, Buffalo, N.Y.. 1984 Crap, Orwell Memorial Gallery, Los Angeles. 1985 LACE, Los Angeles. 1986, 1987, 1990 und 1991 Rosamund Felsen, Los Angeles. 1988 Open Channels Video, Long Beach Museum, Long Beach. 1989 L.A. Freewaves, American Film Institute, Los Angeles. 1990 New California Video, Long Beach. 1991 The Family Romance, Simon Watson, N.Y.; Video Violence, Ars Electronica, Linz; HaHa, Boyd Gallery, Santa Monica; Body and Body, Kunstverein, Graz; The Body, Video, Peter Pakesch, Wien. 1992 Helter Skelter, MOCA, Los Angeles; Post Human, Lausanne, Turin, Athen, Hamburg, Max hetzler, Köln; Daniel buchholz, Köln; Strange Developments, Gallery anthony d'Offay, London; LAX, Galerie Krinzinger, Wien; Spielhölle, Akademie der Kunst, Frankfurt/Main. 1993 Luhring-Augustine, New York; Galerie Krinzinger, Wien; buchholz und Buchholz, Köln; Trancesex, Los Angeles; The Language of Art, Kunsthalle, Wien; The Uncanny, sonsbeek 93, Arnheim; Aperto 93, Biennale Venedig; Figure as Fiction, Cincinnati Contemporary Art Center, Cincinatti; Sampler: Southern Californian Video Collection, D. Zwirner, N.Y., Guenzani, mailand, Buchholz, Köln. 1994 Studio Guenzani, Mailand; George-Philippe Vallois, Paris; Air de Paris, Nizza; FRAC Poitou-Charentes: Bains-Douches, Chauvigny u. Hôtel St. Simon, Angoulême; Outside the Frame of the Object, Cleveland Center for Contemporary Art, Cleveland, und Snug Harbor Cultural Center, New York; Babies & Bambies, amsterdam; Galerie K, Oslo; (Cut), Los Angeles; 90'ernes Kunstscene, Kunstforenigen, Kopenhagen; Dirty, John Good, New York; Hors limites, Centre Pompidou, Paris.

DAVID MOISES
1973 in Innsbruck geboren. 1984-1988 HTL/Informatik (abgebrochen); bis 1991 Lehre als Typografiker, danach Arbeit als Schriftsetzer. 1994 Schnittstellten-Operator bei Melzer in Wien; seit 1995 Studium an der Hochschule für künstlerische und industrielle Gestaltung, Meisterklasse für Experimentelle Visuelle Gestaltung, Linz.
Ausstellungsbeteiligung: „Pronoia in Exnerland" mit les new petits, WUK, Wien.

CHRISTIAN MÖLLER

1959 in Frankfurt am Main geboren; studierte Architektur in Frankfurt und als Stipendiat an der Meisterschule Gustav Peichl an der Akademie der Bildenden Küsnte in Wien. Nach seiner Mitarbeit im Stuttgarter Architekturbüro Behnisch und Partner begann er als Gastkünstler an peter Weibel's Institut für Neue Medien der Städelschule in Frankfurt. 1990 gründete er ein Architekturbüro mit eigenem Labor für Elektronische Medien- und Softwareentwicklung in Frankfurt. Seit 1995 leitet er als Gastprofessor und künstlerischer Leiter das Architekur- und Medien Institut „Archimedia" der Hochschule für künstlerische und industrielle Gestaltung in Linz.

Ausstellungen (Auswahl): 1992 „Space Balance", Ars Electronica, Linz; Kinetische Lichtplastik, „Kunst im öffentlichen Raum" (zusammen mit Rüdiger Kramm), Zeilgalerie, Frankfurt. 1993 „The Virtual Cage", Theater am Turm, Frankfurt; „Im Rahmen der Bilder – Kapitel 3", Karmeliterkloster, Frankfurt; „Chronolyse", Intermedienschauplatz Lindentunnel, Berlin; „Ebenen variabler Visibilität", Galerie Stadtpark, Krems; „Algorithms Creating Space", Siggraph 93, Los Angeles; „Light Blaster – Design Horizonte 93", Naxoshalle, Frankfurt; Audiovisualisierung mit Trautonium (mit Oskar Sala), „Design Horizonte", Frankfurt. 1994 „Interaktive Architektur", Galerie Aedes, Berlin; „Electro Clips", „Electronic Mirror 2", „Netzhaus" (zusammen mit Joachim Sauter), Theater am Turm, Frankfurt und Ars Electronica, Linz; „Audiopendel", ISEA 94, Helsinki. 1995 „Electronic Mirror – Between Seduction and Disbelief", Galerie Power Plant, Toronto; „The Party Effect", Audioinstallation im öffentlichen Raum, Museumspark, V2, Rotterdam; „Prototypen und Projekte – Innovatives Oberösterreich", Design Center, Linz; „Das Akustische Notenblatt", Audioinstallation mit Archimedia, Figarohaus, Wien. 1996 „Autonomous Mirror", Exit Festival, maison des Art, Paris; „Voyage through the Human Body" und „Autonomous Mirror 2" mit Archimedia, „Wunschmaschine – Welterfindung", Kunsthalle, Wien; „The thrid dimension of ‚Ritratto di Gentilurno' und Mozarts Piano Fugus, opus 154" mit Archimedia, Siggraph 96, Museum of Contemporary Art, New Orleans.

FRIEDERIKE PEZOLD

In Wien geboren.

Ausstellungen und Beteiligungen (Auswahl): 1969 Haus der Kunst, München. 1970 Künstlerhaus, Wien. 1971 Modern Art Museum, München; Fine Arts Center, Davidson/USA; Kunsthalle Baden-Baden; Künstlerhaus Graz. 1972 Galleria Numero, Venedig und Rom. 1973 Steirischer Herbst, Graz; Kunstverein Wolfsburg. 1974 Kunstverein Köln; Museu de Arte Contemporanea, Sao Paulo; Institute of Contemporary Arts, London; Kunstmarkt Köln, Castelli & Sonnabend & Wewers. 1975 9. Internationale Biennale, Paris; Museé d'Art Moderne de la ville de Paris; Städtische Galerie im Lenbachhaus, München; Kunstverein Hamburg; Serpentine Gallery / Arts Council of Great Britain, London; Galerie Germain, Paris; palais des Beaux Arts, Brüssel; Haus am Waldsee, Berlin. 1976 Museum of Modern Art, New York; Whitney Museum of American Art, New York; Kunstverein Köln; Frankfurter Kunstverein; Galerie Projektion, Köln; Berliner Filmfestspiele; Galerie Nächst St. Stephan, Wien; Galerie M.L.D'Arc/Ana Canepa, New York. 1977 Documenta 6, Kassel; Staatliche Kunsthalle Baden-Baden; Neue Galerie Sammlung Aachen; Galerie Hetzler und Keller, Stuttgart; Saman Gallery, Genua; Museé National d'Art Moderne, Centre Beaubourg, Paris; Light Gallery, New York; neue Gesellschaft für bildende Kunst, Berlin; Praefekturmuseum, Fukui/Japan; Goethe-Institut, Osaka und Kyoto; Gründung RFU (Radio Freies Utopia), München. 1978 Videofilm „Die schwarzweiße Göttin", WDR. 1979 Berliner Filmfestspiele; Filmfestspiele Wien (Viennale); Kunsthalle Kiel; Cinemathéce Bruxelles; Folkwang Museum, Essen. 1980 Museum des XX. Jahrhunderts, Wien; Galerie Maeght, Zürich; Avantgardefilmfestival Z-Club, Wien; Kunstmarkt Basel, Galerie Nächst St. Stephan; Kunstmarkt New York, Galerie Nächst St. Stephan und Galerie Krinzinger. 1981 Loft, München; Filmhochschule Lodz/Polen; Galerie Magers, Bonn; Kunstverein Bonn; Videofestival Locarno (1.Preis); Filmfestival Seattle/USA; Kunstmarkt Basel; Kunsthaus Zürich. 1982 Preis des BDI für die Videoarbeit „Der Monolog"; „Videokunst in Deutschland", gezeigt in: Kölner Kunstverein, Kunsthalle Baden-Baden, Badischer Kunstverein Karlsruhe, Westfälischer Kunstverein Münster, Städtische Galerie im Lenbachhaus München, Kunsthalle Nürnberg, Nationalgalerie Berlin; Kunstmuseum Winterthur; Museum Moderner Kunst, Wien; 1983 Berliner Filmfestspiele; Maison des Arts, Crétail; Museum of Modern Art, New York; Städtische Galerie im Lenbachhaus, München. 1984 Biennale Venedig; Galleria Communale d'Arte Moderna, Bologna; Sprengelmuseum Hannover; Bonner Kunstverein; Stuckvilla, München; Museum of Fine Arts, Houston/USA. 1985 Museum of Modern Art, New York; Pacific Filmachrives, Berkeley/USA; Max Ophüls filmfestival, Saarbrücken; Stadtmuseum München; Museum der Stadt Dortmund; Würtembergischer Kunstverein; Akademie der Künste, Berlin; Museum des XX. Jahrhunderts, Wien; Galerie Insam, Wien; Kunstmarkt Madrid und Chicago. 1986 Berliner Filmfestspiele; Frankfurter Filmschau; Kunsthalle Hamburg; Kunstverein Hamburg. 1987 Schleswigholsteinisches Landesmuseum; Stedelijk Museum, Amsterdam; Kölner Kunstverein; Kunsthaus Zürich; Centro Videoarte, Ferrara. 1988 Reina Sofia, Madrid; Centre Georges Pompidou, Paris; Tate Gallery, London; Museum voor Hedendaagse Kunst, Gent. 1989 Berliner Filmfestspiele; Museum of Fine Arts, Houston/USA; Filmfestival Cannes; Kölner Kunstverein; Kunsthalle Berlin; Neuer Berliner Kunstverein. 1990 Museum Wiesbaden; Ars Electronica, Linz. 1991 Museum of the 21. Century, Wien; Zentrum für Kunst und Medientechnologie, Karlsruhe. 1992 Lincoln Center, New York; Kunsthaus, Graz. 1993 ARCO, Madrid; Fundació Joan Miró, Barcelona. 1994 Neuer Berliner Kunstverein; Kunsthaus Zürich; Galerie Krinzinger, Wien. 1995 1. Wiener Museum für Videoart &

Bodyart; Centre Georges Pompidou, Paris; Kunst Forum Schloßpark, Aarau; Kunsthalle Krems; Abbaye aus Dames, Caen; Galerie AK, Frankfurt.

ULRIKE ROSENBACH

1943 in Deutschland geboren. 1964-1970 Ausbildung an der Kunstakademie Düsseldorf bei den Professoren Bobek, Kricke und Beuys; Meisterschülerin der Bildhauerei bei Prof. J. Beuys; 1. und 2. Staatsexamen für Kunsterziehung an Höheren Schulen. 1972 erste Videoarbeiten, erste Performance: Beginn von Videoaufzeichnungen im eigenen Studio. 1973 erste Video-live-Aktion/Performance am Kunstmarkt Köln, Präsentation in New York, „112 Greene Street". 1976 Lehrauftrag am California Institute of the Arts, Valencia, Californien, für Videokunst und feministische Kunst. Umzug nach Los Angeles. 1976 Neubeginn in Deutschland, lebt und arbeitet in Köln. Intensive künstlerische Auseinandersetzung mit feministischen Themen. Gründung der Arbeitsgruppe „Schule für Kreativen Feminismus" (besteht bis 1982); Teilnahme an der „documenta 6", Kassel; Arbeit als freischaffende Künstlerin, excessive Ausstellungsarbeit im In- und Ausland mit den Medien Video, Fotografie, Performance. Teilnahme an der „documenta 8", Kassel. Lehraufträge und Gastprofessuren an internationalen Hochschulen. 1989 Berufung an die neugegründete Hochschule der bildenden Künst, Saarbrücken, als Professorin für Neue künstlerische Medien; Rektorin von 1990-1993. Lebt und arbeitet im Saarland und in Köln.
Ausstellungen, Beteiligungen und Performances (Auswahl): 1972 Galerie Ernst, Hannover. 1973 „112 Greenestreet", New York. 1974 „Kunst bleibt Kunst", Kunstverein Köln. 1975 „Biennale des Jeunes", Paris; Oppenheim Studio, Köln. 1976 „Laica", Los Angeles. 1977 „documenta 6", Kassel. 1978 Kunstmuseum Küsseldorf. 1979 Biennale, Sydney. 1980 Stedelijk Museum, Amsterdam. 1981 Galerie Stampa, Basel. 1982 „Videokunst in Deutschland", Köln. 1983 Institute of Contemporary Art, Boston. 1984 Galerie Magers, Bonn. 1985 Kunstverein Oldenburg. 1986 Galerie Meier-Hahn, Düsseldorf. 1987 „documenta 8", Kassel. 1988 „Edge 88", London. 1989 Art Gallery of Ontario, Toronto. 1990 Stadtgalerie Saarbrücken; Stadtgalerie Quakenbrück; Art Gallery of New South Wales, Dydney; „Andernorts", Galerie Bauer, Nürnberg; „Kunst nach 68", Kunstmuseum Basel; „Ressource Kunst", Kunstmuseum Budapest; „Kunstdrachen-Flugobjekte", Kusnthalle Düsseldorf, Museum Tokyo; WDR Köln, Fernsehpräsentation von „Or-Phelia, ein Transformationsstück". 1991 Galerie am Luxemburgplatz, Wiesbaden; Solarwoche, Dillingen; „Geförderte Künstler", Kunstmarkt Köln; Goetheinstitut Paris; Frauenfilmfest Dortmund; „German Video Art", Fukuyama Museum of Modern Art, Japan. 1992 Stadtgalerie, Krems; Galerie Fotohof, Salzburg; Galerie Beck, Schwarzenacker/ Saar; „Force Sight", Galerie March, Stuttgart, Schloß Prestenik; Galerie Kiki meier-Hahn. 1993 Galerie Ulrike Buschlinger, Wiesbaden; „The First Generation", Long Beach Museum of Art, Californien; „Bright Light", Galerie March, Schloß Prestenik; „Tower of Babylon", Videofestival, Helsinki. 1994 Galerie Julia Philipi, heidelberg; Galerie Uli Buschlinger, Wiesbaden; Galerie March, Stuttgart, Schloß Ludwigsburg; Haus der Geschichte, Bonn; „I am You", Goetheinstitute München, international; „Videoskulptur in Deutschland", IFA-Galerie, Stuttgart, internationale Wanderausstellung. 1995 Galerie Weißer Raum, Hamburg; Festival „Bollwerk", Fribourg; St. Petri Kirche, Dortmund; „Andere Orte Überall", Kreuzkirche, Hannover; „Himmel und Erde", Dominikanerkloster, Frankfurt; Videofestival, Freiburg; MMK, Frankfurt; „RAM – Realität, anspruch, Medium", Kunstfonds Bonn, Museum Wiesbaden, Weserburg Bremen, Lindenaumuseum Altenburg, Bonn, Kunstverein Karlsruhe. 1996 Galerie March, Stuttgart; Konversion OberOlmerWald.

LEO SCHATZL

1958 in Obernberg/Inn geboren. 1976-1987 Studium an der Hochschule für künstlerische und industrielle Gestaltung in Linz. 1980 Beginn der Arbeit mit Film (s-8) und Video. 1983-1987 Mitarbeit bei der Kulturvereinigung Stadtwerkstatt Linz. 1985-1987 Mitglied beim Verein Unabhängige Filme Linz. 1984-1988 Zusammenarbeit mit der Musikgruppe Monochrome Bleu.1987 Übersiedlung nach Wien, freischaffend tätig. 1990 Gründung und Manifestation des Künstlerparadieses (Büro Wien). Zusammenarbeit mit diversen Künstlergruppen (Pyramedia, Dead Dog Gallery, Kunstlabor, Lo(o)sgelöst, Contained). Seit 1992 Lehrauftrag für projektorientiertes Film- und Videogestalten an der Hochschule für künstlerische und industrielle Gestaltung in Linz. Preise: 1985 Preis für künstlerische Fotografie (Ca-Bankverein); 1987 Erster Preis bei Kleingraphikwettbewerb (Österreichische Ex-Libris Gesellschaft Wien). 1990 Eines von drei Stipendien für Projekt im Südwesten der USA (OÖ. Landeskulturbeirat); Talentförderungsprämie der OÖ. Landesregierung. 1992 Stipendium für grenzüberschreitende Kunst (BmfUK). 1995 Stipendium für künstlerische Fotografie in Now York (BMfUK).
Film- und Videovorführungen u.a. in Linz (Stadtwerkstatt, Querspur, Ars Electronica, Neue Galerie), Wels (Östereichische Filmtage), Graz (Forum Stadtpark), Inbruck (Tropic Filmfestival, Komm, Akt), Wien (Stadtkino, U4, Fotogalerie, Medienwerkstatt, B.A.C.H.), Osnabrück (Medienkunstfestival), Oberhausen (Kurzfilmtage), Luzern (Videotage), San Francisco (Nite Club Video), Boulder, Budapest (Kunstpalast), Zaragoza (STI), Istanbul (Bogazici Uni), New york (128-Gallery), Denver (Art Broker), Boston (M.I.T.), sowie Beiträge zu diversen Videoeditionen (Infermental Nr. 9) und Fernsehsendungen (ORF-Kunstsücke).

RUTH SCHNELL

1956 in Feldkirch geboren. Studien an der Hochschule für Gestaltung in Linz, an der Akademie der bildenden Künste Wien und an der Hochschule für angewandte Kunst in Wien. 1987 Lehramt für Kunsterziehung. 1988 Diplom für

Visuelle Mediengestaltung. Lebt und arbeitet als freischaffende Künstlerin in Wien. Seit 1987 Lehraufträge für Video und Neue Medien an der Hochschule für angewandte Kunst in Wien, Meisterklasse für Visuelle Medien. Seit 1990 Lehrauftrag an der Hochschule für Musik und darstellende Kunst, Abteilung Film und Fernsehen, Wien. Im WS 1994/95 Gastprofessur für Neue Medien an der Akademie für bildende Kunst in Bratislava, Abteilung für Visuelle Medien. Permanente Installationen: „Wasserzaun", interaktive Wasserinstallation, Zollabfertigungsanlagen Karawankentunnel, Kärnten, 1990/91; „Virtual Terms", Lichtinstallation, NÖ. Landesakademie in St. Pölten, in Planung.
Ausstellungen und Beteiligunen (Auswahl): 1984 „!984", Museum des 20. Jahrhunderts, Wien. 1989 „Im Netz der Systeme", Ars Electronica, Linz. 1990 „Vom Verschwinden der Ferne", Deutsches Postmuseum, Frankfurt/Main. 1991 „Les Images en Follies" Martigny, Schweiz (Assistenz: Kike Garcia Roldan); „Kunst Schau Fenster", Dornbirn, Co-Produktion mit Kike Garcia Roldan. 1992 „Babel", Kunsthochschule für Medien in Köln in Zusammenarbeit mit UNESCO. 1993 „Kunst – die halbe Miete", Bludenz; „Beyond the Screen", allerArt Galerie, Bludenz. 1994 „Kunst und Stadt", Feldkirch; „Lokalzeit – Wiener Material im Spiegel des Unbehagens", Strohal, Wien; Galeria Moderna, Ljubljana. 1995 Fundazione Querini, Venedig; 46. Biennale di Venezia, Österreichischer Pavillon, Venedig. 1996 „Reaching Out" Österreichisches Kulturinstitut New York und Galerie Gritta Insam, Wien; „Österreichische Künstler auf der Suche nach Rom", Palazzo Braschi, Rom; „Personale", Galerie Del Cortile, Rom; „Jenseits von Kunst", Jubiläumsausstellung im Museum Ludwig, Budapest; „Personale", Galerie Sechzig, Feldkirch.
Ausstellungen gemeinsam mit Gudrun Bielz (siehe Biographie G. Bielz).
Teilnahmen an internationalen Videopräsentationen und -festivals: Kutscherhaus Berlin, Centre Georges Pompidou Paris, Bologna, Videofestival Locarno, Experimentalfilmtage Osnabrück, Museum des 20. Jahrhunderts Wien, Berlinale Berlin, Long Beach Museum of Art Los Angeles, Museo de Arte Contemporaneo Madrid, Videofestival Sidney, ARCO Madrid, Europalia Brüssel, Museum Moderner Kunst Wien, Donaufestival Niederösterreich, „Circulo de bellas artes Madrid, Technisches Museum Wien.

PAUL SERMON

1966 in Oxford geboren. 1984-1985 Diplom für Kunst und Design am Bedford College of Hiher Education, England.1985-1988 Studium am Gwent College of Higher Education, Wales, Bachelor of Arts. 1989-1991 Post-graduate degree (Master of Fine Arts) an der University of Reading, England. Seit 1993 Hochschuldozent an der Hochschule für Grafik und Buchkunst in Leipzig. Lebt zur Zeit in Berlin.
Ausstellungen und Festivals: 1986 Gwent College of Higher Education; „Fresh Art Show", The Barbican Center, London. 1987 First Biennal of European Art Schools, Toulouse; „Cultura Digitalis", Hochschule für angewandte Kunst, Wien. 1988 „BA Hons Degree Show", Gwent College of Higher Education, Wales, Cleveland Gallery, England. 1989 Zweite Biennale Festival of European Art Schools, Antwerpen. 1990 Oldham Art Gallery, Manchester. 1991 Watershed Media Center, Bristol; MFA Degree Show, The University of Reading, England; Ars Electronica, Linz. 1992 Muu Media Festival, Finnland; Kajanni Art Gallery und Helsinki Telegalleria, Finnland. 1993 Espoo OTSO Gallery und Helsinki Telegalleria, Muu Media Festival ,93, Helsinki; „interActiva", Köln; Unstable Media Festival, V2, s'Hertogenbosch, Holland; Multimediale, Zentrum für Kunst und Medien, Karlsruhe. 1994 Netherlands Design Institute, Amsterdam; „Ik + de Ander", Amsterdam; ISEA 94, Museum of Contemporary Art, Helsinki. 1995 CeBit 95, Hannover; Visas 95, Maubeuge, Frankreich; „Images du Futur", Montreal, Canada; Museum of Science and Industry, Manchester; ICC, Tokyo. 1996

LYDIA SCHOUTEN

1948 in Leiden geboren. 1967-1971 Studium an der Freien Akademie der Bildenden Künste in Den Haag. 1971-1976 Studium an der Akademie der Bildenden Künste in Rotterdam. 1975 Maaskant Preis der Stadt Rotterdam; 1981 und 1982 Reisestipendien nach New York des Niederländischen Kulturministeriums; 1985 Artist in Residence an der Satellite video Excahnge Society, Vancouver; Studio am Künstlerhaus Bethanien, Berlin; 1989-1990 Studio am P.S.1, New York. 1980 Co-Organisatorin von „Mixage International", Festival für Performances, Expanded cinema, Installation in Rotterdam, Utrecht und Breda; 1979-1994 Editorin von „Modern Denken", Magazin für Video, Film, Installation und Photographie; 1984 Organisation von „Con Rumore", Veranstaltung für Video, Film, Photographie und Installation an der Galerie Westersingel 8, Rotterdam; 1985 Editorin von „Infermental V"; 1986 Co-Organisatorin von „Reflections", Ausstellung von Videoinstallationen, Skulpturen und Malerei, Museum Fodor, Amsterdam; 1991 Co-Organisatorin von „Erotic Desire" in Photographie, Museum De Tempel, Sittard; 1994 Co-Organisatorin von „Can you always believe your eyes?", Ausstellung im Museum De Beyerd, Breda. 1978-1981 zahlreiche Performances;1978-1988 Fernsehprojekte; zwischen 1981 und 1988 Teilnahme an allen wichtigen Videofestivals.
Ausstellungen und Beteiligungen (Auswahl): 1975 „Salon v.d. Maassteden, Stedelijk Museum, Schiedam. 1976 „Debuut", De Doelen, Rotterdam. 1979 „Emancipatie-aspekten", N.K.S., Holland. 1980 „Zelfbeeld", N.K.S., Holland. 1981 „Not Waving", Palais des Beaux Arts, Brüssel. 1982 ,t Hoogt, Utrecht; „Salon v.d. Maassteden", Stedelijk Museum, Schiedam, Gouda, Den Bosch. 1983 Passionata IBK, Nijmegen; Galerie paladijn, Amsterdam; „Berlin-amsterdam", Berlin; Französisch-Deutsche Jugendgesellschaft, Bonn und Marseille; „9 Artists from Rotterdam", Ferens Art Gallery, Kingston Upon Hull; „Reginale", NL-Centrum, Amsterdam; „Fotografische Zelfbespiege-

ling", Nijmeegs Museum, Nijmegen. 1984 Stedelijk Museum, Gouda; Galerie Perspektief, Rotterdam; Galerie Images Nouvelles, Bordeaux; Nieuwe Kerk, Amsterdam; „Rotterdammers", Museum Boymans van Beuningen, Rotterdam; „The touring exhibitionists, a multi-media extravaganza", Brighton, London, Brostol, Rochdale, Nottingham, Newcastle; „Foto ‚84" Nieuwe Kerk, Amserdam; „The luminous Image", Stedelijk Museum, Amsterdam; „Grenzüberschreitungen", die neue Tat, Aachen; „Videoase", Concordia, Enschede; „Vindsulor Kalejdoskop, Konsthallen, Göteborg; „Talking back to the media", Aorta, Amsterdam. 1985 Academie v. Bouwkunst, Rotterdam; Folkwang Museum, Essen; Torch Gallery, Amsterdam. 1986 Galerie Philomene Magers, Bonn; Galerie Torch, Amsterdam; Kölnischer Kunstverein, Köln; Artfair RAI, Amsterdam; „Dutch Photography", Graz; „Innovation und Tradition", Badischer Kunstverein, Karlsruhe, Budapest; „Fotobiennale ‚86", Enschede; „Fotografie Buffa", Groninger Museum, Groningen; „The Self Imagined", Air Gallery, London; „4 Kreuzen", voormalige bibliotheek, Rotterdam. 1987 Städtisches Museum in der alten Post, Mülheim; Appendix Gallery, Wuppertal; „Over Fhotografie", van Reekummuseum, Apeldoorn; „Das gläserne U-Boot", Tabakfabrik Krems/Stein; „De Rotterdamse School?", Museum Boymans van Beuningen, Rotterdam; „Comic Iconoclasm", Cornerhouse Gallery, Manchester, Circulo des Belles Artes, Madrid; „Fotografie Buffa", Carlisle Museum and Art Gallery, Carlisle, Collins Gallery, Glasgow, Stills Gallery, Edinburgh, Photo Gallery, Cardiff. 1989 Ivan Dougherty Gallery, Sydney; P.S.1, Institute of contemporary Art, New York; Galerie Kaess Weiss, Stuttgart; „25 Jahre Video Skulptur", Kölnischer Kunstverein, DuMont Kunsthalle, Köln, Kongreßhalle, Berlin. 1990 Galerie Wanda Reiff, Maastricht; Galerie Snoei, Rotterdam; Gemeentemuseum, Helmond; „Imago", ArtFair, Amsterdam. 1991 Galerie Verplancke-Van Bavel, Brügge; Galerie Wanda Reiff, Artfair Brüssel, Artfair Basel; „Images of women in the eighties", Tokyo Metropolitan Museum of Photography, Tokyo; Artfair Los Angeles; „Imago", Galerie Wanda Reiff, Budapest, Barcelona; „Künstlerische Konfrontationen", Torún, Polen. 1992 Artfair NICAF, Yikohama; „Imago", Galerie Wanda Reiff, Oporto/Portugal, World Expo Sevilla, Rom; 1993 Lieberman & Saul Gallery, New York; Grey Art Gallery, New York; „Double Dutch", Rom; „Tijdelijk Asiel", Arti et Amicitae, Amsterdam; „En Scène", W139, Amsterdam; „Vrij Spel", Gemeentemuseum, Arnhem; De Sterrewacht, Rotterdam; „Verwandtschaften", De Kunshal, Rotterdam; „KunstRai, Galerie Wanda Reiff, Amsterdam; „Public/ Private", Edinburgh; „Imago", Hara Museum, ARC/Japan; „Ohne Titel", Frankfurter Kunstverein, Frankfurt; „Le Benefice du Doute", Optica Centre d'Art Cont., Montréal; „Imago", Taipei Arts Museum, Taiwan. 1994 Galerie Wanda Reiff, Maastricht; The Photographers Gallery, Saskatoon/ Canada; Houston Center for Photography, Houston; Kulturhuset Toldkammerer, Helsingor/Dänemark; Provinciaal Museum Hasselt/Belgien; Städtische Ausstellungshalle am Hawerkamp, Münster; Southeast Museum of Photography, Daytona Beach/USA; Il Ponte Gallery, Rom; „Downtown", Nederlands Foto Instituut, Rotterdam; „KunstRai", Perpektief magazine, Amsterdam. 1995 „Himmel und Erde", Dominikanerkloster, Frankfurt; „20 Years Galerie Grieze", Tielt/Belgien. 1996 Art Space, Kampen/Holland; „drawing manifestation", Het Wilde Weten, Rotterdam; „MUKA Youth Prints", Wanderausstellung durch Dänemark, Belgien, Deutschland; „Hverdagens Helte og Heltiner", Turbinehallerne, Kopenhagen.

SERVAAS

1950 in Amsterdam geboren.

Ausstellungen und Beteiligungen (Auswahl): 1980 Städtische Galerie im Lenbachhaus, München; ‚t Hoogt, Utrecht. 1981 „News Resoncance", WDR 3, Köln. 1982 Art 13, Galerie Stampa, Basel; The Kitchen, New York. 1983 „Video Roma", Rom; Stedelijk Museum, Amsterdam; Holland Festival, Amsterdam; VPRO television, Hilversum. 1984 „Video 84", Gallery du Quebec, Montreal; Beursschouwburg, Brüssel; De Gele Rijder, Arnhem. 1985 Kölnischer Kunstverein, Köln; Stedelijk Museum, Amsterdam; Fine Art Museum, Fukui City, Japan. 1986 Hallwall Gallery, New York; Folkwang Museum, Essen; „Western Front", Vancouver; Concertgebouw, Amsterdam. 1987 „Reflections", Museum Fodor, Amsterdam; „750 Jahre Berlin", Berlin; Schirn Kunsthalle, Frankfurt; „In Spiral", SCAN Gallery, Tokyo; Galerie Torch, Amsterdam; Palazzo dei Diamanti, Ferrara; Vleeshal, Middelburg; „documenta 8", Kassel; L.A.C.E., Los Angeles. 1988 Fine Art Museum, Fukui City; ELAC, Musee d'art contemporaine, Lyon; Museum of Fine Arts, Houston; Musee de L'Elysee, Lausanne. 1989 „Video 1963-1988", Kölnischer Kunstverein; Neuer Berliner Kunstverein, Berlin; Gemeentemuseum, Arnhem; Mousonturm, Schirn Kunsthalle, Frankfurt; Gallery Torch-Onrust, Köln; Folkwang Museum, Essen. 1990 „Schräg", Rheinisches Landesmuseum, Bonn; Kasseler Kunstverein, Kassel; Museum Fodor, amsterdam; „For Real Now", Hoorn; Torch Gallery, Amsterdam; Galerei Schultz, Köln; 8th Biennale of Sydney, Sydney. 1990 Galerie Torch, Amsterdam; Galerie Onrust, Amsterdam; „Order Now", Stedelijk Museum, Amsterdam; Kunstverein, Hamburg; „Op water gebouwd", Goes; Felisenum „Stof en Geest", Velsen; Museum het Prinsenhof, Schrag, Delft. 1992 „Imago", Oporto, Sevilla; Museum van Bommel-van Dam(Mubo), Venlo; La Verreine, Barcelona; P.P.O.W. Gallery, Now York; Sala 1, Double Dutch, Rom; „Impresse mediali", Galleria Forum, Rom; Städtische Kunsthalle, Düsseldorf. 1993 de La Tour Gallery, Basel; Galerie Wassermann, München; Groninger Museum, Groningen; Hara Museum, Tokyo; Robert Bermann Gallery, Los Angeles; Galerie Torch, Amsterdam; Galleria Civica d'Arte Contemporanea, Termoli; National Museum of Contmporary Art, Tapei, Taiwan; „The Fi$h-mobile", Art Cologne, Köln; Studio d'Arte Contemporanea pno Casagrande, Rom. 1994 Galerie Beatrice Wassermann, Köln; „Größenwahn", Kunstprojekte für Europa; Triple X Festival, Amsterdam; „B.A.S. projekt", Hogeschool voor de kunsten, Arnhem; Fi$h-mobile city tournee in Europa; Galerie De La Tour, Amsterdam; Art Basel, Basel; Studio d'arte contemporanea Pino Casagrande, Rom. 1995 „Art is what you Eat", RKS, Rotterdam; Galerie Torch, Amsterdam; Galerie Beatrice Wassermann, München; „Art Eat", Berlin; Groninger Museum, Groningen; Kunsthaus Zürich; Don Lake Gallery, Toronto; „Het bulderbos, grond tot kunst", Schiphol; „Espace 251, Brüssel; TEU, Wien; „BAS project 95", Arnhem; „War Mobile 2", Kölner Messe, Köln; Kunsthalle Bielefeld.

ANDREA VAN DER STRAETEN
1953 in Trier geboren. 1972-77 Studium der Germanistik, Kunstgeschichte, Theaterwissenschaften in Köln, Germanistik und Politikwissenschaften in Marburg, 1. Staatsexamen. 1979 Mitbegründung des Medienzentrums „Bildwechsel" in Hamburg (Produktionsbereiche: Video, Fotografie, Grafik; Video-Verleih und Archiv; Organisation von Ausstellungen, Kursen, Film- und Videoveranstaltungen), Mitarbeit bis 1986. 1981-86 Visuelle Kommunikation an der Hochschule für Bildende Künste Hamburg, Diplom. 1979-96 Kurse, Workshops, Vorträge und Veranstaltungen mit/für Organisationen wie dem Kommunalen Kino Hamburg; Fotografische Auftragsarbeiten für die Berliner Architekturzeitschrift „Bauwelt" und für „Die Zeit" (zusammen mit Doris K. Künster). 1987 Jahresstipendium für bildende Künstler des DAAD für Wien, Hochschule für Angewandte Kunst, Animationsfilmklasse Maria Lassnig. 1990/92 Studien/Arbeitsaufenthalte in Rom und in den USA. 1992 Arbeitsstipendium der Stadt Hamburg für bildende Künstler. 1988-92 Redaktionelle Mitarbeit bei Zeitschriften in Wien „Der Kairos der Fotografie, „MOZ", „Moderne Zeiten". 1993 Artist in Residence bei United Media Arts in Durham, Kanada; Studienreise nach Tokyo im Rahmen des österreichischen Künstlerprojektes „Die Reise zu den Quellen", museum in progress. 1994 Arbeitsstipendium des BMUK für Rom. 1993/94 Gastveranstaltungen/Vorträge an der Akademie der bildenden Künste Wien, der Schule für künstlerische Fotografie, Wien und der Hochschule für Angewandte Kunst, Wien. Seit 1995 Vertragsassistentin an der Hochschule für künstlerische und industrielle Gestaltung Linz, Meisterklasse für Experimentelle Visuelle Gestaltung bei Prof. Herbert Lachmayer, sowie freie Mitarbeiterin beim Österreichischen Rundfunk.
Ausstellungen und Beteiligungen (Auswahl): 1985 Bildwechsel, Hamburg. 1986 Bildwechsel, Hamburg; Folkwang Museum, Essen; Kunstverein, Hamburg.1987 Künstlerhaus, Hamburg; 1988 Galerie Faber, Wien; Fotogalerie, Wien. 1989 Arsenla, Wien; „60 Tage Österreichisches Museum des 21. Jahrhunderts", Wien. 1990 Adelhauser Kloster, Freiburg. 1991 Galerie Faber, Wien; Secession, Wien; Forum Stadtpark, Graz; Galerie der Künstler, München. 1992 Österreichische Triennale der Fotografie, Maribor; Kunstraum Freihaus, Wien; Kunst auf Kampnagel, Hamburg. 1993 Museum am Ostwall, Dortmund; Kunst auf Kampnagel, Hamburg; Österreichische Triennale der Fotografie, Graz; United Media Arts, Durham/Kanada. 1994 Neue Galerie Graz; Forum Stadtpark, Graz; museum in progress, Wien. 1995 Kunsthalle Palazzo, Basel. 1996 Centre national de la Photographie, Paris.
Beteiligung an internationalen Film- und Videofestivals.

BILL VIOLA
1951 in New York geboren. Studium an den Experimental Studios am College of Visual and Performing Arts, Syracuse University, New York. Seit 1995 dessen Ehrendoktor. 1980 Japan/U.S. Crative Arts Fellowship; 1982 Video Artist Fellowship der Rockefeller Foundation; 1983/89 Visual Artist Fellowship des National Endowment for the Arts; 1984 Polaroid Video Art Award for aoutstanding achievement; 1985 Fellowship der J.S. Guggenheim Memorial Foundation; 1987 Maya Deren Award des American Film Institute; 1989 John D. and Catherine T. MacArthur Foundation Award; 1991 Intercultural Film/Video Fellowship der Rockefeller Foundation; 1993 Skowhegan Medal; Medienkunstpreis des Siemens Kulturprogramm und Zentrum für Kunst und Medientechnologie, Karlsruhe.
Ausstellungen und Beteiligungen (Auswahl): 1972 „St. Jude Invitational Exhibition", De Saisset Art Gallery and Museum, Santa Clara, Californien. 1973 Everson Museum of Art, Syracuse, New York. 1974 The Kitchen Center, New York; „Project '74", Kunstverein, Köln. 1975 Everson Museum of Art, Syracuse, New York. 1975-1977 „La Biennale de Paris", ARC, Musée d'Art Moderne de la Ville de Paris. 1975-1987 und 1993 Art, New York. 1977 The Kitchen Center, New York; „documenta VI", Fridericianum, Kassel. 1978 „International Open Encounter on Video", Tokyo. 1979 The Museum of Modern Art, New York; „Everson Video Review", Everson Museum of Art, Syracuse, New York. 1980 Long Beach Museum of Art, Long Beach, Californien. 1981 Vancouver Art Gallery, Vancouver, Canada; „International Video Art Festival", Portopia '81, Kobe, Japan. 1982 Whitney Museum of American Art, New York; „60'80 attitudes/concepts/images", Stedelijk Museum, Amsterdam. 1983 ARC, Musée d'Art Moderne de la Ville de Paris; „Video As Attitude", Museum of Fine Arts, Santa Fe, New Mexico. 1984 „The Luminous Image", Stedelijk Museum, Amsterdam. 1985 Moderna Museet, Stockholm; „Currents", Institute of Contemporary Art, Boston. 1986 „La Biennale di Venezia", Venedig. 1987 The Museum of Modern Art, New York; „Avant-Garde in the Eighties", Los Angeles County Museum of Art, Los Angeles. 1988 Contemporary Arts Museum, Houston, Texas; „Carnegie International", The Carnegie Museum of Art, Pittsburgh, Pnnsylvania. 1989 Fukui Prefectural Museum of Art, Fukui city, Japan; „Einleuchten", Deichtorhallen, Hamburg; „Image World, Art and Media Culture", Whitney Museum of American Art, New York. 1990 Fondation Cartier pour l'Art Contemporain, Jouy-en-Josas, Frankreich; „Passages de l'image", Musée National d'ARt Moderne, Centre Georges Pompidou, Paris,

Centre Culturel Fondation Caixa de Pensions, Barcelona, Wexner Art Center, Columbus, Ohio, San Francisco Museum of Modern Art, San Francisco. 1991 „Metropolis", Martin Gropius Bau, Berlin; „Opening Exhibition", Museum für Moderne Kunst, Frankfurt. 1992 Institute of Contemporary Art, philadelphia, Virginia Museum of Fine Arts, Richmond; Städtische Kunsthalle, Düsseldorf; Moderna Museet, Stockholm, Museo Nacional Centro de Arte Reina Sofia, Madrid; Musée Cantonal des Beaux-Arts, lausanne; Whitechapel Art Gallery, London; Tel Aviv Museum of Art, Israel; „Pour la suite du Monde", Musée d'art contemporain de Montréal, Canada; „documenta IX", Kassel. 1993 Musée d'art contemporain de Montréal, Montreal, Canada; „New World Images", Louisiana Museum of Modern Art, Humlebaek, Dänemark; „American Art in the 20th Century", Martin-Gropius-Bau, Berlin, The Royal Academy, London. 1994 Centro Cultural/Banco do Brazil, Rio de Janeiro; Salzburger Kunstverein, Salzburg; Madison Art Center, Wisconsin; „Beeld/Beeld", Museum Van Heedendaagse Kunst, Gent; „Landscape as Metaphor", Denver Art Museum und Columbus Museum of Art, Columbus, Ohio. 1995 Biennale von Venedig, United States Pavillon, Venedig; Kestner-Gesellschaft, Hannover, Arizona State University Art Museum, Tempe, Arizona; Institute of Contemporary Art, Boston; Van Abbe Museum, Eindhoven; „Video Spaces: Eight Installations", The Museum of Modern Art, New York; „Rites of Passage", Tate Gallery, London; „3e Biennale d'art contemporain de Lyon, Musèe d'art contemporain, Lyon. 1996 Savannah College of Art and Design, Savannah, Georgia; Lannan Foundation, Los Angeles; Durham Cathedral, Durham, England; „Portrait of the Artist", Anthony d'Offay Gallery, London; „Foreign Bodies", Museum für Gegenwartskunst, Basel; „Mediascape", Guggenheim Museum, New York; „Along the Frontier", Center of Photography, New York; The Russian Museum, St. Petersburg; Galerie Rudolfinum, Prag.

VA WÖLFL
1943 geboren in Mortnaumont (F). 1961-1966 Studium an der Akademie Salzburg bei Oskar Kokoschka und Slavi Soucek; 1966-1972 Schüler bei Otto Steinert an der Folkwang-Schule in Essen
Ausstellungen und Beteiligungen:1966/67 Universität Ohio; Galerie Caltanisetta, Sizilien. 1968/69 Galerie St. Barbara, Washington; Erfindung des „Latenten Bildes, New York. 1971/73 Atelier Essen (Aktionen). 1974 Kaufhaus Neckermann, Dortmund (Aktion). 1976 Galerie Becker, Bochum; Museum Fokwang, Essen; Galerie im Rick, Essen-Kettwig. 1977 Kunsthalle Recklinghausen (Aktion mit Reinhild Hoffmann und Hubert Kretschmar). 1978 Eintagsatelier Scheidtsche Tuchfabrik, Essen-Kettwig (Aktion). 1979 „Essener Kunstszene 79", Essen; Gruga, Essen (Aktion). 1980 Museum Bochum. 1981 Galerie Brusten, Wuppertal. 1982 „Erweiterte Fotografie", Wiener Sezession, Wien. 1984 Städtische Galerie Schloß Oberhausen; Museum für Kunst und Kulturgeschichte, Dortmund. 1985 „Kunst in der Bundesrepublik Deutschland 1945-1985, Neue Nationalgalerie, Berlin. 1987 Museum Folkwang, Essen. 1988 Kunstpalast Düsseldorf; „Junge Kunst in der Bundesrepublik Deutschland, Warschau, Belgrad, Zagreb. 1989 „Nibelungen – Niegelungen", Kunstraum Wuppertal. 1990 Galerie Schneider, Frankfurt a.M.; „Lichtbild", Galerie Karin Bolz, Köln. 1992 Galerie Roeder, New York. 1994 Galerie Roeder, New York; Galerie Bolz, Köln.
Arbeiten für das Theater: 1977 Bühnenbild und Kostüme für „Masada" von Israel Eliras, choreographisches Theater von Hans Kresnik, Theater an der Wien, Wien. 1978 Bühnenbild und Kostüme für „Magnet" von Wolfgang Bauer, Ballett von Hans Kresnik, Theater am Goeheplatz, Bremen; Regie mit Hans Kresnik; Ausstattung und Kostüme der Oper „Representatione di Anima e di Corpo" von Emilio de Cavalieri, St. Peter-Universitätskirche, Theater der Stadt Heidelberg; Libretto „Ich will, daß es dir gut geht" für das Ballett von Youri Vamos, Bayerische Staatsoper, München. 1979 Inszenierung und Ausstattung mit Youri Vamos, „Die Kaiserin von Neufundland" von Frank Wedekind und Henning Brauel, Bayerische Staatsoper, München. 1980 Darsteller und Mitarbeiter am Film „Ulisses" von Werner Nekes; Videoperformance „Jahrhunderthotel" für die Angestellten des Kaufhauses Beck, München. 1982 Inszenierung mit Hans Kresnik; Ausstattung und Kostüme für „Sacre" nach der Musik von Igor Strawinsky, Theater der Stadt Heidelberg. 1984 Skulptur und Kleidung für das Ballett „Thron" von Dansgroep Krisztina de Chatel, Amsterdam. 1985 Choreographie mit Susanne Linke „Schritte verfolgen", Essen. Seit 1986 Choreograph der Freien Gruppe „Neuer Tanz" mit Wanda Golonka. 1987 „Caspar de la Nuit", Darstellung in der Zeche Carl, Essen. 1995 „High Fidelity", Choreographie mit Wanda Golonka für das Bayerische Staatsballett, München.

LANDES GALERIE

Kataloge des OÖ. Landesmuseums
Neue Folge Nr. 108
ISBN 3-85474-003-4

Medieninhaber:
Land Oberösterreich / OÖ. Landesmuseum
Museumstraße 14, A-4010 Linz

Direktor: Dr. Gunter Dimt

oö. Landesgalerie: Mag. Dr. Peter Assmann

Konzeption und Kurator der Ausstellung:
Gottfried Hattinger
gemeinsam mit Peter Assmann

Organisation: DI Martin B. Atzwanger

Katalogredaktion und grafische Gestaltung:
Gottfried Hattinger

Übersetzungen:
Englisch: Aileen Derieg
Französisch: Ingrid Fischer
Italienisch: Rainer Weißengruber

Fotos:
Eduardo Calderón (Viola)
Denis Farley, S. Steal (Servaas)
Clemens Gießmann (Berghold)
alle anderen von den KünstlerInnen

Abbildung Umschlag:
Susan Alexis Collins, „Touched"

Repros: Krammer, Linz
Druck: Estermann, Aurolzmünster

Verlag:
publication N° 1
© Bibliothek der Provinz
A-3970 Weitra
02815 / 35594

ISBN 3 85252 135 1

Diese Publikation erscheint anläßlich der Ausstellung „Objekt:Video" in der oö. Landesgalerie vom 10. Oktober bis 17. November 1996

OÖ KULTUR

LEIHGEBER:

Air de Paris, Paris
Martin Fritz / Franco Kappl, Wien
Galerie Eigen+Art, Berlin
Ydessa Hendeles Art Foundation, Toronto
Kulturabteilung der NÖ. Landesregierung
Rijksdienst Beeldende Kunst, Den Haag
Stedelijk Museum, Amsterdam
Ing. Andreas Unterpertinger, Wien

KOOPERATIONEN:

Archimedia, Linz
Canon Art Lab, Tokyo
Epidemic Association, Paris
Galerie Hofkabinett, Linz
Kunsthochschule für Medien, Köln
Montevideo, Amsterdam
Österreichische Bundesbahnen, Hauptbahnhof Linz
Karin Pleinschek Seidenblumengeschäft, Linz
Soros Center for Contemporary Art, Prag

SPONSOREN:

Allgemeine Sparkasse, Linz
Cancom, Linz
Firma Köck
Megatechnik, Linz
Oberösterreichische Versicherungs AG, Linz
Sharp Corporation, Linz
Spitz Hotel, Linz
The British Council, Wien

The British Council

Allgemeine Sparkasse Oberösterreich

CANCOM

Megatechnik

SHARP

köck

Keine Sorgen
Oberösterreichische
Unsere Versicherung hält